W9-BYL-032

Women Who
Love Sex

Books by Gina Ogden

Safe Encounters* (co-author)
Sexual Recovery
Food for Body and Soul
When a Family Needs Therapy (co-author)

*Available from POCKET BOOKS

Women Who Love Sex

Gina Ogden, Ph.D.

POCKET BOOKS

New York   London   Toronto   Sydney   Tokyo   Singapore

WOMEN WHO LOVE SEX is based on real conversations with hundreds of real women in a variety of settings over a span of twenty years. Identities of these women have been concealed by changing details, and certain women are composite creations and not actual women, although the words ascribed to them are those of actual women.

POCKET BOOKS, a division of Simon & Schuster Inc.
1230 Avenue of the Americas, New York, NY 10020

Copyright © 1994 by Gina Ogden, Ph.D.

All rights reserved, including the right to reproduce
this book or portions thereof in any form whatsoever.
For information address Pocket Books, 1230 Avenue
of the Americas, New York, NY 10020

Library of Congress Cataloging-in-Publication Data
Ogden, Gina.
    Women who love sex / Gina Odgen.
        p.   cm.
    Includes bibliographical references and index.
    ISBN: 0-671-86550-1 (hardcover)
    1. Women—United States—Sexual behavior. 2. Sexual behavior
surveys—United States. 3. Sex. 4. Sex (Psychology) I. Title.
HQ29.038   1994
306.7′082—dc20   —dc20
[347.73′75]   [347.30775]   93-40883
                                                                          CIP

First Pocket Books hardcover printing May 1994

10 9 8 7 6 5 4 3 2 1

POCKET and colophon are registered trademarks of
Simon & Schuster Inc.

Printed in the U.S.A.

Material in this book has appeared in other forms in the following publications:
    Archives of Sexual Behavior, Berkshire Women's News, the Boston Globe, Changes Magazine, Contemporary Sexuality, Focus Magazine, Hartford Woman, Medical Aspects of Human Sexuality, Sexuality Today, and Women and Therapy.

From THE TAO OF LOVE AND SEX by Jolan Chang. Copyright © 1977 by Jolan Chang. Used by permission of Dutton Signet, a division of Penguin Books USA Inc.

From SASSAFRASS, CYPRESS, AND INDIGO by Ntozake Shange. Copyright © 1982 by Ntozake Shange. Reprinted with permission from St. Martin's Press, Inc., New York.

The author will donate a portion of her proceeds to causes promoting women's health and freedom of expression.

*To the creation of a world
in which women can safely choose
to love sex*

Contents

Contents

On the maps made by men there is an immense white area, terra incognita, where most women live. That country is all yours to explore, to inhabit, to describe.

—Ursula LeGuin

Opening Thoughts

WHAT IS SEX? Ask this question of the next ten women you meet and you may find descriptions varying wildly. Depending on personal experience and the current trend, you may hear that sex is an outflowing of passion, an affair of the heart, a comfort, a dalliance, an experiment, an economic necessity, or perhaps a social construction, a reproductive imperative, a need for intimacy, a search for love.

If you ask women to think beyond the conventional images of sex—the sensational tabloids, the glossy photos of bodies doing "it"—if you ask them to think about their own lives (or what they wish for their own lives), they will tell you that sex is more than just a genital act or a mad dash to orgasm. Often they will tell you that sex is more than physical. If it is joyous and satisfying, women may describe sex as an opening up of vital energy. They will say that their sexual responses lead them to a sense of wholeness— a connection of body, mind, heart, and soul; a sense of oneness with their partners, with the universe.

When women say they love sex, this does not imply that they love it "too much." Nor does it imply a polarization with women who, for whatever their reasons, love it less or maybe not at all. There is no one right way for women to love sex. And there is not one all-encompassing reason that they love it. Women love sex because it helps them escape from their ordinary routines. They love it because it connects them with their inner beings and because it

1

leads them to romance, love, and intimacy with partners, men and also women. They love it because it feels good, sometimes good enough to change the course of their lives.

There have always been women who love sex. They have loved sex even though it may have caused them heartache and, in many cases, abuse, deprivation, even death. For most of the world's women, over most of recorded history, love of sex has been accompanied by some kind of shadow: control, objectification, abuse, abandonment. Too often, women have had to pay for their sexual pleasures with shame and ostracism, unwanted pregnancy and disease. The last ten years have brought a raised awareness about sexual abuse and the victimization of women. Today's news media abound with stories of women violated by harassment, incest, rape, the deadly gift of HIV, to the point where you wonder whether this is a further abuse of women, hyping their miseries to sell more papers and boost TV ratings. But although there is great openness to exploring in minute detail all of the pain attributed to sex (the televised Anita Hill hearings is only one case in point), there is not yet a reasonable counterbalance—the permission to explore the positive possibilities of what sex means for women who love it, actively and safely.

Sexual energy is connected to the core of all of women's energies. Because sex has been regularly used as a tool for social control—proscribed, propagandized, rationalized, and institutionalized to keep women in their place—it has political ramifications even at its most intimately, succulently personal. What women do with their sexual energy, their conscious and unconscious choices, affects them far beyond the moment. Think about it. For women to love sex and also love themselves creates a new balance, a new set of images about what is "real," not to mention about what is "normal" or "hot." For women to love sex and also define sex in their own terms—frame it positively, beyond ownership, media hype, violence, or the porn debate—shifts the sexual ecology by removing the historical filter of male domination.

But this degree of affirmation presents challenges. "How do I even begin?" women ask. They stumble over a learned doublethink that tells them the full scope and depth of their experience is not valid. The language we associate with *human* sexuality is the language of *man*. It is the joke, the testosterone thrust, the so-called objectivity of science. Even more basically, for women to act honestly on what they want means reassessing their sense of affiliation. Just what does it mean to *belong?* Women are used to squeezing or stretching to adjust, used to conforming to attract—even when their partners are women. Our wishes for something more in bed never seem to be the right size or the timing is off. We begin to question if we ought to want what we want, if our wishes are normal. Before we know it, we can find our sexuality framed in the language of pathology or self-help. Women who are judged to be too randy or too cold or too demanding risk losing the right to a relationship.

This book proposes a new theory of sex. Based on the premise that women's stories are valid, it takes women's stories seriously as they are without reducing them to statistics. Based on the assertion that sex begins long before women enter the bedroom and reverberates long after, it provides contexts for a full rainbow of positive experiences. It focuses on the meanings of sexual satisfaction as well as the searches for it. It offers images for sexual health and empathy and focuses on the process of sexual image making. The personalities in this book are women, the theory of sexuality is human.

What makes this approach drastically new is that it asks for your involvement. It asks you, the reader, to broaden your definitions of sex to include your own desires and behaviors. It asks you to envision a sexual response cycle that flows directly from (and to) all kinds of life situations rather than one that revs up with vaginal lubrication, climaxes, and finally rolls over on its side and falls asleep. It asks you to acknowledge the sexual intelligence of your entire body, even beyond the genital "homing sites," and to explore the mysteries of a mind–body connection. It asks you to incorporate intimacy as a part of your sexual expression rather than apart from it. It asks you to factor in time, memory, and all the particular conditions that make sex alive for *you*. In short, it asks you to ask your own questions and to think wholly and optimistically.

To each woman reading this book I want to say: Listen to yourself as well as your partner, if you have one. Tell the truth (where it is safe) and nurture a sense of humor. Your sexuality is layered, complex. It informs the whole of your being. Your innate cycles of response are not necessarily the physical ups and downs and explosions you've been led to believe.

To each man reading this book I suggest: Be open to surprise. You may not yet know that listening to women is in your best interests. Listen. You may find yourself expanding your own capacities. Maybe you'll find pleasures you didn't know existed.

The new perspectives offered here are framed by stories of women who love sex, hundreds of women with whom I have talked and worked and empathized from the mid-1970s to the present day. In thinking about how most accurately to present all their voices, I reflected on their major message: Healthy sexuality is not a diversion, it is part of the whole story, integral to the quality of life, adding dimension and purpose. It seemed too piecemeal to pile up case studies—the usual lineup of subjects trotted out to illustrate a point—and too pruriently boring to report endless snippets of disembodied conversation that had little connection to the lives of the women speaking them.

I have chosen instead to create a few composite women to convey the spirit behind the words. The Alice, Maya, and Iris of the chapters that follow speak the insights and actual words of many individual women while not necessarily

4

being exactly like any one of the women. This device serves to protect the identities of those involved in the various phases of research. It also allows me to enter actively into their conversations—to show that researchers are human, too, and that the questions we ask affect the outcomes of research. In proposing a new theory of human sexuality, it is important to convey the notion that I was always there with these women, exploring the depths of their feelings, the layers of their experience, rather than remaining the "objective" observer behind a white lab coat and a computer. The conversations we had helped equalize our roles and allowed glimpses of the complex lives that inform and are informed by the sexual energy of women who love sex.

A remarkable, shining fact remains through all these years of interviewing and thinking and writing, and it is the major theme of the pages that follow. Despite the risks and dangers; despite the possibility of brutalization somewhere along the line; despite the challenges, taboos, and misunderstandings, there are women who continue to love sex. Women for whom sex, by their own definitions, is a source of connectedness, health, and personal power, for whom sex is a route to ecstasy.

Who are these women? What moves them? What is it about sex that these women love? What do they have to teach us?

That is the story of this book.

1

Portrait of
a Feminist
Sex Researcher

While the term male sexuality *conjures up powerful images of men's desire for women, the phrase* female sexuality *conjures up only visions of women's wombs and vaginas, graphic illustrations of women's reproductive systems as depicted in the sea of textbooks in the health section of the library or bookstore. But few female voices speak out to describe their pleasure,* to *define precisely what feels good and what does not. . . .*

—*Dalma Heyn*

I AM A WOMAN who loves sex, so I am going to start with my own story. Love of sex has moved me to experience many surprising relationships in my life. I'm not talking about sleeping around. Far from it. In terms of personal partnership, I'm what you might call a commitment bore.

Love of sex has led me into the profession of sexology, a discipline that includes sex therapy, education, research, and the more far-reaching study of how attitudes about sexuality affect the course of human behavior. So loving sex has expanded my universe by bringing me into contact with people and situations I would never have known had I loved, say, driving race cars or selling real estate. I have met teachers and students, colleagues, and clients, and once

Portrait of a Feminist Sex Researcher

I started writing, agents and editors. Most recently it's led me to the edges of the talk show circuit—the land of jokes and assumptions about what it takes to make women tick in bed.

Love of sex has even moved me to take a course in Empowerment Through Effective Public Speaking. I was so paralyzed with fear the first time I appeared on TV to talk about sex, actually my research on safe sex, that my brain seemed to turn to batter. I opened my mouth and smiled broadly. My eyes darted about, but no words came out. Years of therapy, self-help, and psychodrama had proved useless in counteracting those early messages that gripped my throat in public situations: *Nice girls don't. They don't even talk about it.*

The Effective Speaking program promised to change all this, and it did, but not in quite the way it promised. To illustrate one of the assigned weekly speeches—An Object I Use Frequently on My Job—I stood before the class and pulled out of my pocket one of the tools of my trade as a sex educator in this age of AIDS: a condom. To demonstrate its strength and resiliency, I blew it up until it was bigger than my head and bounced it smartly against the wooden podium. The instructor catapulted down the aisle, beating her ear with her clipboard and shrieking, "OH MY GOD, A CONDOM!" The hall full of students (mostly grandmotherly telephone operators and budding male executives) began to stamp and ululate like teenagers at a rock concert. I felt my voice expand to greet the din. I finished out my allotted two minutes with a flourish. A public speaking nightmare had finally occurred and it had not devastated me. To the contrary, it had energized me, even invested me with a measure of spontaneity and wit. My terror of standing up and speaking to strangers (about sex, anyway) has permanently disappeared.

Perhaps most consistently of all over the years, love of sex has impelled me to talk with women—hundreds of women, thousands if you count the brief, intense connections made

7

in conferences and workshops all over the country. I talk with these women in an attempt to understand how sex affects them. How sex touches their emotions, thoughts, and spirits, as well as bodies. How it permeates their pasts, presents, and futures; ranges back into the caverns of memory; reverberates in every facet of their relationships. These women tell me that sex is not a separate entity, but an integral part of their whole lives. Because of them, I no longer see sex as a specific set of physical behaviors. I now see sex in the round.

Finally, love of sex has brought me into a surprising relationship with myself. For me, sex has always been more than a thing of the body, although sensuous pleasure is crucial to my well-being as it is for many of the women who have talked with me. Strands of sexual imagery have braided themselves into my emotional life as causes for passion, rage, terror, longing, tears. Sexual images in many forms inhabit my mind and certainly my relational self: wishes, hopes, notions of beauty and fairness. Each time I take a step toward spiritual wholeness and intimacy, I recognize yet another connection with my sexual self.

It wasn't always so. I grew up in Back Bay Boston at the tail end of the Great Depression. "Banned in Boston" was the buzzword of the times, and as far as I could tell, sex had been banned there well before I was born. Looking back, it seems the closest the Bostonian WASPs who brought me up got to enjoying sex was joking about a night habit they had called *mothing*, where you walked down Beacon Street and peered into people's lighted windows to see what was going on. During my adolescence, I mothed diligently several nights a week on my way back from doing homework with my best friend, but there was never anything juicy to see. This left me knowing there must be something vital missing, not only behind those staid Beacon Street windows, but in my own life. I was possessed with an insatiable curiosity about what it might be, but I lived in a lonely household. My father, the handsome portrait painter, had long disappeared in quest of other women, and my mother was too ravaged to focus on anything but her own pain. So I learned never to ask about anything, especially sex, and it was not until years later that I developed the knack of asking. My own life unraveled when it began to replay my mother's. My husband began to have affairs, and in the excruciating process of searching for my own being amid the tangle of hurt and memory and rage, I discovered a profession that allowed me to ask all the questions I wanted. I became a psychotherapist.

My original training was in family therapy. As an intern sitting in on ten or fifteen intakes a week, I heard client after client voice concerns and confusions about their sexual relationships. I recognized the concerns and confusions because some of these were ones I shared in my own life. I especially shared concerns about what I now understand to be "disorders of desire," both the lethargic lack of sexual energy and its opposite, the outlandish lust that makes you act like a warthog in rutting season. But none of the therapists who were training me was able to deal directly with these clients about the sexual concerns they brought into the office—any more than my alcoholic, bipolar mother had been able to address the questions I'd wanted to ask or my husband had been able to tell me what had been missing from our marriage bed. I rushed to the family therapy literature for guidance. Sex wasn't even listed in the indexes of the books. I felt a mission coming on. I sought specialized training in sex therapy.

"Our Research Protocol Doesn't Include Females"— The Double Standard in Sexual Science

It was as a doctoral student in sexology in the late 1970s that I became acutely aware of the male bias in both sex therapy and research. I loved student life. It was exhilarating to be able to discuss sexual issues out loud. It was eye-opening to learn how sexual repression affected virtually the whole world, not just Back Bay Boston. But listening to experts (female as well as male) lecture on sexual politics and religion, medicine and law, and reviewing the literature on sexual attitudes and behaviors as they ranged over history and across cultures, I began to feel as if all this was somehow preprogrammed. I felt as if I was peering at the complex, flowing, ever-changing subject of sex through a kaleidoscope, one that focuses only on male genital needs and constructs. No matter which way I twisted and turned the material or faced it toward the light, the little pieces inside always seemed to reconstruct into the shape of a penis.

There was one incident in particular that jolted me into acknowledging the gender gap in the study of sex. An expert in animal behavior showed us laboratory films of how he had disturbed the social order in a macaque monkey troupe to create sexual dysfunction. No longer motivated to hump and cuddle at will, the formerly manic monkeys skulked in corners, isolated and ungroomed, knuckles dragging on the cement. How like home, I thought. How like the therapy room. Dysfunctional dynamics cause sexual dysfunction.

Then the animal expert went on to show us techniques for curing the dysfunction—in the male monkeys. Only the *male* monkeys? Women in the class became agitated: "What about the females? What did you do in the lab for them?"

"Nothing," he replied. "We don't know whether the females experienced sexual dysfunction or not. We don't know whether or not female macaques even come to orgasm. Our research protocol doesn't include females."

The animal expert's admission underscored what I was beginning to see was true of virtually all establishment sex research: It doesn't include females.[1] And even when it seems to, it doesn't really. I began to notice that there is a kind of old-boy/old-girl agreement among sex researchers that encourages a double standard based on *male* norms.

Moreover, the linear methods of scientific research seemed incompatible with the spherical, lyrical way women were telling me they experienced sex and lovemaking.

I came to a radical conclusion back in the '70s, a conclusion that still holds true today: Most sex research and much sex therapy actually oppresses women, that is, if it doesn't dismiss them entirely. This is especially true if women are not young, white, middle class, and squeaky-clean heterosexual. The so-called scientific study of sex is characterized by:

- Quantitative inquiry, mostly about dysfunction.
- Gender-loaded norms.
- Heterosexual norms.
- White, middle-class, able-bodied, youthful norms.
- Goal-oriented standards of satisfaction, especially the orgasm standard.

In short, mainstream sex research and therapy deal mainly with how often and how successfully young (but not too young), white, middle-class, able-bodied, heterosexual couples complete the act of intercourse. It consistently isolates sex as something separate, self-enclosed, physical, focused closely on a few magic inches of mucous membrane. It engenders those terms we all know well, like *foreplay*, *dysfunction*, and *achieving orgasm*, as if orgasm were an assault on Mount Everest, complete with ropes and pickaxes.

Establishment sexology presents a far narrower range of positive experience than women clients, friends, and colleagues have reported to me over the last twenty years. "What's most important about sex for me is a sense of connectedness" is the essence of what these women have told me. They say they cannot separate physical pleasure from their emotional feelings, their relationships, and their life situations, including their dreams and passions, fears and memories, needs, even their economic realities. And with this sense of connectedness comes release. In the words of Maya, friend and colleague, ecologist, philosopher, mother, and formidable aunt, who at the age of seventy has finally earned herself the title of Wisewoman, "Sexual ecstasy is a joy. It's letting go. That sphincter hold you have on life lets loose for a moment."

In the years when I was doing wall-to-wall therapy, it was hard to find sex-positive, *woman*-positive books I could recommend to clients. Only a handful of writers draw their basic information directly from women's experience, most notably, Betty Dodson (*Sex for One*), Shere Hite (*The Hite Report*), Lonnie Barbach (*For Yourself*, among her other books), Sheila Kitzinger (*Woman's Experience of Sex*), and, for lesbian clients, JoAnn Loulan (*Lesbian Sex* and *Lesbian Passion*).[2] But as I began to understand more of what women were telling me about their sexual experiences, I held the gender-sensitive kaleidoscope to these writers and found that even they sometimes reflected the male bias, not by focusing on pleasing men (all of these authors were obviously writing to empower women), but by basing their major premises on the mainstream definition of sex: Orgasm is queen, and it derives from stimulation that is physical, mainly genital. What's more, they tended to offer little emphasis on women connecting and integrating their sexual responses with the rest of their lives.

There is another curious twist within the positive literature on women's sexuality: a division between lesbians and heterosexuals, as if women are either frogs or toadstools, two separate species with no common sexual epistemology. Arbitrarily separating "the lesbian sexual experience" from the heterosexual one doesn't totally jibe with stories women have told me. It seems like a divide-and-conquer tactic, the kind that's been used throughout history to prevent women from forming powerful alliances with one another. The absurdity of sexual labeling was brought home to me recently as I was moderating a panel on *bi*sexuality. One of the speakers outlined how staunchly the general population (including the Senate Armed Services Committee) denies the existence of any sexual middle ground, and she even cited scientific studies that polarize avowed bisexual women as solidly ensconced *either/or*.[3]

Clearly, lesbian and heterosexual women have differences. For starters, they have chosen to love and make love with separate genders. Bisexual women are special in that they have chosen to relate sexually with both genders. But whatever the orientation, all of these women have distinct similarities. In the words of Maya again, "All of us are socialized as *girls* to grow up as *women*, and we're all born with the same kind of equipment between our legs—you know, that equipment Freud told us was unenviable." That is to say, we all have a particular load of girl–woman baggage about how we are supposed to relate and not relate sexually to women, men, and the universe. This holds true whether we are Catholic or Jew, African-American or Native American, Asian-American, Latina, or (Maya reminds me) Proper Bostonian.

But even beyond the biological imperative, I have found that whatever their orientation or cultural differences, there are similarities in how women who love sex talk about their positive sexual relationships. Call it energy, call it soul, call it mind–body connection, women who have talked with me seem to share a positive sexual core. These women have found direct access to their sexual selves, but they agree that there does not always seem to be adequate language to describe those selves with accuracy and detail and feeling.

"Sexual Pleasure Is the Enemy"— The Victim Standard in Politically Correct Feminism

In my greening as a feminist sexologist, there was another turning point. This one encouraged me to examine my own prejudices and to stay open to surprises. One April weekend in 1987 I attended two sexuality conferences. On the Saturday was an annual scientific meeting whose purpose was to present learned papers in the sex field. The male keynoter and president-elect of the organization announced to the membership that a feminist critique had no legitimate place in the scientific study of sex.[4] On Sunday, by contrast, was a rude and radical feminist conference that blasted the misogyny of scientific and liberal sex researchers, so aptly epitomized by the keynote speaker of the day before.[5] I don't know at which conference I felt most uncomfortable. After squirming through the pronouncements of the "liberal" scientist, I had looked forward to the feminist group as an antidote, an escape, or at least the sense that I was among kindred spirits. What I found on that Sunday, however, was not positive direction, but hard-boiled negativity. One speaker categorically maintained that all intercourse was rape. She was followed by another who spoke of sexual pleasure as the body's way of betraying a woman. Another characterized women as victims in *all* sexual encounters, therefore (she maintained) consent was meaningless as a sexual term. Heterosexuality was a trap. Men were the enemy in the war against women. And by association, sexual pleasure was an enemy, too. At this conference, it seemed as if sex negativity was almost a standard for satisfaction—antipleasure, antiorgasm, antiintimacy. There was a plethora of problems but no solutions. Tables in the hall were spread with a smorgasbord of pamphlets from organizations *against*—from Women Against Pornography to Women Against *Sex*.

I learned that even women dedicated to making the world a safe and empowering place for other women are not all-knowing, at least where sexuality is concerned. The women at this conference were superbly conscious of important issues like race, class, age, and ability. But in the course of battling patriarchy as the oppressor, it seemed that they had become pleasure police, turning with venom on sex as the oppressor. In the sorely needed effort to rid sex of its centuries of sexism, subordination, slavery, addiction, rape, battering, and incest and in the politicizing of women around these issues, I could see that something essential was being thrown out with the bathwater—many somethings: humor, play, comfort, softness, the transformative possibilities inherent in ecstatic sexual relationships.

Separating women from a basic source of energy and pleasure only serves to further discount and oppress. Certainly it makes it less possible for women to love sex. Certainly it confuses those who do. The hard-line, negative approach to sexuality is characterized by:

- "Politically correct" norms.
- Focus on violent and destructive aspects of sex.
- Denial of positive sexual possibilities.

In the dichotomies of this weekend of experts dictating women's sexual norms, I had seen a need for a dramatically new approach. I envisioned research that would help bridge the gaps between main-line sexology and hard-line feminism by shedding light on the full range of women's positive sexual responses. I envisioned research that would allow women to say what they felt about their own positive experiences rather than having these experiences interpreted for them by others with agendas. I envisioned research that listened to women rather than seeking to control them.

The Search for a Positive Direction

Even long before this crucial April weekend, it had become clear that my doctoral dissertation would involve interviews that allowed me to ask all the questions I ever wanted to ask women about their sexual responses, questions that remained unanswered, and even unasked, in science, feminism, porn, pulp, or pop.[6]

15

Specifically, I wanted to know how women who considered themselves to be sexually satisfied describe their *own* peak sexual experiences. What kinds of stimulation *really* turn women on? What are the basic ingredients of their peak experiences? Do women always need a partner or can they do it better themselves? How do women respond to touch? What kinds of touch? And where on their bodies besides their genitals? Do they need touch at all or can they be aroused by fantasy alone? How are their physical responses colored by their ideas, their feelings, their needs for meaning and connectedness? What about the vast spectrum of emotions and spiritual meanings, the variables so often left out of sex research entirely because they are unmeasurable by any yardstick scientists can recognize? What about imagination, love, romance, commitment, nurturing, intimacy? Is orgasm all it's cracked up to be? What *is* an orgasm anyway?

These were some of the questions. Who would I ask? I figured the obvious population to explore was women who love sex, for this group would be willing and able to shed light on the positive aspects of sexual experience. My interest was further piqued by the knowledge that women who love sex had never before been the subjects of serious sex research. To satisfy academic requirements, I chose the term *easily orgasmic women*. (Kinsey had used orgasm as a measure of sexual health and my dissertation committee was headed by Dr. Wardell Pomeroy, one of the authors of the *Kinsey Reports*.) Although *easily orgasmic* does not describe all the women in the world who love sex, I was only going to interview fifty, so I felt it would do just fine.

Where would I find a research population of fifty easily orgasmic women? I figured *everywhere* (this was 1980, before people knew about AIDS, before the pursuit of sexual pleasure had become a matter of illness and death as well as excitement and life). My original plan was to spend a few months traveling around the country talking with women I'd always wanted to meet—writers, artists, sociolo-

16

gists, sexologists—asking them hundreds of questions about their peak sexual experiences. Who would be able to resist such a request from an earnest doctoral candidate with highly developed interviewing skills?

But my travels got no further than a conference in Pitts-field, Massachusetts,[7] where I spoke on sexuality the spring just after I had passed my qualifying exams. I mentioned that I would be conducting two-hour interviews in the fall with women who identified themselves as easily reaching orgasm, both with masturbation and also with a partner. I invited the participation of anyone in the audience who felt she fit the description, expecting that a courageous few of the hundred or so women present would sidle down to the podium at the end of the talk to sign up. Instead, there was something like a stampede. When the dust had cleared, I had my entire research sample of fifty.[8] This one lecture had produced not a random sample, representative of the country as a whole, but a very convenient "convenience" sample, diverse in some ways, albeit limited in others. The women were housewives, mothers, teachers, nurses, writers, artists, executives, business owners, therapists, psychologists, doctors, cooks, restaurateurs. They were women in uncommitted relationships, married women who had had only one partner in all their lives and had never talked with anyone about their sexuality, and a former swinger who had had countless partners, male and female. White, middle class, and mostly professional, their ages ranging from twenty-four to seventy, these women were heterosexual, bisexual, lesbian. All of them considered themselves to be easily orgasmic—and thoroughly *normal*. And to their delight, and mine, they were willing to tell me their stories.

Equally important research underlying this book involves many more women than the Pittsfield fifty who stormed the podium to partake in the structured interviews in 1980. The stories of women who love sex range over a period of twenty years, from my early training until the present day. They come from a more diverse background than the original research sample, including women from seventeen U.S. states, three Canadian provinces, England, Ireland, Italy, and India; some women who are African-American, Native American, Latina; women who are working class; women who grew up in brutal families and others who were raised by virtual angels. Some women were clients, more were and are friends or colleagues. All of them wanted, like the Pittsfield women, to talk in depth about *their own* responses to sexual stimulation, not necessarily their partners' responses: "I want to tell you about me, so you'll write about it and tell others." One of the identifying features of women who love sex, it seems, is a willingness to share the wealth, to spread the good news so that other women can have positive information, too.

The process of gathering information has been scientific in the sense of seeking knowledge, but not in the sense of reducing it to numbers, except in a very few instances for purposes of startling comparison. The voices of authority in the book are the voices of the women themselves.

Some of these informal pieces of research are fresh in my mind. I can remember scenes from my sexology training that moved me to challenge the existing definitions in the first place. I remember Cynthia, a studious, no-nonsense Freudian therapist in her midforties. She attended a weekend massage workshop in the Berkshires and during the final session, she astounded a roomful of professional bodyworkers by coming quietly and gracefully to orgasm as the masseuse continued for several exquisitely protracted minutes to work not on any recognized erogenous zone, but on her left heel.

I remember Joanna, a young but determined nurse-practitioner in our doctoral study group who first demonstrated for me the powerful phenomenon of spontaneous orgasm. This occurred during another group massage-training session: An intense knot of sexology students hovered around Joanna as she exhibited for us the outward signs of full-body climax in response to no stimulation except for a surefire fantasy of her own making. In some awe, we watched her breathing quicken, her muscles tense, and her chest and neck glow rosy and bead with sweat. With a "Whoo-ee!" she let us know she was beginning to experience the vaginal and uterine spasms that heralded her orgasm.

I remember sitting in a San Francisco restaurant with other Ph.D. candidates in sexology eating spaghetti and talking shop. Elaine, Sylvia, Phyllis, and Marian had joined me for dinner. We ranged from our late thirties to early fifties, each of us with complex lives, growing children, and growing therapy practices. Even before our food arrived, we had noted with distress that with all of our combined life experiences of 223 years we still did not understand the parameters of orgasm. As we sought meaning, we found ourselves moving away from all those "objective" criteria, describing responses beyond the muscle spasms, flushed skin, and hot, heavy breathing. We told each other of flashing light and color. Of bonding with our partners. Of shifting planes of consciousness. We were laughing, crying, pouring out our own stories—whole-woman experiences that connected body, mind, heart, and soul. We found ourselves describing sexual ecstasy.

A very recent memory is set at the reedy edge of a Minnesotan lake almost at the headwaters of the Mississippi. It was a week-long camping experience. We were not to know it was going to rain for seven straight days, but right from the beginning the women voiced a need to gather on a regular basis. When they heard I was writing this book, they said, "Oh, good. Let's get together and talk about sex!" So each afternoon until the men and children descended to interrupt, we huddled on the screened porch of the old lodge and we talked. Mostly we talked about our bodies, probably in an attempt to keep them warm. We talked about body size and praised the goddess proportions of Avis and Marge, massive, comfortable women, both. We talked about the intelligence of the body: Maureen lay on the damp floor and showed us the stretches she practices even before she gets up each morning. Edith told us she had cancer. She wept tears of gratitude about her new husband, about how he touches and adores her body in spite of the disease, in spite of chemotherapy. Betsy is a minister, for whom sexuality is an integral part of her whole being: "I can't separate my body from my spirituality or any other part of me."

She helped us laugh about sexual guilt, *"Lutheran* guilt," she called it. All of the women on the porch groaned and tittered nervously.

"What's the difference between Lutheran guilt and Catholic guilt?" I asked. (I felt I understood something about Catholic guilt from having grown up in Boston. Whenever you were feeling anything sexual that meant you were impure.)

"I think Catholics have a lot more fun!" said Maureen with a little shimmy.

"They get to drink and have parties," said Marge, the goddess.

"Catholics can do whatever they want and then they go to confession and unload it all on the priest," said Edith. "We have to hold it all inside."

Betsy, the minister, offered the final word as we watched sheets of rain lashing the reeds at the lake's edge, "I guess you'd say Lutheran guilt is kind of like living in a Bergman movie." Her meaning was clear. Sexual guilt is a state of mind. If you can remove yourself from it, you don't have to take it seriously. Like a brooding cinematic image, it, too, can pass.

Toward a New Theory of Human Sexuality

My ongoing research was begun almost two decades ago, but the questions it addresses are far from out of date. Perhaps they are more relevant than ever as I write today. Despite the advances of sexual science and the women's health movement, there is still precious little information about the full range of women's sexual function. Even pop star Madonna with her stunningly frank, in-your-face photobook, *Sex*, portrays only the most physicalized aspect of erotic power.[9] As a participant in a recent workshop in rural Maine put it to me: "What I want to hear you talk about is the whole spectrum of women's sexual practices: How far out is far out and how constrained is constrained?"

The large-scale national sexual surveys from 1948 to 1993 have asked thousands of women hundreds of questions about what they do, when, how much, and with whom— from their age of first masturbation to the frequency of their extramarital affairs. These are authoritative tomes bursting with graphs, tables, and narrative analyses. The latest is *The Janus Report on Sexual Behavior*,[10] publicized as bringing the forty-year-old Kinsey statistics into the twenty-first century. What's missing? Why isn't all this enough to satisfy the curiosity of my down-Maine workshop participant? Aside from the *Hite Report* (which establishment sexual scientists have criticized for shoddy methodology), none of these surveys allows women the space to elaborate on what activities give them the most pleasure and why. None deals with the complexities of women's sexual relationships or dives deeply into the rich, murky areas of feelings and meanings. Not a single one of these panoramic surveys asks women to define what *they* mean by sex.

To ask relevant questions of women, first we have to reexamine what we mean when we say "human" sexuality. At least three sex researchers have already called for the necessity of redefinition from a woman's point of view.[11] Still, none has ever spelled out a definition of sex broad enough to allow for the whole spectrum of women's experience. Nor has any suggested a continuum of pleasures or a sexual response cycle that is more attuned to women's experience than the big-bang model popularized by Masters and Johnson. As a result, attitudes are still entrenched. I know this

21

because women still call me for therapy appointments saying they are desperately confused about their various "dysfunctions." A generation after the so-called sexual revolution, I am still listening to them sob that they must be abnormal freaks because they don't enjoy sex the "real" way, as coitus. In the enlightened '90s I am still hearing them accused (and self-accused) of the F word, frigidity, because they don't respond with lubrication and orgasm to partners who don't know how to make love to them.

A new take on sexuality can inform women like these that they don't have to continue to be victims—either by submitting to abuses or misdiagnoses or by letting sexual pleasure pass them by. Hearing how other women—women who *love* sex—relate to the sexual opportunities in their lives offers new models. I've witnessed it happening in groups and workshops where women talk and listen and begin to define their own experience. I know that there are active ways for women to respond to their sexual situations, strong ways, delightful ways. To women reading this book I say: Your sexuality belongs to *you*. This message is not original to me, but it deserves restating until it works its way deeply into the national consciousness. My hope is that today's winds of social change will allow it to travel a wide course and take hold at long last.

After listening to so many stories of women who love sex, I have begun to think that the medium itself may be a sufficient message. Perhaps in response to the questioner from the Maine workshop who wanted to hear about the whole spectrum, it may be enough to tell and listen without speculating about change. It may be enough simply to enjoy the stories of women who love sex. Enough to bear witness that women have experiences that warrant celebration as well as crisis intervention, that pleasure is not necessarily a plot of the patriarchy, that women's orgasms may be gifts from the Great Spirit and not part of a score like a slam dunk in a basketball game, that sensuous play can deliciously satisfy by itself and not always need to sandwich itself around a main event of intercourse, that sexual function can depart from textbook definitions and not be discounted as immature, immoral, or kinky.

As I continue to listen closely to interviewees and clients, colleagues and friends, I find myself looking at sex through a new kaleidoscope—a colorful women's one, with no two patterns coming up exactly alike. Yet taken together, there is an overall pattern to these women's stories, and it holds a crucial message for women and for the partners who love them: Sexual pleasure is good. More than good. It is life enlarging, particularly as women become more adept at exploring the vast arena that pleasure *is*. Sex is a source of energy that radiates beyond this or that randy encounter. Satisfaction leads to personal integration and rewarding relationships of all sorts. To celebrate the erotic, to feel motivated by satisfaction rather than by guilt and suffering, is a radical reframe for many women. It means women don't have to give up sex in order to be safe. It means they can orchestrate the positive instead of mustering all their energy to block sexual pain—danger, abuse, manipulation, inequality. It means shifting from control—the ability to say "No"—to power—the ability to say "Yes."

This is a benign kind of power, this active energy born of women who love sex. Seen through my newly found kaleidoscope, it doesn't aim to gobble men up. Rather, it means sharing responsibility for initiating, for setting goals, for enjoyment. Such sharing encourages compassion and love, and this is true whether your sexual partner is a man, a woman, or, for that matter, your own mind or your own hand. By taking this kind of power women may be able to narrow the gender gap. With sexual self-ownership comes voice. Dialogue can ensue. There can be a closer meeting of minds and bodies, hearts and souls.

What specifics have I learned from listening to these women who love sex? I have gained a number of system-shifting facts and insights. These have helped me reframe the story of human sexual interaction into a new story, from physical lust all the way to the tenderest intimacies.

Lust—Broadening the scope of sexual desire. The women who talked with me hardly ever mentioned physical stimulation alone as the most important route to sexual desire and arousal. Although the mainstream researchers' magnificent obsession is to catalog the exact kinds of physical stimulation, how much, how long, with whom, and so on, they have left out what may be most important to many women. The women who love sex said that the body's lust most often has to do with the feelings of connectedness in their relationships—heart to heart, soul to soul, even mind to mind. This degree of connectedness starts with a woman recognizing those connections within herself.

Satisfaction—Envisioning an alternative sexual response cycle. The women's descriptions of sexual satisfaction in their peak sexual experiences often went beyond the details of physiological orgasm as described by Masters and Johnson and other titans of the sex field.[12] The women who love sex did not report sexual satisfaction as a predictable, time-limited stereotypical event. They spoke of it as a flowing continuum of pleasure, orgasm, and ecstasy. For them, satisfaction was not a one-shot, two-dimensional occurrence. It was more often a four-dimensional experience affected by desires, partner involvement, and memory as well as the present moment.

Extragenital stimulation—Exploring the riches that lie beyond the vulva. The women in my dissertation study reported that 70% of their pleasure responses during the peak sexual experiences they described came from stimulation all over their bodies—fingers and toes, hips, lips, neck, and earlobes, as well as the genitals from clitoris to G spot. (The interview questions are on pp. 249–56, along with a chart of popular extragenital locations.) Perhaps even more

24

remarkable, 52% of these women affirmed that (like Cynthia, the no-nonsense therapist with the sensitive left heel) they were able to experience orgasm from extragenital stimulation alone, with no touching of the vulva. There is nothing in the sexological literature with which to compare these figures; extragenital orgasm is virtually unresearched in sexual science. Moved by the specter of AIDS, however, researchers, educators, and therapists are finally beginning to explore pleasures beyond the genitals. But true to the male bias in the sex field, these explorations are aimed more specifically toward heating up the experience for men than toward validating ways women can say yes to pleasures that are physically and emotionally safe.[13]

Spontaneous orgasm—Extending dimensions of the mind–body connection. Sixty-four percent of the women in the original research study said they were able to experience orgasm "spontaneously" without any physical touch at all, like Joanna, the nurse in our study group. This is an astounding figure, even if about a third of the women's orgasms were from so-called wet dreams and even if several of the women reported exercising a great deal of control over their waking and so-called spontaneous orgasms. This represents another almost unresearched area. The major mainstream statistics on spontaneous orgasm appear in the *Kinsey Report*,[14] which indicates that 2% of that sample of women could come to orgasm "on fantasy alone," and in *The Hite Report*,[15] which indicates 1%. Years after this study of easily orgasmic women, I collaborated on a laboratory project to determine the physiology of spontaneous orgasm.[16] Thereby hangs another tale in the life of a feminist sex researcher (see Chapter 5).

Sexual nurturing—Validating the sensuous possibilities in attachment and altruism. Arousal and satisfaction evolve not only from receiving sexual energy, but also from the lusty joy of stimulating one's partner. So say most of the women

25

with whom I have talked over the last twenty years about their positive sexual experiences with partners. Balancing their need to give with their need to receive was essential to their enjoyment of sex. In Chapter 6, Molly calls this balancing act "a dance of give and take." This notion of balance calls into question the well-publicized dichotomy between sexual assertiveness and the dreaded phrase *loving too much*. In the current self-help literature, these concepts are portrayed (indeed cartooned) as polar opposites: the aggressive dominatrix versus the self-effacing caretaker who services her partner without regard for her own needs.[17] But such labeling is simplistic if not downright pathologizing and blaming of women.[18] The women who talked with me were neither power-crazed monsters nor Pathetic Pearls. They were simply reporting the whole range of their ecstatic experiences without trying to categorize their responses or force them into rigid frameworks.

Sexual intimacy—Integrating romance, love, and commitment. Most of the women stated that warm, loving connections with themselves and with their partners were essential to and inseparable from the experience of sexual ecstasy even though the male medical model persists in seeing sex as separate from intimacy.[19] Specifically, these women said, these intimate connections provide the acceptance to help reevaluate crippling morality messages, the support to move beyond abusive memories and behaviors, the optimism to counter the dread of pleasure. Perhaps most significantly, sexual intimacy provided a sense of safety for the women with whom I talked. Although *safe sex* is a term usually associated with AIDS prevention, emotional and spiritual safety are also crucial to women. Without this safety, women remain armored in the relationships that are supposed to be the closest and find themselves disconnected even when they are most physically vulnerable to their sexual partners.

Portrait of a Feminist Sex Researcher
What's Normal?

The reports of the women in the research study, together with the variety of other women who love sex, have thrown into question some popular notions of sexual normality. These women may not represent all women the world over, but they do represent themselves and show that there are healthy women whose positive sexual experiences do not fit the norms commonly assigned to sex. And although fifty or even several hundred and fifty is a relatively small number, it has been sufficient to change my thinking permanently. As Kinsey and others have stated, one-on-one in-depth interviews provide an unparalleled opportunity for listening carefully to women and hearing the complexity of their responses.[20]

I have been moved over the years to ask just what it means when a behavior is called "sexual" for women. Does *sexual* mean genital? Coital? Physical? Orgasmic? In reporting overwhelmingly positive responses to extragenital stimulation, the women who love sex have led me to understand that the conventional view of sexuality is severely and needlessly limited. They have suggested that we can broaden our view of what is sexual to include a variety of stimulations that evoke responses of satisfaction whether or not the stimulations center on the vulva or lead to coitus or orgasm.

These reports have moved me to ask just what is meant for women by the terms *sexual desire* and *satisfaction*. What is meant by *sexual function* and *dysfunction*? Further, how—and by whom—are these defined and measured? In reporting a continuum of pleasure, orgasm, and ecstasy, the women have pointed out that physiological orgasm is too narrow a concept to hold as a criterion, or even the major criterion, of women's function and satisfaction. Women who love sex have suggested that we can broaden our definitions to include emotional and spiritual dimensions of the personality. They suggest that we can include the mind.

27

Their words bespeak the power of self-evaluation and self-definition rather than evaluation and definition by others—partners, doctors, or researchers. They suggest that we take some of the findings of sexual science with a massive grain of salt and that we discount the moralizing, nay-saying, maneuvering, and mixed messages embedded in the culture. Women are able to express and evaluate their own experiences of function and satisfaction without the sanction of outside experts.

Finally, and of prime importance, the responses voiced by these women who love sex have potential value for other women as information, as role-modeling, as power, as hope. Until there can be open dialogue across the genders, it is necessary to honor women's need to gather positive context from other women in the time-honored way: word of mouth. Perhaps when enough stories are told from enough points of view, critical mass will be reached. Women who love sex will become a norm.

These are extraordinary stories of ordinary women who are seeking new ways to look at sexual relationships, enjoy them more, and incorporate them into their everyday lives.

Let's listen as the women speak for themselves.

2

Alice

Lust and Connectedness

Sexuality offers us the opportunity to learn to move grace-fully between desire focused in intense body experience and desire infused with concern for the other.

—Judith V. Jordan

ALICE IS ONE of the clients who makes being a therapist both an honor and a delight. She walked into my office one day looking for help and by the time she walked out for the final time months later she had ended up teaching me as much as I had taught her. Maybe more. She appeared a number of years ago, just as I had completed the extraordinary interviews with the original fifty women who love sex. She was a research librarian searching for information about herself, and working with her helped me begin to channel the flood of interview information into an orderly flow of ideas. Alice's story is here because it exemplifies so clearly the distinctions between the disconnections that accompany low sexual desire and the feelings of connectedness that are crucial to developing ease with your sexuality.

Alice is a woman who loves sex, but she doesn't know it when I first meet her. Her presenting problem is that she is unable to experience sexual desire no matter how many

29

books she tries to read on the subject or how many hours she spends locked in her room with mood music and a vibrator. Moreover, lack of vaginal lubrication makes intercourse physically painful for her: "Sometimes it feels like I'm being sandpapered." She is seeking professional help for her desire problems because marital arguments are threatening to rock her bedroom door off its hinges.

Her opening words to me are the cry of a woman trying to save her marriage: "I've already been to sex therapy and it didn't work. I don't want to lose my husband just because it's no fun, you know, going to bed with him. We've been married nine years and I love him. We like living together. He's my security. He's my safety. And he's the father of my children."

Taking her at her word that this is a relationship worth fighting for, I ask what it is about the sex, and the former sex therapy, that hasn't worked.

Alice sits in the chair opposite mine, her head down and her face shaded by hair that hangs to her chin. She looks up briefly as she describes the Friday night coupling in bed that Frank requires. The set of her jaw and the darkness behind her pupils speak eloquently of her rage and humiliation. In a reedy little girl's voice, she complains of her lack of power to change the situation.

There is no detail of this coupling that Frank does not control (and in the next session he proudly corroborates her). "He likes the lights turned low, we have low lights. He likes me to wear black lace, I wear black lace. He likes consistency, we go at it every Friday night at eleven."

These obligatory interactions always begin with Frank fumbling to unhook the "Friday night bra" that contains Alice's breasts. Dependable as the Pony Express, neither rain, sleet, nor gloom of night can stay him from his appointed rounds.

Frank sets the rules, and sex for Alice means only one thing: intercourse, or "the Big I" as they have nicknamed it because it is difficult for either of them to say any explic-

30

itly sexual word without making a joke out of it. On further questioning, Alice affirms that before her marriage to Frank she had defied her Roman Catholic upbringing to try out sexual relationships with three other men. All of the sex had had the same focus: the Big I. Never in her thirty-eight years, before her marriage vows or after, has she stopped to think about what it is that she wants in bed let alone how she might enjoy going about getting it.

In one of our early sessions, Alice states, "All of my life men have been saying, 'This is the right way. Hurry up. You're on the wrong track.' And I've just this minute understood that that was because they operate like trains, going forward and back on a set track, and I've been trying to please them by staying on this single track even when it doesn't make any sense to me. I'm not like that. I think I'm more like a helicopter, which can go forward and back and sideways and up and down. My vision operates through 360 degrees. I want more than he does. I want more than the Big I. I want mobility and fun. I want a *relationship* in bed. I want to have the Big *R*."

The information from my interviews on peak sexual experiences is fresh in my mind. I think some of what the women have said can be of help to Alice. Like many clients who present with desire problems, Alice has had little practice talking about sexual feelings or even facts. There is a preadolescent innocence about her as if she has never quite joined the twentieth century, never read a woman's magazine, never fully participated in messages her body beams to her.

It is a joy for me to be able to cite the interview women not only as role models, but as experts. Perhaps most notably at first, talking about their experiences gives me a chance to use a variety of explicit words, cheerfully and casually. Alice can see for herself that when we converse about this taboo subject the ground does not open up and swallow us both. For instance, the women had told me exactly where on their bodies they liked to be touched; among other places, they mentioned fingers and toes and earlobes; lips, breasts, and nipples; clitoris and vagina. As I speak of these various body parts, Alice witnesses what for her is a startling phenomenon: absence of cataclysm. There is no thunderbolt from the heavens, the pictures do not even shake and rattle on the walls. She finally admits that the nuns in her parochial school must have been misinformed.

"But even so," Alice says, "hearing you say those words in such a normal, everyday way feels very strange."

Indeed, she is shaking. Her body is beginning to express what she is not yet able to put into words: a shaking off of her training that talking about sex is a venial sin, maybe a mortal one. She agrees that her body is also shaking off the belief that intercourse is all there is to sex: "In all my life and in every book I've read this is what happens. Now you're telling me it's possible for women to feel something else—all over their bodies?"

Equally groundbreaking to Alice is hearing that so many of the women had found emotional closeness to be essential to their enjoyment of their peak sexual encounters. The men who had dictated Alice's sexual experiences had left emotion out of the equation. From them she had learned that sex was a relentless dash for orgasm, no more, no less.

"You mean I'm not the only one!" she exclaims, beginning to lift her head from its perennial kowtow. "What I wish is that Frank would look at me and listen to me. I wish he would just lie around with me afterward with his arm around me and talk. I thought women who come to, you know, who get satisfied so easily, I thought these women would only be interested in the physical part—the way Frank wants me to be."

Alice is riveted by what several of the women had to say about training their ordinary partners to be great sexual partners. I relate to her the story of Rosemary, another woman brought up as a Roman Catholic, a woman who had loved sex enough to risk breaking some taboos of her own.

"Actually, I guess you could say I'm a *recovering* Catholic," Rosemary had offered during the interview. "When I first married Sean, he wouldn't look me in the eye or speak to me once we had our clothes off. It was absolutely weird. Like I was the Virgin Mary or something and he was so wound up with having to perform his marital duty thing with a holy icon.

"On our wedding night," Rosemary continued, "he actually got out of bed after we had sex and sacked himself out in the bathtub. I thought my world had come to an end. Here I was joined for life to this handsome person who changed personality in the dark. And the sex *hurt*. I'd waited my whole life for the magic moment and it *hurt*, and my husband of six hours was snoring away in the hotel *bathtub*.

"We got through the honeymoon by drinking a lot and spending hours on the beach *not* talking about *it*. But every night it was horrible again. He'd get tense and weird and I'd cry and we'd drink till we passed out. I mean I was excited by Sean in the daytime, but I couldn't imagine what it was that was so great about having sex. That first year I developed a lot of headaches and he spent a lot of nights out bowling with the guys. My mom tried to help. She said to keep hanging in there. But I thought, I don't want to end up like my mom—all martyred and looking so old at fifty.

"I realized here I was talking about all this with my mom over the ironing board, but I wasn't talking about it with Sean. So one night I just asked him not to go bowling. I'd bought a real trashy nightgown and I put it on and asked him to take a good long look. I wanted him to see me, see my body. And then I said, 'We've got to start talking.' And he was really grateful, because he'd been feeling terrible about it, too. He thought he was supposed to know how to do everything, and he felt like such a klutz. He *was* a klutz, but I loved him. I had really grown to love him in that first year despite it all. So I took off my trashy nightgown and said, 'Let me be your coach.'

33

"It turned out he was a real fast learner! And so was I. That was nineteen years ago, and we're still learning. You know what our nicknames are to this day? Coach. Sometimes the kids call us that, too. We tell them you can't make the people you love guess what you want, you just gotta tell them."

Rosemary's story seems to speak directly to Alice. That kind of direct communication is what she longs for with Frank. The idea that she might be able to intervene in their predictable pattern of Friday night coupling had never occurred to her. "Coaching. It's going to be like learning a new language," she remarks. "It seems like such a lot of work, such a struggle." A smile spreads over her face and her eyes brighten as if thunderheads are parting. "And the amazing thing is that when I say this I feel like laughing myself silly."

Alice understands that to begin a coaching career she will have to arrive at a more precise sense of her own sexual self. There will have to be a period of unlearning her old rigid notions (and Frank's Pony Express, goal-orientated notions) about what sex is supposed to be. As she had foreseen, the struggle is not all drudgery. Choosing from the banquet of possibilities suggested to her by Rosemary and the others in the interview sample and also by the how-to books she is reading with new eyes, she begins to reflect on her present lovemaking process in a constructive way. She is able to start separating out the parts that feel like pleasure and the parts that feel like pain. She finds, for instance, that Frank's unswerving commitment to her is a quality that moves her deeply, just as his driven, repetitive behavior enrages and bores her.

We begin with the positive, to build a base. I ask her to imagine actions that might feel like pleasure if she were ever able to experience them with Frank (perhaps during the intervals when he has to slow down for a moment to change horses).

"Tenderness and concern," she begins, clearing her

throat several times as if to dislodge whatever it is that is making her voice crack and yodel like an adolescent boy's. "I'd like to be able to talk about my feelings with him. Be alone in a room with him, calmly, without distractions or goals. Just be ordinary together."

These revelations surprise her because they seem to have so little to do with sex, or what she has learned to think of as sex. "What does just being quiet with Frank or having a conversation with him have to do with making me feel more like making love? Maybe I'm missing something."

Finding a Context for Sex

The possibility that there could be more to sex than she has ever experienced so far causes Alice to ask me a radical question one day: "Just what is sex anyway?"

What is sex? I look back on almost twenty years as a sex therapist and researcher, not to mention my own personal experiences, and I still cannot come up with a shining answer. Surely, there is no objective, scientific description of what women mean by really good, satisfying sex, the kind that melts both body and soul. There is no quantitative answer for the feelings, the connections, the explosions of memory bank. No way to measure the reverberations into women's daily lives.

To provide Alice with some kind of positive framework, I turn again to the role models and experts—women in the study who had spoken directly and authoritatively based on their own experiences and observations. Their stories suggest some of the individualized spectrum of desire women can have for sex, disparate views even, rather like blindfolded women describing an elephant. To get anything like a whole picture, you have to listen to a number of the descriptions and then finally put together a picture for yourself.

Women Who Love Sex

One of the women spoke of the quixotic nature of desire and of her own ability to generate it when she feels in tune with herself, as if her sexual energy has no barriers from the rest of her energy. Sondra was a young mother who had just quit her job to go back to school full time. When she talked, her voice was vibrant, reflecting her excitement about her life, her openness to the wonder of new experiences. Sondra's view of sex is far more than physical: "Sometimes I think sex is a state of mind, not skin contact. When I'm in the mood, *anything* is a turn on."

In contrast, another woman said her most ecstatic moments were marked by the sheer physical lust she felt at certain times with a boyfriend who kept reappearing in her life. "We were like alley cats, we couldn't get enough of each other," said Lois, swaying her body lushly as she spoke about a peak sexual experience that had occurred fifteen years earlier. "We have discussed the distinct possibility that we'll end up in the same retirement village and sweep each other right out of our wheelchairs."

Denise described yet another experience of sex. In a twelve-year committed relationship with another woman, she spoke of the emotional pull between her lover and herself as being far more compelling than the physical attraction. "We've been together so long I don't think it's just our bodies making love anymore. What we love so much is how perfectly we fit together. How we fit into each other's lives."

Gayle and her husband had recently taken on joint directorship of a peer counseling program in a college community. She spoke of sexual desire from yet another perspective: spiritual oneness and erasing artificial barriers between men and women. "Sex is a path to the deepest part of me. The part that's open to choice, to possibilities, to moving in any direction. All sorts of things come together for me through my sexuality. Feminism, worship, connection. I see myself embracing the whole universe gen-

36

derlessly. The spirituality of these times has to do with wholeness. Separation doesn't make sense."

As I talk with Alice, I realize that the women's stories keep coming back to a central concept: Sex is much more than intercourse. Sex is connection. Lust for sex is longing to bond with a partner and at the same time yearning to belong to your own self, body, mind, heart, and soul. A greed for "complete satiety," says poet Sharon Olds.[1]

In Alice's search to find answers to her question "What is sex?" she needs more than stories of individual women. To fully understand the differences between her lovemaking desires and Frank's, she needs to recognize just how incongruently women and men are socialized around sex. Now, ten years later, as I reflect on Alice and her question, I think of the relational model of therapy developed during the last decade by the Stone Center at Wellesley College. This model, with its emphasis on healthy interpersonal connection, puts into elegant, scholarly, positive language Alice's longing for the Big R.[2]

With all the clarity of hindsight, I wish I could have referred Alice to Dr. Judith Jordan's paper on desire and sexuality.[3] Jordan points out how the kind of bedroom roleplaying that characterizes Alice and Frank's rigid sex life typifies the different patterns of desire developed by men and women from childhood and adolescence. In Jordan's analysis, Frank's profound sense of sexual entitlement developed from an adolescent pressure for genital release. Alice's profound sense of sexual invalidation and lack of clarity about her wishes is a legacy of a childhood in which time and time again she was "talked out of" her own desires and yearnings.

Let me quote Jordan here, because I think she delicately explains the cultural influence that is at the heart of the condition sexologists grimly label *disorders of sexual desire*.[4] She writes: "Ashamed of their 'deficiency,' many women denied their own experience, adopted male norms or, not surprisingly, withdrew interest in sexuality and lost further touch with their desire. Thus, it is difficult for women to say, 'I want this.' "

Jordan systematically challenges the accepted model of sexual desire in our society that values independence based on individual power. What passes for lust, she points out, is the need for mastery, the need to use another person as a gratification object, like Frank's insistence on Alice dressing in black lace. Jordan proposes that for women desire is not one-sided, but interpersonal. It is the "empathic knowing of the other" that is crucial for full sexual expressiveness. In other words, it takes two to tango.

This is not to say that to feel sexual desire requires that women lock themselves into a codependent two-step with a partner. The relational theory of sexuality is rather a validation of Alice's wish for the Big R: relationship or, as Jordan puts it, the pleasure in being *a part of* rather than *apart from*. For women who love sex, lust, and connectedness are integral pieces of the same pie. The women in the study reported they often entered into sexual relationships through a lust for connectedness.

With these thoughts in mind, we can rename Alice's desire *disorders* as Frank's and Alice's desire *discrepancies*.[5] We can view them as an example of the way the majority of heterosexual couples have been socialized throughout history to respond sexually. Even allowing for a variety of class and ethnic differences, our culture maintains a climate for sexual *dis*connection, just as chaotic a climate as there was for the depressed, knuckle-dragging macaque monkeys in Chapter 1 whose social order had been disrupted expressly to create sexual dysfunction. Such disconnection results in a core of unacknowledged sexual self-denial and confusion for women and a core of knuckle-dragging performance anxiety for men. In short, Alice and Frank.

I believe there is a logic for the desire problems that brought Alice into therapy. Its roots are political and economic, and they go back to the predawn of history. The facts are hard to come by (as Elise Boulding has quipped, trying to study the history of women is like "sampling the invisible"[6]). Nonetheless, it is not hard to imagine that for women in all eras, sex has more often been an issue of survival than an issue of choice and pleasure. Like Alice, most women throughout history have had to depend on men for economic security, protection, and legitimacy. Like Frank, most men have called the shots in the bedroom (or the cave) as they have in other aspects of life.

Sexual ownership of women by their richer, stronger husbands and fathers, the power of men to destroy women whether or not they play by the rules, has turned much of the sexual history of women into a woeful document of displeasure and disembodiment. In the name of sex, women have been abducted, raped, beaten, footbound, and sold like cattle.[7] It is a miracle or perhaps a tribute to the raw power of sexual energy that there are any women at all who have survived to love sex and tell the tale. In every era, men, especially men in power positions, have been encouraged to sow wild oats. But women have had little sanction for acting out lust. We're all familiar with the message *nice girls don't,* meaning even at the dawn of the twenty-first century that if we want to be accepted in society, we'd better adhere to our set roles: virgin, wife, mother, celibate spinster, nun, helpmate.[8] These roles allow no freedom for rambunctious sexual play. By contrast, highly sexual women (or women imagined to be highly sexual) are known by their roles as outcasts: concubine, prostitute, witch, and rude-girl lesbian.

Melting Frozen Feelings and Moving Energy

Hearing this historical context helps Alice feel less isolated, less like the only woman in America to feel turned off and angry in bed even though she doesn't want to end her marriage. She begins to entertain a radical belief: "Maybe it's not my fault. Maybe I'm not a turned-off woman after all." Alice begins to voice the belief that maybe she is a lusty woman in a lackluster situation.

She gets mad. She gets madder. She becomes enraged.

First of all, her rage is about what she has missed. She begins by taking it out on herself. Self-rage is often safer for women than going chin to chin with the people who are tormenting them. Besides, it fits in with the worldview that women deserve to be blamed for whatever goes wrong in paradise.

"I feel so stupid for never suggesting that Frank touch me anywhere else." Alice gnashes her teeth and punches her right knee. I thrust a pillow onto her knee so she can punch without hurting herself.

"Imagine this pillow is you," I say. "Go ahead and hit it. Hit it as hard as you want." I am remembering a woman in a therapy group who had been severely abused as a child: Norah, a compact, athletic nursing student who spoke very little and when she did it was without seeming to move her lips. One of Norah's first actions of liberation from the hurt she had internalized was to feel her rage and begin to express it physically. Not yet ready to direct it at her terrifying father (the very idea of him was terrifying even in the relative safety of the therapy room), she turned on herself. In the group, she took off her studded belt and beat a pillow representing herself until there was nothing left but tiny squares of foam stuffing.

Because of the extent of Alice's disconnectedness and even numbness about sex, I strongly suspect a history of some kind of abuse. Such suspicions and hunches deserve attention and always pose a crucial choice point for me as a therapist. I am acutely aware that the power balance between therapist and client is analogous to the power balance between potential abuser and potential victim. What I mean is, that for me to suggest abuse might create an image of it in Alice's mind even though there had in fact been none. This is one way a well-meaning therapist can actually become a perpetrator. I prefer to wait for Alice to bring up her own memories.

Besides, before her full story can emerge, I know she has to get through the self-blaming part, just as Norah had to do in the group. It is not the moment to bring up the messages she might have received about sex as a little girl nor to search for traumas she might have experienced. Neither is it the time to examine Frank's participation in her desire problems nor the participation of the partners before Frank. Alice needs to express her feelings; she can fine-tune the object of them later. Is her lack of sexual desire a form of self-punishment? Now is not the time to stop and analyze. Better she rip into the pillow and get her energy moving.

But Alice balks and clenches her fists to her chest. "Why in the world are you asking me to hit this pillow? How is that going to make me feel better about going to bed with Frank?" A good sign: Alice isn't letting the therapist push her into something she doesn't understand. How we work this through can serve as a model for her communicating more clearly with Frank and holding her ground.

I describe how moving her muscles to hit the pillow might help to free up some of the sexual desire problems she is experiencing with Frank. The body has revealing stories to tell (I explain), but it is not always possible to access these stories just by talking about them. The discipline of bioenergetics has demonstrated that memories are held in the skeleton, the muscles, even the cells. These body memories are just as real—and just as powerful—as cognitive memories that are stored in the mind. Moreover, body memories go back to preverbal times, before we have learned to order the events in our lives sequentially and to talk about them. In addition, the body is a storehouse for memories that have been, for one reason or another, impossible to talk about or make order of, for instance, traumatic sexual events. The mind may forget, but the body never

41

does. Although some scholars dispute the validity of memory dredged from the depths of consciousness, my therapeutic experience is that these memories can lead in a direction of profound healing.[9]

"Oh," interjects Alice. "Is that why my back aches all the time? Is my back trying to give me a message?" She places her hand just below her left kidney.

"It could be," I respond. "If you're chronically tightening your buttock muscles, your back could be telling you they need to relax."

"You mean my back is telling me I'm being a tight-ass," Alice offers, grinning at me like a cat that has just discovered a platter of sushi. This is the first time she has named a body part below the waist and certainly the first slang I have heard her utter. Perhaps she is beginning to loosen up.

I tell Alice that I often notice her clenching cold, hard anger in her eyes, her jaw, and her fists, as well as her buttocks. I guess this means she is holding onto muscle memories. I also point out to her that for as long as she clenches those muscles in bed, it is impossible for her to be using those same muscles to reach out to Frank, impossible to experience a full rush of lust, or, as Reich called it, *orgone energy*, the excitement that builds to the release of orgasm.[10]

"In other words," I say to Alice, "you can't be both frozen and melting in the same moment of time. By holding back your anger, you're effectively holding back your potential for feeling sexual desire and expressing it. You may even be preventing yourself from lubricating, which is why intercourse feels like sandpaper instead of smooth and flowing."[11]

"So punching a pillow is going to shake loose those old memories that are stuck in my muscles?" Alice pulls the pillow back onto her knees. "OK," she says, "let's do it."

Here is eye contact. It is an agreement of understanding, not of capitulation. We are ready to get on with our work.

*   *   *

Lust and Connectedness

There are a number of sessions where I encourage Alice to physically move those muscles that hold the rage and the memory of rage. However, once her anger has been broached, she ceases being the cooperative, compliant little girl who had walked into my office that first day with her head down and her eyes hidden behind a shock of hair: "I don't want to hit pillows or talk to pillows or stamp around," she fires at me as she stamps petulantly around my office. "I want to feel better in bed. I don't want to be bored and turned off anymore."

"Great!" I encourage her. "Tell me that again! Say it louder! Go ahead and yell!"

Her first yell is barely more than a whine that seems to waver weakly from her sinuses. But she soon discovers the power of her full breath and the muscles of her diaphragm. Just as Norah had begun her healing through testing her strength, so Alice finds a whole repertoire of growls and yells that begin down in the belly below the diaphragm. And she finds that moving them feels good.

Sometimes we participate in an athletic tug of war with the offending pillow. She flings back her hair and glares at me, grunting, exercising arm and shoulder muscles that she has held so tense for so long. These are muscles that, given the impetus of sexual desire, will be the ones to reach out to touch, fondle, and appreciate her husband's flesh and her own. When her energy is alive and moving, Alice's eyes lose their murkiness and flash a clear and spacious gray-green.

As her muscles begin to loosen, her emotions begin to flow more freely. She stops automatically blaming herself for what is going wrong with her flow of desire. Once again, we use talk as the crucial medium for raising awareness. Toward the end of one therapy hour she asks me to describe again what it was that the women in the study said they loved about sex.

I repeat several women's stories, rather in the manner of favorite fairy tales, creating an array of images Alice can

43

choose from. I remind her of Rosemary who had coached her terrified husband, of Sondra, Lois, Denise, and Gayle, who had collectively described desire as a blending of body, mind, heart, and soul. I go on to relate some of the specifics these sex-loving women had mentioned in the interviews: the warm hands on buttocks; the sweet messages breathed into receptive ears; the trancelike, rhythmic body music of lovers passing energy back and forth.

"I love those things about sex, too," she blurts. "I love the tenderness and the holding and Frank's breath in my ear, and I love him complimenting me and I love how strong his arms are."

This extraordinary admission is followed by a rush of tears, deep tears that come from a place of agony. "I love these things about sex because I've never had them," she sobs. "Never felt them. These are all just words. They're faith. These are the things I'd love to love about sex."

Once Alice's frozen feelings of self-blame have begun to melt and spill over into positive longings, it is time to involve Frank in our discussions of her lackluster sexual desire. Although it is Alice who has initially made contact with me for therapy, she is not the only one responsible for their problems. Frank's mail-must-get-through approach to their sex life is a central issue. Frank will have to be an integral part of the solutions.

Couple Therapy and Developing Empathy

Two scenes stand out from the couple therapy with Alice and Frank. One is when I ask them to sit in each other's chairs, reverse roles, and play each other. Their task is to play out the dynamics of how their lovemaking negotiations usually begin. I point out that since they know each other's responses so well, they should have no trouble giving accurate details. Why do I ask them to do this? Alice and Frank have each been counting on the other's predictable responses to keep a stuck system firmly in place, and role reversal can sometimes dislodge an emotional logjam that has been immovable for years.[12]

Alice starts in with gusto. In her role play of Frank, she comes on as rigid, forceful, stern, dunning "Alice" for sex. As Frank, she demands him to wear black lace. Then, as she reaches out to fumble with the make-believe bra, she crumples into tears, which deepen to sobs, the kind that send a current down my spine. As a therapist, I have learned that sobs like these probably signal flashback memories.

When she can speak, Alice's voice is an octave lower than usual, clear and strong: "That was my father. My father did that to me. He used to come into my room and unbutton my pajama top and make me take down my bottoms and then he'd look at me. Just stand over me and look at me naked on the bed. I would lie there with my eyes closed. I was so cold. I never knew how long he stayed there or when he was gone. We never talked about it, and he died when I was twelve."

Here at last is the sexual trauma I had suspected in Alice's life, one that predated by many years Frank and his Friday night demands. Although Alice's "incest" had not been violent in nature, indeed barely even physical, it still had significant earmarks of sexual trauma. It had been a betrayal of trust, confusing and humiliating. It had been repeated. It had been a closely guarded secret. Recent research on incest and its effects indicates that traumatic events experienced in childhood can carry over to devastate a woman's adult sexual responses even if she has no cognitive memory of a trauma having occurred.[13] The official manual used by the psychological community identifies a condition labeled post-traumatic stress disorder (PTSD), that is, the stresses that remain after an original trauma is long gone.[14] What this means for Alice is that in addition to her present problems with sex and pleasure, she is suffering from a kind of emotional jetlag that affects her perception of sex and pleasure as an adult. Because of it, she has little control over some of her emotional and physiological responses. She is confusing past and present, pain and arousal, even preventing herself from lubricating appropriately.

Post-traumatic stress is often characterized by such perceptual telescoping. There are negative flashbacks that Norah from the therapy group had described like this: "When your partner is gently caressing you and whispering sweet nothings, your experience is total panic that your father's big, hairy penis is about to stuff itself into your mouth again." Once Norah had found her voice, she was able to speak eloquently about her situation. She was to reflect at the end of that therapy group: "Trauma is such a powerful teacher. It teaches us to disconnect from what we know so that we can live through the night."

Alice, too, learned to live through those nights of her father's visits and now the Friday nights with Frank by shutting herself down, turning off the knobs so that she didn't feel. By turning the knobs on once more so that she can finally feel the past, she is able to be more aware of her present feelings. An important part in her recovery of sexual awareness is to be played by Frank.

Frank's response is fully as spontaneous as Alice's role play has been. As Alice pours out the secret she has kept buried for almost thirty years, he holds her face in his hands and cries with her. The melting between them has begun.

With his tender reaching toward Alice, Frank's anxiety about sex seems to soften. He ceases to be Alice's adversary in the therapy room, arguing every point like a case lawyer. There are instances during subsequent sessions when he actively takes her part and I can feel them catch each other's eyes and smile. Sometimes, when they walk away from the office they are holding hands like teenagers. Alice reports that his headlong dash for the Friday night Big I and Big O has seemed to slow down and be less controlling.

The second remarkable scene comes about three months further into our work together. One day Alice stands up in the therapy office and asks for Frank's full attention. By this time, Frank is able to stop talking, look Alice in the eye, and listen actively to what she is saying.

"First of all," she explains to him, "you know I care about you. And you know I need you. I need your money and that kind of support. But I need your love and friendship even more. And you know I want to feel sexual toward you, but it's been so hard and now I realize why."

She tells Frank she now understands how shaken she had been by her father's weekly visitations. She describes the mixed messages, the confusion, the burden she had to carry. She was supposed to be both chaste and attractive all at once, a little girl and a substitute wife for her father.

She confesses a truth that had devastated her when she admitted it in an individual session: "I looked forward to my dad's visits. They made me feel special. As if it was my role to make him happy. That had somehow become my reason for living. You know, part of God's plan. And then my dad died. My role in the family changed—totally— overnight."

She relates how she had to be her mother's comforter and confidante while she herself had little comfort in return and absolutely no one to whom she could tell her own complicated secret. The secret had died with her father, who, after his heart attack, was canonized as a family saint.

She adds that at some deep, unaware level she had felt responsible for her father's death: "Maybe I should have been more welcoming to him. Kept my eyes open. Not let myself feel special. . . ."

She describes the heaviness of the guilt she had brought into the bedroom right from their wedding night: "I wanted you so much, but I was so scared that if I allowed myself to want you, you would have a heart attack and die, too."

Having come clean with Frank about her participation in their desire difficulties, she proceeds to outline what she sees as his part. "Please hear this, Frank. Really hear it. Every time you insist on having sex in the same way week after week, those old awful feelings come up for me, not desire to go to bed with you. But I'm not a cold woman. I'm warm and I'm sensual. And believe it or not, after all these years, I'm interested. I want you. The floodgates are opening, so watch out. But the way we go to bed together has got to change."

"What do you want us to do?" asks Frank.

Alice's tone becomes firm as she gathers herself to deliver her major pitch: "I don't care what we do together as long as it's different and it's not on Friday night!"

She presents a list of conditions that she hopes will make sex feel good to her—simple and to the point:

- No more dress-up.
- No more Friday night at eleven. We will vary the time of day, including mornings and weekends.
- You will look me in the eyes, not just look at my body.
- We will touch each other all over, not just on the homing sites.
- We will begin by telling each other how we feel.
- We will be spontaneous—even if we have to plan for it in advance!

This is Alice's recipe for lust. It is a testament to women's need for safety, power, and connectedness. It contains no mention of orgasm, no *Playgirl* centerfold. It is a cry for overall feeling and contact. Connectedness in relationship. The Big R. Not the Big I or the Big O.

This session is remarkable because it seems to be a rite of passage that marks the moment Alice puts away her last vestiges of powerless little-girl behavior and becomes a woman. It also signals the beginning of a new direction in the sexual relationship between Alice and Frank and the eventual ending of couple therapy.

Frank responds to Alice's request like the engineer that he is, weighing each point to see how the stresses might shift. Satisfied that what she has proposed has merit, he nods and says, "Well, let's see what we can do about that."

What they report over the next few weeks is not an instant cure. Alice is not suddenly moved to tear down cement walls to get to Frank's body nor does Frank become a perfectly sensitized lover. Frank and Alice report, instead, a gradual shift in the system.

Alice begins: "We went home and talked. We even talked about the idea of splitting up and trying to find new partners who were more like us. But the more we talked, the more I realized what a good person Frank is and how much I value him as a human being and the children's father. And then I thought to myself, If it's only the desire that's keeping us unhappy, maybe I don't have to be all that excited beforehand to enjoy sex. Maybe I can just relax and take it as it comes."

Frank continues: "And I thought, Why give up everything we've built together just so I can live out an old seduction fantasy that started when I was a teenager. I decided to listen to what Alice wanted. Touch her body and watch for her reactions."

But the path of growth is often a bumpy one. Just as Alice is beginning to let down her guard and trust in the sexual process, Frank, for the first time in his life, begins to experience an interruption in his formidable abilities to perform. He develops erectile problems. As his sexual demands are growing less and less rigid, there is a physical concomitant. His penis is growing less and less rigid during lovemaking: "I *think* I want to make love with Alice," he complains. "But I just can't seem to *will*, you know, an erection. And now every time I'm with her, I'm afraid I won't be able to, you know, get hard."

The focus of therapy turns to Frank.

His anxiety fills the room. It bubbles up through his engineer's facade, quickening his speech, even loosening his ever-present necktie. No longer able to generate his genital responses all by himself, Frank admits that he has to begin to let Alice close enough to affect him. Instead of *thinking* about sex, he has to begin to *feel* it.

"I'm scared," he says. "I'm scared to let anyone near enough to control me. I guess you could say I'm scared of intimacy."

Frank's story unfolds: "I was an army brat. My parents moved sixteen times before I went to college. I never had a chance to make friends, let alone have girlfriends. The one thing I ever wanted was stability, and now it looks like I'm messing up my marriage."

It becomes evident that the core issue is not erectile dysfunction. It is power. *Potency,* as distinct from *impotency.* As we continue to clarify the power dynamics, Frank's emotions surface more and more. In one session he cries the tears of a little boy powerless to keep his parents from uprooting him yet again.

Alice does what is most difficult for her. She allows Frank to feel his pain without intervening and trying to take it on herself. Nonetheless, she feels some of his agony: "It makes me want to hold him and comfort him," she says empathetically.

Their energy has ceased to be used mainly for self-protection. They have both developed compassion. And with compassion begins to come passion, the first moments of the inner fire that has been missing from their bedroom and from their lives. Frank describes reaching over to touch Alice's breasts in the night and her moving under his hands sinuously, "like a beautiful, slinking cat." He grins.

"Sex is something I look forward to now," reports Alice in one of our last sessions. "I look forward to our touching each other. I even look forward to taking off my clothes, as long as I can do it myself without somebody else messing around with the hooks and zippers." She shoots Frank a look and then smiles broadly: "I like our bodies to be naked together."

"There are still times I don't get erections," Frank remarks. "So we do something else. We take a bath together or trade rubs, you know, back rubs. And we're able to play more and laugh a lot. It feels kind of good to slow down. I guess sex is the one thing in life where speed doesn't get you a gold medal."

Alice and Frank spend the final weeks of therapy getting to know each other again in the light of their newly developing sexual habits. They grapple with memories and feelings. They learn to state their wishes. They find they can laugh at themselves and each other without losing dignity. They go away on a vacation without the children. Eventually they announce that they are ready to move out of therapy and into another plane of their relationship.

"What do you love about sex now?" I ask them in our last session.

Frank, wearing an open sportshirt, no necktie to strangle his responses: "There are no more games. Nothing hidden. Nothing covert. There's trust. I don't feel I have to keep things in control anymore. I know Alice will pay attention to me. I love Alice. The whole package, even when she's not wearing black lace. Even when she annoys me. Even when she says no. I like pleasing her." Here, he looks directly at Alice. "And I'll tell you, it's a relief to think about going to a movie or something every once in a while on a Friday night."

Alice, her gray-green eyes clear and focused: "I love sex because it's so new for me. Sometimes it feels greedy and scary. I love the closeness. It's been so many years coming. Sometimes the thought of going to bed together to make

51

love still feels like work, but when I curl up in Frank's body now I feel safe, as if I've come home."

I ask her to describe what sexual homecoming feels like to her.

"You mean tell you the details?" she asks.

"Go for it," I urge.

"Well, that feeling has to do with finally being able to open up to him—the whole length of his body—without always having to go further, you know, worrying it's always going to lead on to something else. It means lying up against him every night and curling my legs around his and reaching for his toes with mine. It means my head on his chest, breathing with him, holding his heart under my hand. I can relax with him now. That's what feels so much like home to me.

"You know, Frank never used to touch me unless he wanted that old Friday night routine. Now he has a way of touching me just if he's walking by my chair. And sometimes he kisses me for no reason at all. Sometimes he calls me from work. Or I'll find a message on the machine when I come home from a day at the library: 'Just don't forget that I love you,' he tells me."

She shifts her focus and speaks directly to Frank. "I look forward to the cuddling and comfort—and knowing you're there for me—for always. See, that's what makes me want you. I can't even imagine life without you now. Sometimes I wake up in the middle of the night and just look at you— the way we used to check Bobby and Hannah when they were small. It seems like such a miracle that there you are, next to me, that we're still together and able to be so close after all these years and all our troubles. And I love it that you talk to me now. That you can even cry. It makes me want to cry just sitting here thinking about it."

Alice dabs at her nose and sniffs. Not the quiet, ladylike sniffs she brought with her into the therapy room so many months ago, but spacious, sinus-clearing ones.

I ask her if there has been any time or event, something

she did or thought, that has seemed like a turning point for her, when she knew things were going to be different forever. I was mindful of stories other women who love sex had told me about ecstatic experiences that had changed their sexual perspectives and responses, their approach to their whole lives.

"For me, I think the big shift came last spring when we took that trip to Lancaster County, remember? The trip without the children. In Mennonite country with the buggies where we got lost on that farm road."

She starts to blush like a young girl and looks over to check out Frank's agreement to go on with the story. He smiles broadly in permission.

We were sightseeing in this incredibly conservative area where it looks like nobody ever goes out of their houses except to go to church or maybe sell bags of grain. It had just finished raining and the bottom of every field was covered in a white mist. The hills were greener than green. There was nobody on the road but us. It felt kind of like Brigadoon, you know, like some kind of magical island, floating.

We were pretty lost and Frank turned the car into a dirt lane. It was called the Farmer's Way. I know that because I was the navigator; we had this detailed survey map he'd gotten for us.

Suddenly he stopped the car. We'd just passed by this farmhouse and I was still reading the map and trying to figure out a shortcut. I guess I actually initiated what happened; I probably had the map in one hand and the other on his knee. I looked up and there was his face, just like that, next to mine, and he was looking at me so intently, and he started stroking my hair and cheek and his hand found this place on the back of my neck that was very, very sensitive.

I have to tell you, I was taken by complete surprise. I thought, This is not the Frank I know. To tell you the

53

truth, I wasn't quite sure what was going on at that point. The suddenness of it—the surprise—it took my breath away. I was gasping. And feeling things I'd never felt before. And I thought, Well, if this is what I've been missing all my life, I'm just going to relax and enjoy it.

I reached up and started to kiss him. What a difference when I began to move instead of just lying there waiting for the inevitable to happen.

This was the first time in my whole life I'd ever felt sensations like that. I wanted to inhale him. He tasted so warm and so, well, wild all at the same time. It was as if my mouth and tongue were drunk on him. I couldn't stop and I couldn't get enough. I was actually panting and drooling. I found myself grabbing his hair and pulling his head down so hard I thought his beard might scrape my skin away. But it felt so good I kept pulling harder and wanting more. Then in the next minute we were just as gentle with each other as if we were dancing to violins. I never knew there were so many different moods a kiss could go through.

Then in the middle of all that, there it was in my hand. His penis—growing—as if I'd picked a flower. Except it was warmer than a flower and so alive. You know, I never knew what one really felt like. Can you believe I'd never touched Frank in all our years together?

Knowing Alice, the research librarian and sheltered wife with her strict Catholic upbringing and her heavy loads of personal fear, this degree of sexual innocence is something I can well understand. I look over at Frank and he is beaming like a lottery winner. I encourage her to go on.

I realized even when it's hard it's so soft. Soft and, well, silky to the touch. My heart opened up to it. I felt I wanted to make up to it for all those years of not noticing. I didn't want it to feel alone anymore. I leaned down and began to kiss it. It tasted warm and sweet and salty

Lust and Connectedness

to my tongue—kind of nourishing, when you think about it. I'd never done such a thing before. It was as if I'd finally lost my virginity, after two children and how many years of marriage? Maybe the place truly was enchanted. It seemed we were both acting in completely new ways.

Then I realized we'd somehow lost most of our clothes! They must have come off bit by bit as if by magic. Mind you, here we were in a place where I'm sure it was a sin for a husband and wife to undress in front of each other. My shoes were behind me in the back seat, Frank's pants were down around his knees. My sweater was suddenly in a soft ball behind my head. Everything seemed to be swirling around like the mist in the fields. Then the seat seemed to lower itself into a bed. For a queen, I thought. For me—I am queen of this magical isle. I must have been really into it by then.

Alice turns in her chair and laughs, catching Frank's eyes again. Frank is still grinning his megabucks grin.

By then it was all in slow motion. He climbed on top of me, though looking back, it seems impossible—it's only a small car, a little VW Fox. I had no idea Frank was so athletic. Somehow he managed to fold his legs in under the dashboard so that his head was right up here (she places both hands on her breasts). I used to resent all that time he spent at the health club. But if it keeps him in good shape like that, I won't resent it nearly so much anymore.

And I had no idea I was so agile, able to move my legs in unusual positions. I was doing all kinds of things while he was kissing me up there—completely hugging his body with my legs, enfolding him. I felt like one of those women in a Chinese print, you know.

Alice as a kimonoed concubine is a stretch for my imagination. Yet as she describes the scene—the urgency of de-

55

sire, the soft palette of textures and colors, the grace of motion—I can see similarities. A major difference (I think to myself) is that Alice's feet weren't bound. Even in the confines of a compact car and the heat of passion, Alice and Frank were playing out a way of relating together that gave choice and freedom to them both.

You know what's so amazing? I never once thought about that dumb bra Frank used to want me to put on all the time or what my underwear looked like—whether it was lacy enough for him or not. It was all so spontaneous, I don't think either of us really knew exactly what it was we were doing until a string of those black buggies came clip-clopping by and we suddenly remembered we were parked right next to a Mennonite farm where this sort of thing is, well, it's just not done. We started giggling like teenagers caught necking by the police. Frank was still on top of me. He couldn't move; I was gripping him with my thighs. We sort of clutched for our clothes. I pulled his jacket over part of us and he grabbed for something; it turned out to be my slip which ended up over his head.

Then suddenly it wasn't funny anymore. My eyes were still shut, but I could imagine exactly what was out there. In every window of the car there were going to be men leering at us. Standing there, watching and leering. Stern men with beards.

Oh, the vulnerability of abused women. At the instant that she is finally enjoying her first, tenuous unfoldings of excitement, Alice faces yet another reenactment of her childhood trauma. This ring of bearded elders could knock her capacity for sexual desire back into hiding for another thirty years.

Frank must have understood what I was going through. He stroked my face and whispered, "It's OK, you can open your eyes." When I got up the courage, I couldn't believe what I saw. Nobody was looking in, and if they had been, they couldn't have seen anything. The inside of the car was completely steamed up. We were making such body heat and breathing so hard with all our exertions that there was nothing but fog. The buggies had driven on down the road. We'd been carrying on right under their noses in total privacy!

The scene Alice describes is stunning to me. If I'd been a sorcerer, I couldn't have conjured up a more healing incident. In a single afternoon's roadside romp, she had experienced newborn lust and disenfranchised old family ghosts. She could now view sexual desire as her ally, safe as well as exciting. This experience had created its own curtain of steam that vaporized invaders, present and past.

I ask her what she has learned from this episode.

"Maybe that we're beyond romance. Romance is when things are perfect. It's when the toast doesn't burn and the eggs don't stick and the kids don't need braces on their teeth. We've been together too long for that kind of romance. We're beyond romance, but we're not too old to play. After the buggies went by, Frank got out and picked a bouquet of wildflowers for me. Can you believe I still have the buttercup he held under my chin? I guess I learned I can feel like a teenager and a grown woman, too.

"I learned I can want Frank. I learned I can flirt with him and that he knows how to pay attention to me, not just to what I'm wearing. I learned I don't have to control everything. That I like to be surprised. Whenever I go for a drive now, I remember. Just the smell of the car is enough to do it. There's Frank with my slip on his head looking like one of the nuns in school. I laugh. I get excited. I just can't be timid around him anymore."

There is silence in the therapy room when Alice finishes. Her story, in all its directness, feels like a gift to be appreciated for a long while. It is a testimony to planned spontaneity, to the casting out of stultifying rules, to the return of desire. It is a testimony to the healing properties of lust when it is infused with concern for the other. With this trip to Brigadoon via Lancaster County, it seems that the tenderness taboo between Alice and Frank is finally, irreparably, broken.

Alice has kept in touch over the years by writing me periodic notes. In these notes she has spoken of the therapy as an initiation ceremony in which she had been able to visualize a new future. Memories of satisfying sex—like the caper just described—are now replacing most of her old tapes of abuse and fear. Her last report stated, ". . . more happiness than we had ever felt possible, and still deepening, even in the bedroom."

Where Desire and Relationship Meet— Reframing Sexual Function

The therapy sessions with Alice were completed ten years ago, but the problems of desire with which she presented are just as relevant for women today. They are especially relevant for women whose sexual responses have suffered because of some kind of abuse. As I work increasingly with women who have been incested, raped, and otherwise brutalized, I find that healing their sexuality may be crucial to healing the rest of what is out of joint in their lives. For some women, it is the final piece of the puzzle, the last frontier.

Using a relational model as a clinical basis for dealing with the desire problems Alice brought into therapy departs from standard sex therapy, which focuses on specific goals in the bedroom, like more frequent orgasms and more enjoyment of intercourse. But I knew from Alice's first session that standard sex therapy had not been a good match with her—she had reported up front that a prescribed daily hour of so-called self-pleasuring had done nothing to move her toward sexual enjoyment.

In my experience over the years, I have found that standard treatment does not speak to all of the women who have come into my office. Even before I met Alice, I had become increasingly uncomfortable with the technical aspects of sex therapy. My discomfort stemmed from the stereotypical formulas that are supposed to differentiate sexual function from sexual dysfunction. The bottom line is that a "functional" woman is one who can successfully complete the act of intercourse with a man; a "dysfunctional" woman cannot.[15]

For instance, it is standard sex therapy to teach women how to "achieve" orgasm through at-home genital stimulation and how to "overcome" disorders of desire through behavior modification and homeplay (never home*work*), like the mood music and vibrator sessions Alice had been assigned.[16] These techniques aim to render women sexually functional, and often they do as long as a woman has an uncomplicated history and her goal is to complete the act of intercourse and experience vaginal spasms at more or less the same time.

But these techniques can exacerbate women's sexual problems as well as help them. Clearly they were not helping Alice. By emphasizing a woman's "adjustment," therapists may be acting out the male medical bias in the sexuality literature rather than acting in the personal interests of the woman. This forces a Procrustean solution. Just as the villainous Procrustes chopped or stretched unsuspecting visitors to fit his guest bed, sex therapy may be altering the woman rather than using her experience to extend the parameters of human sexuality. Standard sex therapy may also be encouraging an unequal partner dynamic. To have coached Alice in techniques to accommodate Frank's anxiety and neediness would have been to suggest, in effect, that he remain on top of her in perpetual missionary position.

I have found, in fact, that standard sex therapy causes some women to feel and act even more turned off, even more confused. To teach women how to use fantasy to disconnect from their memories and feelings does not necessarily empower them, especially those women who are suffering from any degree of dissociative disorder as a response to abuse. Nor does it necessarily improve women's lives to teach them how to alter their parasympathetic responses—to relax and lubricate—so that they can tolerate the kinds of stimulation and penetration that the literature labels sexual. In terms of Frank and Alice, it is as if the Pony Express is not considering the health of the pony. *The mail must get through.*

Long after Alice's therapy, her question continued to haunt me. What *is* sex? As the interview material had helped Alice see more and more possibilities, she had freed up layer upon layer of her own connectedness. I felt that what had been true for Alice might also be true for other women, even women from different economic, racial, and ethnic backgrounds.

I began to picture a way of thinking about sex and relationships that included a woman's point of view and also a process point of view, a way of thinking that does not depend on goals, norms, and measurements. Suddenly I had hopped off the one-track sexology train and into Alice's four-dimensional helicopter, maneuverable in every direction including memory. With four-dimensional vision I began to see a picture of sexuality that is uniquely women's. Not a glossy centerfold or a diagram of disembodied genitalia, but more a map of the dynamics. How sex connects with the rest of women's lives.

What is sex? According to the women who love it, it includes all of our senses, and it also includes how we think and put information together, how we feel about what is happening and what it all means to us. If a partner is involved, it includes how we respond to our partner's sensations, thoughts, emotions, and meanings. Moreover, our sexual relationships occur in time, a time present that includes both time past and time future—memories and dreams, terrors, anxieties, hopes, anticipations.

What is sex? It has become clear to me that if sex is healthy, it feels good—whether or not it is genital and whether or not it has the official stamp of orgasm on it. It stems from balanced relationships with oneself, with a partner, with a whole coordinated team of factors in one's life and the universe. Conversely, rotten sex feels bad or makes life beyond the bedroom feel bad. It stems from imbalance. How can a woman have a delightful sexual experience, for instance, when her primary sexual relationship is with an unbidden ghost—in Alice's case, an ogling, dead, and sainted father? Yet it is possible for Alice and other women to put these ghosts into enough perspective to allow another primary (and chosen) partner to move in close. It is possible to create lust from connectedness. And connectedness can certainly grow from lust.

For women, sexual function is more than a set of actions, more than the physiological events scientists know how to measure in the laboratory. It is more than turning on to incense, feathers, and cucumbers. It is more than what happens Friday night at eleven after the children are asleep. It is a function of women's whole *lives*.

Women's sexual pleasure has to do with openness and connection and growth fully as much as it does with measurable specifics of physiology, such as genital touch, arousal, and the spasms of orgasm. Think about it for a moment. In the heat of passion do you find yourself stopping to count your muscle spasms or take your pulse rate? Not if you're like the women who have talked with me.

Take Naomi. She is typical of the other women in the interviews and also of the many other women who have spoken with me over the years about their sexuality. When asked what details she remembered about her peak sexual experiences, her observations were decidedly subjective rather than objective: "Well, I remember *living* those details, not *measuring* them." Naomi couldn't tell me exactly how long her orgasms lasted, but she could recount with utmost clarity how they felt: "As if I had been invested with some pulsing sea creature, alive and wild and glowing with brilliant blue light." Naomi couldn't tell me the exact number of breaths she was taking per minute during arousal, but she could describe, as if she were still there, how hot she was, how active, how released, how loving, and how loved. "What I remember most is my partner's tenderness and smell and how we laughed. We were both so open and silly. There was moonlight filtering through the hairs on our wrists."

Naomi and the other women who talked with me about sexual ecstasy reported total concentration on what felt good. They reported daring to be vulnerable to a partner and also to themselves. They reported bonding. They reported deep sexual satisfaction as a sense of waking up from a trance that surrounded their daily routines. They noted greater enthusiasm, more attention for their children, more creativity on their jobs, more zest for living—one of the earmarks, according to Jean Baker Miller, of that illusory concept called health.[17]

These women were reporting an energetic definition of sex that moves beyond the bedroom, beyond their temporary responses, to touch every aspect of their lives.

Alice's story is not all there is to say about sexual desire and sexual connectedness for women. Each woman's story is special. There are details of Alice's story that would be dramatically different were Frank alcoholic or physically violent or if Alice were Jewish or African-American or Latina or Asian or Native American with another set of culture-bred rules about her role in his life. Or were she stuck with Frank against her will for reasons of economic survival. Details would be different if Alice were lesbian or infected with HIV. But Alice's story is a start. Even though she is a woman of relative privilege, at least privileged enough to be able to locate and afford therapy, she is none-theless a victim of cultural oppression. She was victimized as a child, and as an adult she was encouraged to become a willing volunteer, contributing to her own lack of sexual luster. That she reaches out for therapy doesn't mean that she is crazy or at fault. That she heals and changes doesn't imply permission for the abuses that abound at every level of society.[18]

The moral of Alice's story is that to regain our zest for sex we first have to listen to ourselves, present, past, and future. Then we have to understand which knobs we have turned off for the sake of survival or for propriety, which may be another level of survival, or because we simply didn't know any other way. Then we have to learn to sur-render. Not surrender to an ogling father or the wishes of a rigid partner. Not the kind of surrender that means giving up. The kind of surrender that means *giving in*. Giving in to our memories, our outrages, our hungers for pleasure. Giving in to our desires and asking for what we want from a partner who is willing to hear.

What is sex? For Alice and some of the other women who love it, perhaps sex boils down to courage and a capacity for surprise. Because when a woman has the courage to open up those deep, vulnerable layers of her being and to speak truth in her relationship, there's no telling what that may lead her to next.

3
Maya

Pleasure, Orgasm, and Ecstasy

Real satisfaction is not enshrined in a tiny cluster of nerves but in the sexual involvement of the whole person. . . . Women must hold out not just for orgasm but for ecstasy.
—Germaine Greer

I MET MAYA at a workshop in the Berkshires in December 1978 on the night of a full and frosty moon. She was, and now in her seventieth year still is, one of the most sex-loving women I know. Sex loving in the sense of welcoming joy in all her senses. On a scarf around her waist that night she sported a brass pendant that spelled in cutout letters: TO HELL WITH HAPPINESS I WANT ECSTASY.

It was the kind of workshop where the procedure was to stand up and announce your sexual orientation. (This was still the 1970s; nowadays in groups, people announce their addictions.) We did the rounds of the room: "I'm heterosexual through and through." "I'm a full-blooded lesbian." "I'm bisexual—a 3 on the Kinsey scale."[1] When Maya stood to be counted, to the delight of all, she called out loud and proud, "I'm *tri*sexual—I'll try anything."

Maya and I became immediate friends and colleagues, a

64

bond that has remained through her move to a mountain-top on the West Coast and mine to the East Coast city of Cambridge, Massachusetts. Once every year or so, I visit her in her crystal-hung aerie with its 360-degree outlook over the sensuous California landscape. We sip juice and talk about hills and sky and our ongoing research on women's sexuality—mine as a therapist and author, Maya's as a former therapist and now as a philosopher and healer with a sense of humor. With Maya I can always be assured of the big view, the generous vision.

On this trip I resolve to ask her to help me make sense of some ideas precipitated by talking with Alice and other women who love sex. Were these ideas outlandish? Or were they eminently sensible, even groundbreaking? Who knew? There has been so little research focusing on how women perceive pleasurable sexual feelings that the ideas still felt slippery. I was unsure of how to assess them.

What I did know is that when women described their peak sexual experiences, the language they used was quite unlike the language in the sexuality literature. The words may not have been so dramatically different, but the emphasis, the images they evoked, invited an entirely new look at the concept of sexual satisfaction.

The women had spoken of their sexual responses not as predictable treadmills of physiological cause and effect, but as flowing sequences of perceptions that shift and change and overlap. They had spoken of sexual satisfaction as complex and relative, as a constellation of factors that touches their whole lives rather than as a specialized, time-limited, physical something that occurs under the covers in bed and then—zap!—is over. As I listened to the words *ecstasy, pleasure*, and *orgasm* braid themselves over and over again through their conversations, I realized that these women were talking about states of sexual being—processes, actually—that were undeniably distinctive yet just as undeniably connected to one another.

They were describing a continuum of sexual response. Of

65

pleasure (the awareness of heightened sensation and all-over well-being), of orgasm (the experience of physical, emotional, and spiritual release), and of ecstasy (the altering of consciousness that informs a peak sexual encounter and may last long beyond it to alter the course of a woman's life.)

I had never heard anything like such a continuum articulated in scientific terms or in any other terms for that matter. My mind raced with questions: What is this pleasure–orgasm–ecstasy continuum? How does it play itself out in the experience of women who love sex? How do these women think and talk about what they experience? For it is in the thinking and talking (the "re-membering" as feminist theologian Mary Daly calls it)[2] that we name the experiences, *own* them, invest them with meaning beyond the moment. This is how traditions develop. Myths, if you will. So far, the myths about what women like in bed have been habitually determined by men.

When I arrive, Maya says she has a surprise for me. She leads me out onto the deck and introduces me to her nieces, who are visiting from Wisconsin. I have heard about them both for years. Maya had all but adopted them when her own daughters were grown, and it seems that they are a challenging mixture of rock-solid work ethic from having been raised on a dairy farm and free-spirited sense of adventure from having spent vacations on the West Coast with Maya. Lorie is thirty-two, a bookkeeper, and just engaged to be married. She proudly displays her ring, a tiny diamond set in a delicate gold band. Jan is a graduate student in women's studies. She wears shorts and a tank top and looks much as I imagine Maya must have looked at age twenty-six: light, slight, with quick, purposeful movements, like a deer. I am delighted they are present. For one thing, their voices will help bridge the age gap in our talks. Now we will span three generations—Maya's and theirs with mine somewhat in between.

Pleasure, Orgasm, and Ecstasy

"That is, if you're interested in talking about sex and pleasure and all that," I add, offering them a way out.

"Are you kidding?" Lorie grins at me. "I'm the one who's about to be married, you know. I can use all the advice I can get!"

Jan piggybacks on Lorie's comment: "This isn't such a totally big deal if that's what you mean. Auntie M, well, she was the one we always came to when we had any questions."

I like that they call Maya Auntie M. It adds a homelike, Midwestern quality to her character as well as an Ozlike quality to the afternoon.

"So, then. Let's just take it from the top," I begin, outlining my need for a reality check of my new concepts. "How do good sexual feelings work in women's lives? How do women put the information together? What does sexual satisfaction actually *mean* for women?" I remember Maya's pendant that proclaimed TO HELL WITH HAPPINESS. . . . "Is sexual ecstasy something special?" I look at each one of them. "Is it more complete and powerful than pleasure? Or orgasm? Or is it just part of the whole picture?"

"Yes, certainly, all those things," answers Maya with her quirky little smile as she sits sunning herself crosslegged on a canvas chair. "Ecstasy includes all those things. The problem is, we don't have a way to talk about it that says what it really is." She winks at her nieces, who are giggling, but who make no move to dispute her statement.

Even though Lorie and Jan have bravely offered to contribute to my research, I am acutely aware of how skittish they are acting and note that it's not easy for most women to carry on a conversation about sexual satisfaction and ecstasy whether they are seventy or twenty-six. There doesn't seem to be adequate language. The language of science doesn't offer women an expansive syntax; it reduces sexual function and satisfaction to a few inches of mucous membrane. "The language of therapy explores what's wrong with women, not what's right," Maya points out.

Lorie adds, "Our mom taught us a lot of things, but she never told us about any language of pleasure."

"Most moms don't," I find myself responding somewhat defensively, remembering chances I had missed with my own daughter. "They're too busy trying to protect their little girls from being hurt or provide them with survival skills."

"Come on, wasn't there some kind of stock advice mothers used to give Victorian brides on their wedding nights?" asks Jan, the women's studies student. "I got it—this one's for you, Lorie—it goes 'Just close your eyes and think of England!'" Although Jan may be somewhat giggly about the subject matter, I realize she has read a great deal and has much to offer, including her youthful perspective. And like Maya, she is blessed with a sense of humor.

Maya breaks in: "Speaking of language, women don't even have a sexy locker room banter. Certainly it can't compare with those scoring rituals the boys have after the game is over. So—" she focuses on me, warming to her subject now—"you're looking for the words women use to express what happens outside and inside of us. All that feeling that carries over into power and changes our lives. To express the aftershocks, the incredible reverberations, that connect us to the universe."

"That's pretty spacy stuff, Auntie M," says Jan, helping herself to a glass of apricot juice.

Lorie elbows her sister. "Hey, let's listen; we might learn something."

Maya plows ahead, smiling benignly at her girls, as she fondly calls them. "Shall we say we're searching for the ecstasy connection?"

The Ecstasy Connection—
An Alternative Sexual Response Cycle

It's a spacy phrase, perhaps, as Jan is quick to point out. But "ecstasy connection" nonetheless aptly describes peak experiences of women who love sex. Clearly, it describes some of the most moving phases of Alice's journey to sexual wholeness—Alice, who was finally able to feel the full rush of sexual desire for her husband only when she had remembered and re-owned her long-ago volcanic feelings for her father. Ecstasy connection. Like Alice, many of the women who love sex had asserted their own versions of this, describing sexual encounters that left them feeling stronger, healthier, more whole and up-to-date, with a new sense of personal freedom: "wings to fly."

I relate how I was coming to understand that this kind of ecstasy connection—the essence of satisfaction—could simply not be crammed into a Masters-and-Johnson-type definable event or set of physiological responses. For the women I had interviewed, it was something larger, more diffuse, less definable and measurable. It involved passions and meanings and relationship as well as body sensations. It involved pleasure as well as orgasm. Sometimes it involved a wordless, transformative experience whose aura lingered into the future to create new thought patterns, seemingly new wrinkles in the brain. The ecstasy connection involves an entire continuum of positive sexual responses.

"A continuum. You mean one with a beginning, a middle, and an end? Like a ruler?" asks Jan.

"It's more like one that never ends," answers Maya. "Because it's made up of energy."

"Energies—make that plural," I suggest to her. "At least if you listen to enough women."

"OK, energies. And these constantly dance around and through each other. They change their size and shape and importance depending on what's happening in bed—or out of bed—or wherever it's happening! This is a continuum that's made up of memories. And anticipations for the future. It moves and dances in time as well as the here and now." She rises from her lotus position and begins to waft about the deck as she demonstrates the fluctuating, self-renewing, four-dimensional quality we are trying to understand.

"I see," Jan teases her. "This is why we don't have a written language of ecstasy? Because it's a dance, not a bunch of nouns and verbs?"

Watching Maya's movements, I am reminded of an ancient tantric metaphor for ecstatic states, *skydancing*.

"Well," I argue, "we may not be able to come up with *the* word right away, but we can try to reach some agreements about the concept and how we communicate about it."

"You're right," says Jan, by now also thoroughly engaged in the conversation. "After all, Eskimos have how many words for snow? Fifty-two or something. But they all know what snow *is* and how to shovel it. Hey, it's part of their lives."

In the process of our discussion I begin to understand one of the givens of Maya's notion of ecstasy connection. The term cannot be considered "scientific" because there is no way to take measurements or make quantitative judgments about the relative merits of pleasure, orgasm, and ecstasy. These are energies that seem to possess potentially equal value in the whole scheme of sexual functioning. Whereas some women say they move through pleasure and orgasm to a peak experience of ecstasy, there are others who describe orgasm as the peak. And there are still others who say that all the energy flows together in a deep and endless river they call pleasure.

Maya catches Lorie's eye. "And then there are those of us who don't have any words to describe the feelings, just incoherent sighs and murmurs. But seriously, Lorie, you can't tell me your orgasms are higher quality than your pleasures or that you can feel ecstasy without feeling the whole bunch. I mean, which do you value more as you go about your daily life: your heartbeat or your breathing?"

"Yeah, OK, I get it," says Lorie thoughtfully. "They all

depend on each other. But are you saying you can't have one without the other?"

"I think they sort of come in waves or layers," Maya answers. "For me, orgasm or pleasure or ecstasy—none of these even has to start out being sexual, I mean sexual in the sense of physical behaviors. I can peel back the layer labeled sex, and the feelings are still there through all the other layers of me. Sitting on this deck, feeling the sun, watching that hawk over there circling around for mice in the sagebrush—these are connection, these are pleasure, these are ecstasy. I feel them in my soul. I feel them in my body. I have actually orgasmed many times watching a rainbow spread across that bowl of mountains."

Lorie and Jan stare at their aunt.

"That's awesome," says Jan.

Lorie breaks into a grin. "So that's what could happen if I just let myself get into it. I'll have to suggest going for a nice long walk in the rain sometime when Doug comes out to visit."

Granted, Maya on her mountaintop is an original, whose sexual responses defy traditional definition, but many of the women who have talked with me are sexual originals, too, even though from the outside they may look like regular housewives, teachers, CPAs, social workers, businesspeople, or whoever else they happen to be. Perhaps originality is another identifying mark of women who love sex. They have learned to peel off all those centuries of definition by others. To trust their own experiences as sources of information. To dare reach out to make contact. Perhaps, as Maya suggests, these acts of originality are the language of ecstasy. The self-definition and the trust and the daring, these are the dance. And the dance is the language, the ecstasy connection.

"I guess I still don't totally get it," complains Jan. "That continuum you're talking about, I mean."

"Let me show you," I offer. I have a sense of Jan as a

woman for whom intellectual understanding is a significant form of control.

There is a sandy path leading off the deck. With a stick from the underbrush I scratch out something that looks like a hieroglyph. "This isn't very artistic, but it's a version of the Masters and Johnson sexual response cycle.[3] See how it says you begin at ground zero and then whip up into a frenzy of excitement until you explode in orgasm, and then collapse into a heap—the French call it *la petite mort*—the little death."

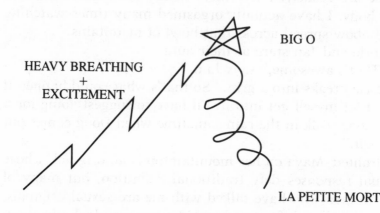

**CONVENTIONAL SEXUAL RESPONSE CYCLE—
PEAKING AT ORGASM, THEN RUNNING OUT OF ENERGY**

"Now let's look at an alternative model, a model based on an energetic definition of sex rather than sex as an action or a set of physical responses. This is a model that allows for feelings beyond just your sensations of the moment." With the stick I draw a circle. "Let's call this circle pleasure, OK?"

Jan steps off the deck to watch. I trace three circles in all, intersecting one another: pleasure, orgasm, and ecstasy.

"So these represent the continuum," says Jan.

"Right. Now comes the creative part. You have to imagine these aren't just circles scratched in the sand. Let yourself see them as spheres, dancing spheres of energy. Of pleasure, orgasm, and ecstasy. Constantly moving and shifting their size and shape. And shifting in time to incorporate memories and fantasies of the future. See them as the sexual energy that connects a woman with her own insides. And with her partner."

"And with all the rest of her universe," adds Maya, indicating the sweep of hills and sky.

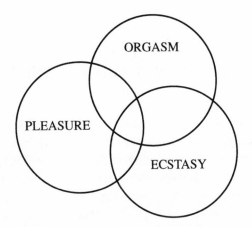

**ALTERNATIVE SEXUAL RESPONSE CYCLE—
AN ONGOING CONTINUUM OF PLEASURE, ORGASM,
AND ECSTASY**

I look at Maya, wishing that this diagram could move fluidly like she does to show the fluctuation, the complexity of the dance, the scope of it.

"That's OK," says Jan, putting up a hand to stop Maya from wafting around the deck again. "The diagram you drew is awesome. I can see the interrelationships. I really can."

As we hover over the stick drawing, we feel somewhat like early hill dwellers struggling to decipher the mysteries of life. Finally, Jan remarks that ecstasy, pleasure, and orgasm seem to be far from a hierarchy of terms. Rather, they suggest groups of potentially equal issues.

"You mean we can feel all these things at once," says Maya. "That may be true, but we can't talk about them all at the same time. That's one of the limitations of having to communicate, you know. You got to start somewhere and that's tough when there's no real beginning, middle, or end."

"Pleasure's a good place to begin talking," I say. "What do you think of when you think of sexual pleasure?"

Pleasure: The Power of Affection, Skin Hunger, and Well-Being

"Touch. Lightness. Body music," begins Maya. "Sexual pleasure is attraction. Interest. It's arousal and wetness. A part of all the wonderful energies that connect my being with the universe. It fills me with a sense of enthusiasm. My nerve endings wake up and say, 'Hello, world.' And just for the record, that's something that's still there for me after menopause. And it's there even without hormones. Without a partner. It's not like I have to depend on anything else."

"To me," says Jan, "sexual pleasure means having fun. It's not any big explosion or anything. Maybe not even making out. It means flirting or dancing or eating pizza together, you know, with eye contact. Or having my back rubbed when I have my period. It's a different thing from orgasm. You can do it for a long time without getting whacked-out tired. And it's not like ecstasy. It's easier to deal with. It doesn't stay with you in the same way and force you to change."

"Doug and I run together," says Lorie. "And sometimes that feels sexual 'cause we're so conscious of our bodies.

Then there's the warm bath together and the body hug, where we look at each other and feel each other's skin."

Is pleasure always the same? Is it something you always respond to in the same way? I ask them.

"Not at all," answers Maya. "Kissing, for instance. Kissing is something that's definitely a pleasure for me—or it was when I was having partners. But if I have a sore throat, I don't feel much like kissing that day, and it certainly would not be a pleasure to give my germs away as nasty little door prizes. I'd rather curl up with a cup of hot tea or have a massage to soothing music. So pleasure is not always the same. It's relative. It fluctuates depending on the situation. And it's self-perpetuating. The better I feel, the more open I am to feeling even more pleasure."

Maya has by now spread herself full-length on the deck so that her whole body is absorbing the afternoon rays of the sun. "And I think it's important to mention that pleasure is healing. I find this in my work with people, don't you?" She looks up at me. "Helping them notice what feels good to them is usually the missing link. Anyway, it's a big step in getting well."

Pleasurable activities like laying on of hands, massage, meditation, music, bathing, and a reasonable amount of lying around in the sun can indeed be healing as well as arousing. They are among the oldest of medical prescriptions, and even contemporary science often agrees that these can help prevent and treat all sorts of somatic and psychosomatic imbalances, including cancer.[4] But in the world of sex therapy and research, the concept of pleasure is routinely referred to as sensate focus or foreplay, a second-rate activity that precedes the "real thing."[5]

Maya warns Lorie not to let Doug push any goal-oriented ideas on her. "Tell him *foreplay* is a golfing term men shout out as they're preparing to tee off. Tell him what you love most is the feeling of soft, lazy touching all over your body, not just on your genitals."

Lorie's eyes soften, then she twirls her engagement ring and looks sideways at her sister.

"Hey," Jan reassures her, "take it for all it's worth. Here's your wedding-night advice on a platter. And it sure beats 'Close your eyes and think of Wisconsin!' "

"Skin hunger!" Maya calls out. "That's what I think of when you ask me to think about pleasure." She is not the first person in the world to have had this revelation; according to researcher Ashley Montagu, the sense of touch is the primal sense, the first of the five to activate when we are born.[6] Maya regales us with her delight in remembering her daughters when they were tiny: "That soft, silky skin, and those wiggly little bodies. I don't know who enjoyed the cuddling and hugging more, my babies or me."

"Was breast feeding part of that enjoyment?" I ask her.

"An incredible turn-on! I mean of course with my babies I never acted sexual. But the whole breast thing was certainly a sexual pleasure. Without doubt—how else can you describe it? The milk streaming into your nipples, that wet little pink mouth sucking, those little fists pumping away. It's as if your body exists only to satisfy hunger, like a mama cat or goat. I think Nature does that to keep mothers on the job. You can't wait for the next feeding time to roll around because it's not only the baby you're feeding. You're feeding your own hunger, too."[7]

Maya's delight in her babies was a life-affirming one. In order to thrive, human beings (indeed, all mammals) need pleasurable skin sensation from the moment of birth. Jan speaks up, in what I am coming to recognize as her scholarly voice: "Don't studies show that babies who are left alone and untouched for hours and hours, in orphanages, for instance, don't those babies get sick and die mysterious deaths right in their cribs?"

"Yes," I answer, citing research.[8] "And for our whole lives, human beings retain their skin hunger—their need for affectionate touch. As we grow up, every single one of

the senses yearns for pleasure. In the course of a lifetime"—
I look at Jan—"you might shuttle back and forth between
touching, tasting, smelling, seeing, listening."[9]

"You might even shuttle minute by minute," Maya points
out, "depending on what you're up to in bed—or wherever
it's happening." She shoots me a look.

"When you say pleasure, I mostly just feel anxious,"
Lorie says. "Right here in the pit of my stomach. I mean,
we're living together and getting along in bed great now.
Everything's wonderful. It's almost too good. But suppose
after we're married I can't come through for him the way
he wants."

Lorie with her premarital jitters is voicing a fear that
women have voiced for centuries for one reason or another.
Turned the other way around, the fear reads: "If I show
pleasure in my own pleasure—if he can see how good I
really feel—will he still accept me?" I am especially sympathetic to Lorie because I see so many women in my office
who seem to be scared to death to feel good. It's almost as
if they'd rather feel pain, depression, and dysfunction for
the rest of their lives than risk figuring out how to feel
whole and sexually alive.

"They're afraid they're going to be called trollops or
whores or whatever people call loose women nowadays,"
offers Maya.

"They're afraid they'll get hooked into crazy relationships
they can't get out of, that's what," says Jan with the air of
one who's been through it. "I had this roommate who could
only get a real sexual hit by being with a guy who was
totally a drunk and didn't care about her. She just couldn't
seem to think a guy was cool if he treated her like a human
being. It was like she was being forced to make this
choice—either hang out with someone boring who loves
you or some dude in a leather jacket who turns you on.
Either way it was a horrible, awful choice, and she got very
depressed and finally flunked out of school and left."

Wilhelm Reich was the first to recognize and label the fear of feeling good as a cultural phenomenon. He called it *pleasure anxiety*,[10] and he pointed out how Western society is organized around controlling our pleasures rather than around teaching us how to enjoy them. Reich was especially wary of how the families of his native Germany between the two world wars trained children to become—in Maya's words—"puritanical little prigs." He called these families factories of repression, and he noted that in these families, as everywhere else in the culture, girls and women were pleasure-repressed even more than the boys and men were. "But that was then and this is now," says Maya. "We're not Puritans any more. Translated to post–cold-war America, pleasure anxiety means what?"

It means we desperately want sensuality and tenderness in our lives, but we may never feel satisfied because we're seeking them outside our bodies, outside ourselves. It means we've developed a junk food mentality about sexual pleasure, objectifying our needs as a need for commodities instead of a hunger for personal connection. Pleasure anxiety means being scared of any sexual encounter that is more than casual, that threatens to have deep emotional impact and meaning.

"You mean instead of getting nervous about getting married I can just go to the mall and pick out clothes and stereos and stuff?" says Lorie. "I guess what pleasure anxiety means for me, is that I seem to be real good at taking care of business, but not at listening for human needs—the ones deep inside. And that's what worries me." She confesses how her impending marriage has focused her on her engagement ring and wedding dress, as if she is being moved by status rather than intimacy. "Sometimes I wonder if I'm marrying Doug just so I can afford to own a house."

"I wonder why you're marrying him at all," blurts Jan. "Like, he's a *hunk*, but do you have to get *married*? You've already moved in with him. What's so special about formalizing it with a ceremony?"

"I want something more than just being roommates. See, it really is more than the dress and the ring and the house. I want the sense of permanence that comes with making this kind of commitment. I want to start a family. But I am scared. Scared we'll get tired of each other. I read married couples are supposed to get restless after four years or seven years and start making out with the neighbors."

As I listen to Lorie's fears, I am struck by how much she personifies the flip side of Alice, whose struggle was to regain a sense of sexual desire with her plodding but faithful husband. Here is Lorie, bursting with desire for pleasure but torturing herself with anxiety about losing it. She is only a few years younger than Alice, yet she seems to be from a completely different generation, more knowledgeable about her sexual feelings. Still, Lorie has reason for her anxiety. There's nothing in the culture that says marriage makes sexual attraction and pleasure grow richer over the long haul; in fact, the high rate of affairs, divorces, and domestic violence might indicate just the opposite.[11]

The good news for Lorie, however, is that she has resources, including some that Alice lacked. She can bank on the farm upbringing that taught her the kind of steadiness and effort that can make commitment work. And she can bank on the influence of Maya: "One thing you've always taught us, Auntie M, is to appreciate, to feel. I never got that other places. It was always more like 'Hurry up, get on with the job.' Or 'If you get too close to somebody, you'll drop dead.' Even simple stuff, like holding someone's hand or cuddling. That was supposed to lead to something bad, like 'going all the way'—whatever *that's* supposed to be."

The fact is, for Lorie, Alice, and many other women (and many men, too), simple acts of pleasurable connection can be complicated and scary. Perhaps that is why pleasure is so vastly underrated in the sexuality literature. Also, as Maya states, "You pointed out already that you can't really measure it. All by itself, it isn't something that shows up as high drama on the sexual Richter scale."

Interestingly, though, the women I interviewed about their peak sexual experiences reported more pleasure responses than they did responses of orgasm and ecstasy. They reported craving nondemand comfort and sensuality as part of their sexual encounters—flirting, playing, teasing, nuzzling, hugging, full-body snuggling, sweetly scented backrubs, rocking, and holding like a babe in arms. Michelle, who was one of the women in my original study, had a special take on her pleasure responses: "As a practicing bisexual, I find it's a lot easier to tease and snuggle with women lovers than with men. It kind of happens all during the day. There's a lighter touch. A mutual understanding. Not so much pressure to turn a little eye contact into genital seduction."

The women who love sex described all kinds of sexual pleasures with words that bubbled over with feelings of optimism and well-being: "energizing," "connecting," "serene." They talked about physical sensation, yes, but they also talked about spiritual nourishment. Poet Gioia Timpanelli underscores the importance of pleasure for vitality and connectedness of body and soul: "The most holy thing you can do is live with pleasure. Enjoy your food, enjoy your sex. It's where the life force is."[12] Theologian Elizabeth Dodson Gray concurs and urges us to "go for it," as Jan would say: "We're all told to prepare for an afterlife. Well, my greatest fear is that in the afterlife I'll meet the Great Spirit who will say, 'I hope you enjoyed the life you just lived because that was *it*.' "[13]

Is pleasure enough? Mainstream sexology doesn't think so, but many of the women who love sex feel that pleasure can be complete and satisfying in itself. They agree with Maya as she answers Lorie: "I don't always need fireworks going off. Sometimes for me pleasure *is* all the way."

Making a commitment to sexual pleasure is a powerful step for women to take in this pleasure-negative society that undervalues women. It means, like Lorie, coming to terms with pleasure anxiety. It means, like Maya, honoring the positive energy, including the sexual energy, that flows through every aspect of life. But she would be the first to wag her finger and say that pleasure is more than simply acting out your turn-ons.

"Don't forget about responsibility," she says.

"Doesn't that take all the spontaneity out of it?" asks Jan.

"It doesn't have to," says Maya. "But it does mean spending some time thinking about it beforehand."

"You mean laying in a supply of feathers and cucumbers?"

"Definitely that, too, along with a basket of strawberry-flavored condoms. But I was thinking a little more generically. I was thinking that responsibility for pleasure means knowing how to create it, prepare for it, pay for it, and pick up after it. In other words, learning how to take care of your self—inner child, adult child, uppity woman, and all."

"Maybe that's the answer," says Jan. "I see women getting so hurt. Freedom and playing around are groovy, but what happens after the good times roll? Like who gets to go to the abortion clinic or take care of the baby for the next twenty years?"

Responsibility for pleasure also involves learning what expressions of it are appropriate where, when, and, perhaps most importantly, with whom. Jan warns, "We can't just go out into the world with all our sexual vibes exposed. We'd get killed, hurt, ruined."

Her warning is real and immediate. The world of sex is not a safe place for girls and women. If we need evidence, she points out that all we have to do is look at the appalling statistics about incest and rape. Although there is no way of gathering accurate figures, some researchers assert that one out of every three little girls in the United States is sexually abused by the time she becomes a teenager, and that is only the tip of the iceberg. Numerous studies show that approximately one out of every four grown women experiences sexual assault.[14] The jury is still out on how many women are affected by less documented forms of sexual harassment, from being leered at on the street to being propositioned at the office water cooler to being stalked and attacked in their own bedrooms and kitchens. Even when women assertively choose their sexual partners and interview them closely, there can be no way of knowing everything about those partners' motives and sex histories. There is still the risk of exploitation. And of diseases from herpes and chlamydia to AIDS.

"But if we button up our sexual energy, we dry up like little prunes all wrapped up in our cellophane packages," exhorts Maya. She has deftly outlined a crucial quandary for women who love sex: We need to have sexual pleasure in our lives, but sexual pleasure can be dangerous for women. What is the way through the quandary? How do we even begin to communicate about it?

"Well," offers Jan. "We can start by acknowledging that we've got a problem."

"Hey, now," counters Maya, "you're beginning to sound just like Droopy the Dog. Why don't we start by helping ourselves feel good. You know," she begins to lecture, "we women have a lot to learn, and one way to learn it is by pleasing ourselves as well as our partners. We have to learn the differences between pleasure and pain. When we know that, then we can model it for our children, too—I mean little men children as well as little women children—so they can learn the differences. So they can learn about sensitivity and tenderness. It's not even so much a physical thing. I think it's more a point of view, a way of seeing the world and of being in it. It's connecting the body and the spirit. It's copping to the holiness of feeling good."

"If all that's the pleasure part of the continuum," says Lorie, "what's orgasm?"

Orgasm and Re-Lease—Expanding the Spectrum of Response

What is orgasm? This is a question women have asked me all through my career—in therapy sessions, in support groups, in teaching situations. Women like Alice have asked because they doubt they have ever experienced an orgasm. Others have asked because their partners doubt that what they are experiencing are orgasms.

"I'm asking you," says Lorie, "because I'm worried about how many orgasms it's OK—I mean *really* OK—to have. And how am I going to be sure they're the right kind?"

I assure her that she can have as many or as few orgasms as she wants: "Only you can be the judge. And there isn't any such thing as a right or wrong kind of orgasm. If anyone tells you there is, tell them they've got rocks in their heads!" Lorie smiles and seems to expand as if she has just had a wonderful gift bestowed upon her.

Lorie and the other women are not the only ones asking about orgasm. Sex researchers are still asking questions, too, and have debated the virtues of vaginal versus clitoral orgasms since Freud first propounded the theory that vaginal orgasm as a result of intercourse with a husband is the only grown-up and normal way for women to experience sexual release. Freud's theory not only reifies male pleasure (the vagina, Kinsey speculated, offers more feeling to a man during intercourse than it does to a woman), but, say political feminists, it also keeps women in their place: on their backs, in missionary position. In the last decades, a clitoral theory of orgasm has challenged the Freudian view, and a G-spot theory has challenged both. Despite extensive, sometimes compulsive inquiry about orgasm and scientists' impressive ability to clock vaginal spasms to the nth fraction of a second, researchers still do not know definitively what an orgasm *is*, and they certainly remain unaware of the full extent of its possibilities, especially for women.[15]

"But even though nobody seems to know what an orgasm is, our bedroom scenes are still judged by what you're calling the orgasm standard," snorts Maya. "It's hard to know what's enough or too much. It can get competitive. Ruin all the fun."

She is talking about performance tripping, the notion that orgasm is a competitive goal to be achieved rather than felt, experienced, enjoyed, savored, shared. I nod and reinforce her statements with comments from other women who have confided that anxiety about achievement has delayed and even damaged their ability to feel sexual pleasure or connection with a partner. I quote from a client, Sarah: "When I was growing up, I learned that sex meant having an orgasm, and if I didn't have one, I'd be a failure. So I learned to fake it so he'd think I was whole. As a result, I got less and less whole and our sex life just fizzled."

Women who love sex may be ordinary women, by and large, but they have some important lessons to teach other women—and researchers—about orgasm. One lesson has to do with gathering data. In the search for what orgasm *is*, it is essential to use a layered thought process that encompasses the whole continuum of orgasmic experience.

"You mean that pleasure is part of orgasm, too," states Jan.

"And so is ecstasy," states Maya.

"What do you think about when you think of orgasm?" I ask the three women. I am interested to learn how they will broaden the concept of orgasm beyond knee-jerk responses to physical stimuli.

Maya: "I think about my whole body—all of me. Orgasm is different from pleasure. Well, there's pleasure involved, of course, but orgasm is a lot more than just here and now sensation. It's about body *memory*. Every time I have an orgasm, it seems to contain the feelings from all the other orgasms I ever had before. It all seems to keep adding up. That's one reason sex gets better and better as you get older." She smiles broadly as she adds this last comment.

Lorie: "Orgasm means something really special. For me, I guess you'd have to say it's mostly about love right now. My orgasms, well, they don't occur in a vacuum. They say something about me, about how Doug and I feel about each other. About the plans we have. About trust. About giving ourselves to each other. About being totally romantic and caring."

Jan: "I think a lot about how good they feel. I look forward to them. Well, OK, I fantasize, especially in this one statistics class that is being taught by a superhunk. So you could easily say my orgasms engage my mind and emotions as well as body."

"Can orgasm can be a spiritual experience?" I ask. All three resoundingly answer yes! "You can't separate sex and spirit," Lorie asserts. "Maybe it sounds trite, but isn't orgasm like a bringing together of body and soul?"

Maya underscores these comments when she says, "For me, sex isn't a search for the great pumpkin. It's more a search for softness, warmth, harmony, pleasure. Orgasm is a crescendo. It's terrific, but it's not everything. As an opera fan, I'd say that sexual experience is just as complex as the Ring Cycle. People say they want to hear Wagner Highlights, you know, the end of the *Götterdämmerung*. Well, how would I enter into a sexual experience if I'm thinking, I just want to get to the exciting part and I think I'll skip over a few measures here and the boring part there where you go to sleep. You've got to hang in with the whole deal if you want to have the whole deal in your orgasm."

According to these women and others who love sex, orgasm fluctuates in size and importance as it relates to pleasure and ecstasy. I remind Jan and Lorie of the stick drawing in the sand. Orgasm can be just a teeny circle, small and discrete. It can be a minor blip on the monitor of perception or it can be a blank, not perceived at all.

"It can be subsumed in a pleasure experience or in ecstasy," adds Maya.

Lorie says, "I don't think I believe in the big bang theory of sex. To tell you the truth, what excites me most isn't putting out or even the climax; it's the intimacy." As Lorie explains her feelings, it is evident that the most satisfying part of orgasm for her is emotional release rather than the pubycoccygeal spasms she has learned to associate with the term *orgasm*.

"Or orgasm can play a loud and flamboyant leading lady." Maya laughs and gestures broadly.

"Right," I agree. "It can go on for hours and hours and blow the door right off the bedroom."

"Orgasm can even occur as a kind of paradoxical sick joke in abusive situations," Maya points out. "Haven't you ever heard of women having orgasms in the middle of a violent fight with a lover?"

Yes, and I have heard women admit feeling genital spasms during a rape at the same time that they were terrified and repulsed.

"Is that really true?" Jan looks stunned.

It is true. In intense fear and anger, there is an adrenaline surge that activates the autonomic nervous system, elevating blood pressure, heart rate, and other signs of orgasm, including, apparently, genital spasms. This may also explain what happens when women chronically cut themselves off from positive sexual feelings; they may turn to pain as a way to stimulate sensation enough to remind them they are alive. Their sexual charge may take a sinister turn in relationships that hurt them in and out of bed. It is as if a woman's ecstasy connection may take a step through the looking glass into a cosmic black hole and express itself in reverse as a continuum of grief, rage, and terror. This dark side of orgasm is compartmentalized rather than flowing. For some women at some times in

86

their lives it is as compelling as joy, yet it is devoid of joyful spirit and connection. It may meet the criteria for involuntary muscle spasms, but according to the women who love sex, it is far from a life-affirming release.

"What about *consensual* pain?" asks Maya. "I know this one woman who just loves being handcuffed to a wall and whacked black and blue with a paddle or a cane. She says you wouldn't believe the orgasms."

"That's gross," says Jan.

Gross or not, Maya is talking about sadomasochism, or S/M, a favored turn-on for some and for true afficionados, an entire lifestyle. These women seek thrilling sensations from the lash of the leather thong, the tweak of the nipple clip. (One enthusiast said if the cuts and bruises last for more than three days, sex play has gone too far.)

"It sounds like abuse if you ask me," says Jan.

But there is an important distinction. Unlike the day-to-day hell of a codependant, battering relationship, S/M is a conscious choice some women make for orgasmic stimulation. Women who love it agree that pain is only a part of the appeal.

"Well, then, maybe it's women playing out their early childhood abuses. Like maybe it's an outlet for post-traumatic stress."

Jan's comment is one I have thought about more than once in connection with S/M. Perhaps, after all, women re-create in bed what they know, in this case, pain and victimization. Or perhaps, to awaken sexual feelings deadened by abuse, women may need extraordinary stimulation.

This may be true of some women in S/M relationships, but it is not the story I have heard from women who *love* this kind of sex. These women do not report that they are driven to S/M out of a need to restimulate old abuses. Further, they point out that there is a buoyant fantasy element to S/M characterized by titillating "scenes" and provocative dress-up—spike heels, feather masks, studded black leather bras with the nipples cut out. Some enthusiasts (gay and straight) say that there is a distinct sense of camaraderie, of belonging to an outrageous, rule-breaking club. The orgasmic stimulation comes not only from physical sensation but from the excitement of living on the edge. Perhaps most important, to make S/M work (that is, to make the orgasms fun for both partners), there has to be up-front communication about the power roles. These have to be chosen and agreed upon. They also have to be temporary. Moreover, there is a mutual "safe word," one that will stop the action if it gets too rough or scary. Unlike some of the unacknowledged dominance and submission roles women may play out year after year in the course of their sexual lives, the major control in S/M is dictated by the "bottom," the partner who is receiving pleasure/pain, and not by the "top," the partner who is so tantalizingly inflicting it.

"That's a whole other sphere of orgasm," I speculate. "It's taking yourself beyond the comfort zone, expanding the sexual limits you impose on yourself. On the one hand, it's role playing: top and bottom. On the other, it's learning to negotiate for pleasure and safety."

"It's learning to give a new meaning to the word *trust*," says Lorie.

"Maybe it's another level of learning to give and receive," says Maya.

Clearly it involves learning to know the difference between not enough and too much. Learning to know what *enough* means. Perhaps the ecstasy connection is always teetering in that delicate balance between pain and pleasure.

Philosophizing about the concept of *enough* brings me to a central question about orgasm, a question that depends on women's individual differences: What do women mean by "easily orgasmic"?

I had asked this of my research sample. Women defining themselves as easily orgasmic had mostly to do with each woman's feelings of pleasure and connectedness and power and less to do with quantifiable data like where on their bodies they were stimulated or how fast they could come or how many times. All the women who had said "easily orgasmic" meant a degree of control. They felt very much in charge of their own orgasms ("I can come whenever I want"). Or they felt in charge of the conditions ("I need a certain kind of mood or stimulation in order to come, but I know how to arrange for that"). Lorraine characterized herself as a compulsive homemaker. For her, taking charge meant setting the scene—changing sheets, lighting candles, choosing the music. Holly was a physical education instructor, a leader of Outward Bound expeditions. "I like making love under the stars," she told me. "I'm always looking for new kinds of places. Not kinky—I'm not into dangling from a rope. But I'm pretty intrepid. I've joined my husband in a few mountaintop experiences—literally."

A few women had said that easily orgasmic was relative. For instance, Pauline described many years of inability to come to orgasm with a husband who was a dogged provider and an excruciatingly vanilla lover. Yet in the six months since she had been living with a woman, she had surprised herself by becoming orgasmic beyond her wildest dreams. For her, "easily orgasmic" meant "I have no problems now in comparison with how I used to be."

But back to Lorie's question, What *is* orgasm? The orgasms the research sample of women had talked about did not always fit into the sexologists' construct of arousal/plateau/orgasm/resolution. Nor did they always fit into the feminists' clitoral norm or the vaginal norm dictated by Freud and Freudians. Some women had been able to locate their G spots, others had not been. Some women had come "instantly" once stimulation started; it had taken others as long as an hour to let go into "a mind-blowing release." The typical number of orgasms during a sexual encounter had ranged from one to "more than I can count." Frequency, duration, and sensation had also varied for each woman and sometimes for each experience. Kinds of stimulation had ranged from the time-tested direct clitoral manipulation by self or partner to an energetic account of a crème de menthe and whipped-cream sundae tantalizingly licked off a woman's abdomen as she lay bound to her lover's bedpost with silk aviator scarves.

Is orgasm essential to the experience of sexual ecstasy? I had expected a resounding yes from each of the women interviewed. But about a third of them had said no, maybe, or I don't know. They had listed other elements as the trigger to ecstasy, elements ranging from an exotic setting to sensuous delight, romance, intimacy, and love. Valerie, who was newly in recovery from alcoholism, said she went through a period as a "conscientious objector," consciously resisting orgasms so she wouldn't feel sucked into a performance trip in bed.

Interestingly, even though some of the women in the sample had said orgasm was not a condition essential for a peak sexual experience, every woman I interviewed reported having at least one significant orgasm during each of the peak experiences she described to me.

"So do you think these women were lying?" asks Jan.

"Or denying?" adds Maya.

I don't think so. I think the discrepancy in their reports expresses the confusion built into the way we have been taught to understand sex and orgasm. As Maya had pointed out earlier, in all of recorded history, women have had no commonly accepted ways to describe the holistic aspects of our sexuality; its physical, emotional, spiritual, even intellectual interconnections; or the relationships of orgasm to ecstasy and pleasure.

Maya says the problem with all the research on women and orgasm is that it has no heart. "What did Freud know? What did those other turn-of-the-century Teutonics know?[16] They didn't even like women. The word *orgasm* doesn't even sound like what it is. I think we should change its name so we can start understanding it differently. It's not

a thing you can measure; it's a beautiful, opening, ongoing *process*."

"What'll we call orgasm instead of orgasm, Auntie M?"
Lorie asks.

Maya stands on the deck and begins to gesture again
toward the hills. "Let's call it *release*. And let's spell it with
a hyphen—re-lease.

"Orgasm is about letting go," she continues. "Orgasm is
also about renewal, self-renewal, recycling energy. It means
taking out a new lease on life again and again with each
sexual experience. It's feeling it in every cell of your body.
It's not just vaginal. It's feeling your *hair* follicles explode
for God's sake."

As Maya waxes eloquent, I remember one of the interview
women, Rosanne, passionately describing whole-body orgasm: "All of me was involved. My breasts felt alive,
streaming sensations in my legs, up my spine to the back
of my head. Everything let go. I moaned, yelled, almost
knocked my lover's teeth out. Finally I cracked up laughing.
Everything seemed so funny and so beautiful and I wanted
to go out and hug the world." This story perfectly illustrates Maya's notion of re-lease: the recycling of physical
sexual energy into emotional altruism. And I remember
Amalie, a violin instructor, telling me of an indelible moment of sexual intimacy with her husband of twelve years:
"The two of us were so close it felt more like a love orgasm
than a sex orgasm. I felt it in my heart. My whole chest
opened up and I let go in a flood of tears that felt so healing." Again re-lease, this time moving emotional energy
into a cleansing of the physical body.

Listening to Maya, Jan, and Lorie, I realize that their
ideas about orgasm are consonant with the stories of other
women who love sex. For all of them, orgasm may be about
emotional re-lease as much as it is about physical re-lease.

"What about spiritual re-lease?" I ask the three women.

"It's only a whisper away," says Maya. "But now I think
we're getting into the realm of ecstasy."

Ecstasy—Exploring the Quantum Qualities of Sex

Ecstasy. Here we are back to where we started on this glorious, sunny day on Maya's deck. The third link in the trinity of sexual connectedness. "What do you think it is?" I ask.

"Ecstasy is about *knowing*," says Maya. "It's knowing that you're one with the sun and ocean and every blade of grass and pine needle. It's relaxing all over. It's joining the pulse of the universe. It's the feeling of being breathed. It's joy. It's letting go. That sphincter hold you have on life lets loose for a moment."

Again, Maya gives vitality to abstract thought. This time she is posing an intriguing paradox: To experience a magical sense of belonging and connectedness, first it is necessary to let go.

"But what does that all mean?" asks Lorie. "What does letting go really mean?"

"When you know that," answers Maya, "you'll know all you need to know about the ecstasy connection."

Lorie searches for a solid handle to this proclamation. "Do you mean that if you keep hanging onto the rope that attaches you to other people's expectations, all you'll ever have is the rope?"

"That's part of it," says Maya. "It's when you pry your grasping little fingers off—when you let go of expectation— then you feel a surge of belonging—belonging to your*self*. It's when you let go of control that you are filled with power, with passion, with creativity. You see the world differently. You have power to change the world because you're no longer bound to the rope. You're free to move."

Jan adds a missing piece to the power equation: "You mean it's not the kind of power that wants dominion over. It gives energy instead of stopping other people from having it."

"See how important that is for you to know?" Maya says

to Lorie. "Especially now that you're about to marry Doug."

But in attempting to describe ecstasy, we encounter full blast the language barrier Maya and the rest of us had brought up earlier. A primary problem in talking about women and sexual ecstasy is frame of reference. Definitions for both sex and ecstasy are hung on a linear, hierarchical frame that doesn't begin to accommodate the lyrical, spherical experiences of the women who have talked with me. *Ecstasy* comes from a Greek word meaning to drive out of one's senses.

"That's really silly," says Lorie. "I don't feel knocked totally out of it when Doug and I are making love together. I feel totally alive. I'm more *with* it. *Into* it."

"Me, too," says Maya. "I feel driven *into* my senses. Sexual ecstasy isn't about denial. It isn't about *not* feeling, it's about being exquisitely sensitive, exquisitely aware. As if my insides have been rewired by Cosmo the Cosmic Electrician. Every part of me is tuned into the rhythmic, choreographic cycle of the universe."

As Lorie and Maya talk, seemingly across the generations, they are helping me understand that perhaps women do have a language for sexual ecstasy after all, we just haven't always had the opportunity to describe it directly. Throughout much of history, in order to survive in a male-dominated world, women have been forced to cover up the full power of their feelings along with the explicit details. But being resourceful, women have often managed to ferret out indirect, more "acceptable" channels of expressing what sexual satisfaction means.

Two acceptable channels for women have been romance and religion. Both have their limitations, however, aside from being sexually indirect. Both are based on a dynamic of Other worship, what Maya calls "a psychic game of follow-the-leader." They are likely to disconnect women from their sexual power rather than connect them.

The subject of romance usually raises feminist hackles. Robin Morgan, for one, asserts that the myth of romantic love is a dead end, indeed "a stake in the heart" of women's autonomous selves.[17] Mary Daly articulates the feeding frenzy of self-effacement women can fall into: "the rituals of romantic love ... draw women into the 'ecstasy' of Self-loss, the madness which is literally standing outside our Selves, being beside our Selves."[18] Moreover, romance is typically asexual. In the escape-from-reality script, the heroine is a virgin, and she suffers horribly, usually to retain her maidenhead for the hero, who appears at a crucial moment to rescue her so that she can bear sons to carry on his name.

"It's a sexist plot!" sneers Jan. "Codependent heaven. Wipeout time for women."

"Not necessarily," says Maya. "A lot of women get into it for the excitement and drama. Maybe romance is really ecstasy in drag."

Another channel for women's sexual energy has been religious ecstasy, at least from certain religious traditions. And, to follow Maya's line of thinking, perhaps devotional practices are another way of clothing sexual desire in the drag of acceptability. For instance, a woman who breaks out of her marriage to have a sexual affair is labeled a Jezebel; she has burst one of the ancient taboos of our culture. But if she pours her excess energy into worship and good works, she can earn a halo. One of the women from the interviews recounted that she managed to keep a sexless marriage together for years by getting her fix every Sunday passionately singing in a church choir. Another example of permission to express sexual energy can be found in the Father Divine and Daddy Grace spiritual groups. Here, women can sing, scream, shout, shake, roll, lay on hands—all in the name of prayer. They can pass out in the aisle with ecstatic frenzy, and what's more, they can do it in public. Listen to the language of religious ecstasy. Jesus

is no disembodied ghost, but literal lover. He is "keeper."
He is "bridegroom of my soul."

"Religion." Lorie sneers. "Double sexist plot!"

"Or double drag," Maya retorts. "Haven't women poets
and mystics been writing about sexual ecstasy forever in
one form or another?"

In fact, both romance and religion have provided a kind
of code language over the centuries by which women who
love sex could communicate their transcendant experiences
of sexual ecstasy. "Yes," I answer, "and remember that
phrase: 'Anonymous was a woman'?"

"You mean nobody knows exactly who all of those
women were," says Jan.

"Yes, but still they managed to get the message out."

"Jungle drums," intones Maya with drama, "sounding
out messages across time and space."

"Hey, maybe." Jan capitulates. "I was reading about this
amazing lady in a women's history course. A saint. Spanish.
She lived in a convent all her life. In a cell all by herself,
I think. Yet she had these incredibly sexy fantasies. And
she actually wrote them down."

Saint Teresa of Avila. She lived during the Counter-
Reformation and left her autobiography, a remarkable document of religious erotica. I quote a passage about the periodic visitations of a shining angel who appeared to Saint
Teresa to pierce her heart all the way to her entrails with
a flaming golden arrow: "The pain was so great that I
screamed aloud; but at the same time I felt such infinite
sweetness that I wished the pain to last forever. It was not
physical, but psychic pain, although it affected the body as
well to some degree. It was the sweetest caressing of the
soul by God."[19]

Jan looks at me. "That just about sums up how a lot of
women feel about the agony of bliss—how sometimes it
hurts so good."

Lorie agrees. "And about how sex and spirit—how you

can't separate them. They really are part of the same thing."

Like Jan and Lorie, I am struck by how the same ideas keep popping up, time after time, in almost the same words to describe women's ecstatic sexual experiences. I remember a woman from the interview sample rhapsodizing about a white night with her lover. Interestingly, her name was also Teresa—Terry. Like Saint Teresa, Terry stumbled and searched for language to describe her experience. She paused between phrases. Her eyes looked down and to the side, a sign, according to neurolinguistic theory, that she was fleshing out the images by reaching deep into her memory.[20] Her voice was soft and electric: "Our lovemaking was beyond words. A blending of body and spirit. Exquisitely painful and enlightening at the same time. An opening and cleansing of my soul. I felt whole. I never wanted it to end."

"Wait. We're talking about transcendency here," Maya points out after a thoughtful silence. "But what about the other side of the ecstasy connection? The kind that's rooted in the body. I mean the hot, sweaty sex. The howly-growly stuff that there isn't any words for either but that's moving, that's so outrageous that it moves you into another plane of experience, of knowing yourself."

"That howly-growly stuff doesn't show up in any romantic novels, does it?" Lorie asks.

"But it shows up in other religions," says Jan.

"Look at ancient Egypt and Greece," says Maya. "Look at Africa and India. Europe and Native America ..." She is on a roll.

Indeed, evidence abounds. In the ancient and not-so-ancient past, down-to-earth sexual excess was part of religious ritual. Next to godliness was lustiness along with feasting, drinking, and dancing. Pleasure, orgasm, and ecstasy were not sins, they were routes to the deity.

Sexual ecstasy for women isn't all transcendent either. It has its inside-out twin: the ecstatic overload that works its way deep down into the body until it begins to feel like body memory building on body memory. Women talk about unrestrained sensuality, a flood of response to a deluge of stimulation. Wine, food, music, sex toys. A Jell-O-filled bathtub. A room green with marijuana smoke. Sweat, laughter, noise. "It was sheer gluttony," recalls Eileen. In our interview about her peak sexual experiences, she was remembering the only time in her life she had ever tried group sex: "It was with my husband and two other couples, and we set it up so that each one of us would get all the attention for as long as we could stand it. I had a sore throat from screaming for more. I felt a huge release as if the sound was coming from somewhere else, an incredible sound, deep and roaring like a bear. My release system was changed forever. I'm able to make noise now during sex and ask for anything I want."

Women say that when such gluttonous sexual ecstasy occurs in the context of self-esteem and loving relationships they can incorporate it into their lives as a source of energy and joy.

"That's true for me," says Maya.

Jan and Lorie look cautiously at her and then at one another, as if to say, Do we really want to hear this?

"It's OK," she reassures them. "It's not something that's going to shock you. Honest. Well," she contradicts herself, "it may surprise you a little. See, you've always thought of me as your wacky, free-spirited aunt, but for the first forty years of my life, I wasn't like that at all. I was terrified of ecstasy in any form. I'd bought right into all the good-girl messages. I was a world-class prude; as a matter of fact, you can ask your mother."

Lorie and Jan guffaw in disbelief.

"Well, OK, I was married, but that didn't mean it was any fun. All my life I had craved something I couldn't even name. I can name it now—it was joy. But I wasn't open enough to recognize it then. So I drank a lot and got to craving that instead. My husband was having an affair. He was always having some affair or other—he was that kind of fellow. So when the girls all got into school I took myself out and had an affair, too, just to get back at him. With a college student. He had a flexible schedule so I could pack the kids off and have the whole day to play with him until they got home at three in the afternoon. Oh, God, he was gorgeous. And very athletic. We used to do it in yoga positions in the student lounge, on street corners at high noon, it didn't matter. Once we managed to sneak off for four days together—in a local hotel, where anyone could have found out about us. I remember lugging in a big suitcase full of sex toys and massage oils. The more bizarre, the better as far I was concerned. In fact, I was beginning to get off on the fact that we might be found out."

When women can't have what they really crave, they may begin to crave its opposites. Maya chose alcohol and danger. Other women might be drawn to pain, violence, and addictive uses of drugs. The high from satisfying these cravings masquerades as ecstasy, and it can drive women *out* of their senses, out of themselves—another level of the ecstasy of self-loss Mary Daly talks about.

"But that's absolutely not the effect Eric had on me," Maya argues. "With him, it was as if all the sex finally brought me to my senses—I mean really into my senses— for the first time. I felt like I could leap tall buildings in a single bound. I gave up drinking. After he graduated and left town forever, I didn't go into a decline. I started training as a therapist. I stopped being scared of people. I began to enjoy my children. And finally I did what I should have done all along, I got a divorce. Or rather, you could say I freed both of us to live our lives as they should have been lived—without each other."

Maya's observations on the aftereffects of sexual ecstasy parallels observations of many of the other women who love sex. Not all of them divorced their mates, of course. But whether their experiences were transcendant or centered deep in the body, they reported that something uncanny happened for them. Their self-image improved. They actually saw themselves differently when they looked in the mirror. Their relationships grew more honest, even their job situations seemed to become more rewarding. They were able to ask for what they wanted in a way that enabled them to get it. They reported spiritual movement, sometimes profound enough to propel them to change their lives.

"Mine was profound enough to eventually move me across the country and settle me on the edge of this glorious mountain," says Maya, gesturing toward the sun as it gets itself ready to set over the undulating hills. "I understood that I had outlived the East Coast part of my life and needed to begin a new phase. That new phase is still beginning."

Maya raises a provocative question: "The language of ecstasy really hasn't changed that much over the centuries. Is that because we really haven't come such a long way, baby? Or is it because these words really do describe sexual ecstasy even though they seem to be describing something else?"

In the matter of women and sexual ecstasy, the language that most accurately describes essential details may very well be the language of mysticism and poetry. Knowledge is not always linear, and metaphor can convey layers of meaning that measurements and quantitative analyses cannot. According to some innovative scientists, numbers are not enough even for mathematics and physics. Moreover, they point out what some feminists have long used as a cornerstone of their methodology: the value and validity of first-person storytelling. Anecdotal information *is* scientific information. Indeed, it may be the only information for areas of study that cannot be readily quantified by measurements and numbers.[21]

"So when we're talking about the ecstasy connection,"

asserts Maya, "I think what we're really talking about is a notion of quantum sex."

"Maybe we ought to call it holographic sex," adds Jan. "Aren't we saying that any part of pleasure, orgasm, or ecstasy can stand for any other part?"

"Yeah. Well, sort of," says Lorie. "But that's only the mental part of it. You know when I asked those questions about letting go? That was because I still don't understand it with my head. But I think I get it on some other levels. It's the closeness I feel. The closeness is how I really let go sexually—I mean so I'm on another planet. Maybe there is an ecstasy connection or a quantum leap involved or some kind of miracle, because I've always been kind of a mousy, timid person. I'm like Mom, not like you." She looks at Maya, then at Jan. "I've always been jealous of you from the moment you were born. You always seemed to know exactly what you wanted. I felt I was missing something that you knew about and I didn't. But I just don't feel scared and mousy and jealous anymore. Suddenly I feel like an incredibly loved and loving *woman*."

Jan reaches up from her cross-legged position and grabs for Lorie's hand.

Lorie continues. "I had this dream a few nights ago. It was really bright and lifelike. First I was in bed with Doug." She laughs broadly and blushes the color of the sunset, which is by now beginning to spread a glow over the ocean beyond the hills. "There was this sense of moving, of us being absolutely joined and moving slowly, as if we were porpoises underwater, as if we were the same body, so close and connected. Then the dream shifted and I was in this massive crowd—like in India or Africa—on this sort of never-ending journey. I'm walking along in the dream, moving and humming with thousands and thousands of other people. It's not dusty or smelly or anything. There's this feeling of almost being in the ocean—on a wave—and being washed clean." Lorie pauses to glance at us and sees that we are listening attentively, waiting for her to finish. "I woke up from that dream and suddenly I knew I was ready to meet the world. I didn't have to be jealous anymore. I didn't have to feel second best. And most of all, I didn't have to be scared of marrying Doug. I woke up and knew I was ready to get married. To take the risk. I still have questions. And I don't understand it all in my head. But I guess you could say after this dream I was finally beginning to breathe."

Maya laughs and flings her arms around her. "You got it!" she crows delightedly. "You have your whole life to understand all that in your head. You understand it in your body."

Lorie hugs her aunt, and there are tears of relief in the corners of her eyes, as if this statement has moved her from a position of questioning to a position of affirmation and power. Lorie is no longer attempting to control her passion by saying no or maybe. She is allowing herself to say yes to the prospect of sexual ecstasy.

"You let go!" says Maya, hugging back. "And you discovered the most valuable lesson of all: Letting go is connection!"

Lorie and Maya are talking about a kind of transformation—a growth that is indeed a quantum leap. It is what Shakespeare calls a sea change. New Age physicist Fritjof Capra calls it a systems shift or paradigm shift.[22] Psychologist Abraham Maslow describes its effects by coining the term *self-actualization*.[23] Spiritual feminist Charlene Spretnak writes of a "postorgasmic mindstate." This, she says, is "something quite different from what males have described as *la petite mort* (the little death); rather, the boundary-less, free-floating, nondiscriminating sense of oneness that females experience could more accurately be called *le petit satori* (the little glimpse of enlightenment)."[24]

In fact, women do have a language to describe sexual ecstasy along with orgasm and pleasure. But it is not the detached, linear language of science. As Maya, Jan, and

101

Lorie have helped me articulate, the syntax of the ecstasy connection comes from the inside, born from the turmoil of individual experience, from doubts and questions, even from the nervous giggles with which Lorie and Jan began our conversation. Given the chance, they and other women who love sex know how to say with eloquence how ecstasy makes them feel, and thanks to documents like the autobiography of Saint Teresa, we know they have been saying so for centuries.

By whatever names women have chosen to call it, sexual ecstasy can precipitate a seemingly magical and permanent transformation. After all is said, the continuum of pleasure, orgasm, and ecstasy means satisfaction. It means sexual involvement of the whole person, body, heart, soul, hair follicles, and all. Sexual satisfaction dives deep, and it can surface in surprising facets of women's lives—no matter what age the women may be. Sexual ecstasy has moved both Lorie and Maya to change their lives, each in very different ways. They have no way of determining what effects it might eventually have.

Audre Lorde gives us a taste of the possibilities: "Moved by the erotic," she writes, ". . . I become less willing to accept powerlessness, or those other supplied states of being which are not native to me, such as . . . self-effacement, depression, self-denial. . . . Women so empowered are dangerous."[25]

Sexual satisfaction may indeed be dangerous, at least to the status quo, for joy and spontaneity can disturb our daily routines. Feeling powerful can disrupt our relationships, most certainly the ones that depend on women erasing themselves. Doubtless these are some of the reverberations Maya had in mind all those years ago when she donned her brass pendant that read TO HELL WITH HAPPINESS I WANT ECSTASY.

4

Iris and Company

===

Adventures Beyond
the Jade Gate

===

Too much of a good thing can be wonderful.
—Mae West

IN MY INTERVIEWS of easily orgasmic women, I asked each
one a basic question about her sexual response, a basic
question, but one virtually never explored in research: Are
you able to come to orgasm on extragenital stimulation
only, without touching any part of your vulva? An
astounding 52% of the women said yes.

Iris was one of these women. "I don't know where on my
body I'm *not* orgasmic," she told me. "I think I need to
be mapped."

Of all of the women who have talked with me about loving sex, Iris is among the most dedicated. Her sexuality,
like Maya's, is a part of her spiritual growth, intricately
woven together, like the threads of the many-colored poncho she wears. She is a sculptor, a family therapist, a
mother of two adolescent boys, and an active member of
the local school committee. She has been solidly married

for sixteen years and knows how to make that kind of relationship work.

Like so many other women who love sex, Iris defies the textbooks. In this instance, the books she is defying are the ones that offer up the homing site theory of orgasm, the same theory that served to keep Alice and Frank locked for many years in a sexual stalemate. This is the notion that to excite a women to climax, a partner must zero in on the clitoris, vagina, and G spot and never stray more than three or four inches from home base.

I am suspicious of the homing site theory. It seems like another one of those myths devised by science to keep sexual behavior closely bound by the phallocracy. Perhaps it is another attempt to squeeze women into a fixed sequence of sexual responses. In my more forgiving moments I guess the motive to be less sinister. Maybe it is simply that sex researchers lack the imagination to venture beyond the vulva.

The extragenital routes to orgasm stray well beyond conventional paths. But if they are roads less traveled by, they are also powerful routes to pleasure and ecstasy, the whole whirling continuum of satisfaction described by Maya on her mountaintop overlooking the Pacific. (The more I talk with women, the more I understand that the term *orgasm* almost always stands for pleasure and ecstasy, too.)

Before describing these routes, let me make an important disclaimer: Just because Iris and others thoroughly appreciate the riches that lie *beyond* the vulva, that doesn't mean they don't also enjoy the vulva itself as a source of great excitement and joy. All the women who love sex indicate that they are extremely fond of their vulvas—their sweet shell-like lips, their clitorises bundled up in whisper-soft hoods, and their G spots, those inner buttons of exquisite sensation.

The fact that these women can talk about their vulvas—their genitals—so lovingly says that the world has moved many degrees away from the Victorian dark ages when women's "private parts" were hidden away, never to be seen, let alone touched, except oh so briefly in the act of procreation. Even during childbirth our grandmothers and great-grandmothers had to be heavily draped *down there,* and an attending physician was forced to grope blindly under sheets, blankets, and layers of muslin petticoat. To touch one's own genitals for pleasure was considered to be "heinous"—a sin, a sickness, or a crime depending on whether judgment was delivered from a pulpit, doctor's office, or courtroom bench.

That some women are able to hold a mirror squarely to their genitals these days, appreciate them, touch them guiltlessly and with satisfaction, and even talk about them is a tribute to the women's health movement, to books like *Our Bodies Our Selves,* and to consciousness-raising groups that have encouraged women to look self-lovingly where former generations didn't dare. Alice Walker even skyrocketed the vulva to the *New York Times* best-seller list. *Possessing the Secret of Joy* is a story of the agonies women— indeed a whole continent of women—experience as a result of clitoral mutilation; the book's dedication is "With Tenderness and Respect to the Blameless Vulva."[1] That more and more women can relate to their vulvas with tenderness and respect is also a tribute, at least in part, to a stalwart handful of researchers over the years—those who have put the clitoris and G spot on the scientific map.[2] One of the most pioneering spirits of all researchers belongs to Betty Dodson, whose paintings, books, videotapes, and Bodysex workshops have liberated thousands of women to notice and touch themselves *down there* and revel in the experience.[3]

So let us acknowledge that it has taken a raised consciousness and almost a hundred years of sex research for the glories of the vulva to come to light beyond Freud's "maturity" myth of vaginal orgasm. And like Iris in her handwoven poncho, let us also acknowledge the complexity of wholeness. Let us appreciate that our clitoral, vaginal, and vulval experiences are a crucial part of our sexual experience. But then let us acknowledge that these parts of our body are not all there is. There is more to women's sexuality than what happens between the legs.

In searching for a way to encourage women to talk further about the taboo topic of sexual stimulation beyond the vulva, it occurred to me to form a discussion group of women who love sex. I ask Iris if she is willing to meet with several other women to talk about extragenital response. Rita, Rachael, Mary-Jo, Faith, and Tony are among those who had asserted that they could find sexual satisfaction with extragenital stimulation, and all are ready to tell their stories.[4]

We introduce ourselves around the room. Iris begins. "I'm an unabashed sensualist," she says, sitting cross-legged on a ziggurat of pillows like a tribal queen and fingering the fringes of her flowing poncho. "I like touching. I like everything I can do with my hands, whether it's weaving or throwing clay pots or making love. I think it's important for women to find a way to talk about these things."

Next to her is Rita, whom I first met a couple of years ago when she signed up for a women's personal growth weekend. Judging from outward appearances, Rita's personal growth is moving along at a heady clip. Originally, she had driven up to my office in a bright orange Ford Mustang with a license plate that read UPPITY. Now, she is driving a sky blue Chevy and has changed her plate to GAIA-OM. "I'm here as an out lesbian," she offers. "My lover and I have experienced some very wonderful things together that don't involve penetration, and I hope we can talk really openly."

Rachael slouches beside Rita on an adjoining pillow. She introduces herself as hungry for love and emotional involvement. Her husband has left her for a younger woman, and at age thirty-nine, she is suddenly feeling fat, vulnerable, and unwanted. She says she is a writer who does free-lance public relations and fund-raising to keep herself and her nine-year-old daughter in Reeboks. "If I didn't have a killer sense of humor," she observes, "I'd be a vegetable right now. A carrot probably. Or a turnip. Anyway, something that grows underground. Please forgive me if I talk about sex in the past tense, because it's certainly not happening for me right now. But some of the memories are great!" She lunges toward the box of Kleenex and scoops it closer to her pillow, "so I won't have to reach so far when I start wallowing in self-pity."

Mary-Jo is dressed for speed in a pink jogging suit with satin racing stripes. "I own a restaurant, an African mask collection, and a German shepherd puppy," she announces. "I'm a reformed sex addict and a recovering narcissist. I'm actively searching for a man to set up permanent housekeeping with so that I can start a family. I'm not looking for Mr. Handsome or even Mr. Eveready Hard-On. Just a nice guy who can give me the affection I need and do the dishes because I'm overdosed on KP at work, and God, how I hate to face a sinkful of dirty dishes in the morning."

Faith speaks with the inner vibrancy of a soul who has been on this planet many times: "I work with people's bodies as a masseuse and a bioenergetic therapist. Everybody and every *body* is so special. I believe that if we breathed fully and were able to tune in to our body's sensations at all times, we would just about always be on the edge of orgasm." She smiles benignly at the other women, who nod back and laugh good humoredly. "That would take care of jealousy and wars and all that silliness," she continues. "One of the reasons I'm here is that I want to learn about ways to have more sensations from extragenital touch. For one thing, I'm bisexual and I'm terribly scared of AIDS. I don't want to say no to sex with partners. But I don't want to die before my time either. I'm looking for some evolved ways to have totally safe sex."

Tony is the group ingenue, and at age twenty-four, she is

the youngest in the room. Her statements tend to have a curly tail on them that makes them sound like questions. "I'm an adult child of just about everything?" she tells us. "A year ago I left a man who was abusing me? He was forty-five and had a daughter almost as old as me. But before things got abusive, he was a wonderful lover? He used to tie me down and do amazing things to me and that's where I learned about my body's responses? You might say he brought me to life? I live alone now with my two-year-old Tommy—that's my son—and Emily, our cat, and it's hard—I'm dirt poor and I miss the sex and I'm not sure I want to get into the dating market because of AIDS, but I feel good about starting over?"

To my knowledge, we are at this moment creating sexual history. As far as I know Iris, Rita, and company are the first group of easily orgasmic women ever to get together formally to discuss the subject of extragenital stimulation.

We are meeting in my office overlooking a pond in the Berkshires. It is high spring, June 1987. As we introduce ourselves, the sun smiles on us, the pondside weeds wave magnificently. Through the window I can see a muskrat rooting up grasses from the far bank and paddling to the little island where she is raising her babies; the green streamers must be trailing out six feet behind her. Tony, sitting next to me, spots the swimming greenery and gasps, "Oh my God, an alligator?"

It is not an alligator. It is only Myrtle Muskrat performing her annual rite of spring. But Tony's comment has created a perfect opening for the subject at hand. We segue into the problems of defining women's sexuality and the laughable (and unlaughable) rumors that circulate when outsiders observe and interpret women's desires and behavior. What happens is that these rumors begin to sound like fact, creating a sort of X-rated Ripley's "Believe It or Not." I use Tony's mistaken identification of the nest-building muskrat as an analogy to how suppositions about women's sexuality get carved into stone:

Adventures Beyond the Jade Gate

—Oh, yes! There's definitely an alligator living in a pond in the Berkshire mountains of Massachusetts! I saw it with my own eyes only last spring! It was bright green and it was six feet long and it was swimming like a bat out of hell! It would have eaten you alive if you'd fallen in the water!

—Oh, yes! A ramrod hard penis is definitely what gives women the most excitement and satisfaction in bed. Everybody says so! Besides, I read it in five different books from the self-help section of my bookstore!

But truth is stranger than fiction: "Isn't it a reality that men have always controlled the promo copy on the penis–vagina version of sex?" Mary-Jo calls out. I affirm her question as true, remarking that pleasure, orgasm, and ecstasy by *extragenital* means is virtually unresearched.

"Isn't it mentioned at all?" she asks.

"Well, *The Kinsey Report* talks a little bit about 'full body contact,' " I say, "and *The Joy of Sex* refers to making love 'fish fashion.'[5] But mostly, researchers focus on what they can measure, and other writers don't seem to look beyond their noses ("Or their penises!" calls out Mary-Jo again), except the writers of trashy romances, and then they do another kind of number on women.

"They don't bother with the riches that lie beyond the vulva," I continue. "To them, the sex act means genitals."

"Yeah," says Mary-Jo again, "all you have to do is look in the newsstand." We discuss the fact that contemporary magazines that deal explicitly with sex are full of propaganda about how a woman is at her happiest when there is a large penis inside her. Every issue of *Playboy* and *Hustler* sparkles with passages like "His throbbing engine plunged in and out of her hot lunch box as she gasped for more, more, more!" And if you look back through history, you see variations on this scene repeated over and over again.

Iris breaks in at this point to remark that penis propaganda is not limited to the Western world. "Have you looked at those Japanese prints with their mile-high penises? And what about Chinese pillow books, the ones that give all that advice to the brides?"

Indeed, one of the most creative variations on genital focus belongs to the ancient Chinese *Tao* of love and sexuality, which contains instructions for stimulating wives and concubines. If you think about it, these instructions are not so much about pleasuring women as they are about spreading the penis-vagina rumor—the homing site theory that serves to focus on male pleasure and keep women dependent on men. Of course, in premodern China, footbinding was another way of doing both.

Now that Iris has brought the subject up, I can't resist telling the group the following homing site story, adapted from Jolan Chang's *Tao of Love and Sex.*[6]

Back in the seventh century one of the sure-fire "love positions" was called Turning Dragon. I read from the book: "the man, using his left hand, pushes the woman's two feet up past her breasts. Using his right hand, he helps his jade stem into the jade gate."

Ah, yes, the jade stem. The master, Li T'ung Hsuan, lists six styles of thrusting it into the woman's jade gate. The impersonality of the descriptions rivals anything you'll find today in *Playboy, Hustler,* or, for that matter, *Popular Mechanics.*

Here (I read) is how to do it in seventh-century China:

1. Make contact and press down the jade peak, shuttling back and forth, sawing the substance as though one is cutting open an oyster so that one may reach the sparkling pearls. This is the first style.

2. Thrust down to the jade substance and pull up the gold gully [the clitoris] as though slicing off stones to find beautiful jade. This is the second style.

3. He uses his jade peak to thrust hard in the direction of the clitoris as if an iron pestle is pounding a medicine mortar. This is the third style.

4. He moves his jade peak out and in, hammering at the left and right sides of the "examination hall" [sides of the vulva]. As if a blacksmith is shaping iron with his five hammers. This is the fourth style.

5. He jabs his jade peak back and forth in short and slow thrusts inside the vulva, as if a farmer is preparing his land for late planting. This is the fifth style.

6. The jade peak and the jade gate are grinding heavily and closely, as if two avalanches are mingling. This is the sixth style.

Almost before I can finish, Rita bursts forth: "Most of that jade gate stuff is hysterically funny. But look at what it says about women. It makes it sound as if the only thing we know how to respond to is a throbbing engine or a jabbing peak. What about responding to a hand? Or a mouth? Just about anywhere my partner's hand or mouth happens to land is OK by me."

"Take that a step further," interjects Iris from her throne of pillows. "What about being really creative about flooding the senses? If you're clever, you can eroticize just about anything you find in your bureau drawers, even your broom closet. Have you ever had a silk scarf dragged incredibly slowly across your abdomen or a feather duster flicked up and down your back and buttocks until you thought you'd die?"

"You mean the Leda and the Swan treatment?" asks Rita.

Rita and Iris have opened the floodgates. All the women start talking at once. When the deluge subsides, we take a poll: Both Rachael and Tony, who are presently without sexual relationships in their lives, agree that a penis inside them might feel very good indeed. Mary-Jo and Iris say intercourse is far from the most important aspect of sex. For Rita, who is lesbian, and for Faith, who is searching

111

for totally safe sex with her male partners, a penis doesn't figure in the action at all.

The consensus is that there are many things in heaven and earth that are more sensational in bed than even the most versatile penis. A penis may be able to throb, plunge, pulsate, saw, hammer, grind, ejaculate, sometimes even caress, but it cannot lick, suck, nibble, spank, give a full-body massage, flick like feathers, or vibrate for an hour. And there are many places on the body from which sexual satisfaction can be triggered.

"So what *does* feel wonderfully erotic to you?" I ask this historic group. "What's your biggest extragenital turn-on? Where on your body do you feel it?" I beg them to answer one at a time. The women go around the room:

Rita: "Having my breasts caressed and my nipples gently sucked."

Iris: "A special place on my spine."

Rachael: "Just holding my lover and being held."

Tony: "Stroking my hair."

Faith: "Sucking my earlobes, also my palms and fingers."

Mary-Jo: "Any crevice."

Rita (again): "Mmm . . . popsicle toes."

I ask them to say what it feels like, to say more about their adventures beyond the jade gate.

Rita begins: "Well, popsicle toes is a great start for me. I love to have my lover suck on each toe, one by one, with attention and pleasure. But I don't really care which end of me she begins with. From head to toe seems to say it for me, although actually I am especially fond of my breasts. I could write a poem about my left breast. I think there must be a direct pipeline between that particular breast and the Great Orgasm in the sky. I can't imagine what kind of pleasure it must be like to nurse a baby."

Iris, who seems to be equally panorgasmic, follows Rita: "I respond to soft, tender touch on the middle of my back, on my buttocks, behind my knees, inside my elbows. I can come to orgasm on any of these. When my husband strokes the tender spot on my neck by my carotid artery, I go wild! Also, when my lips are stroked or sucked or when my back is licked or my buttocks are kneaded. The feelings go right through my whole body. The orgasms feel bigger and more complete than direct clitoral stimulation. By the way," she looks at Rita, "nursing my babies was like heaven—this intense sexual stimulation every four to six hours. But you don't respond with sex, you respond with immense love and bonding—and gratitude."

"Hugs are what I love—I mean the really radiant, lingering, full-body ones," says Rachael from her vantage point next to the box of tissues. She has cheered up since the beginning of group and is warming to the task at hand.

"Nobody in my family ever touched each other when I was growing up, but I can remember wonderful hugs as early as sleep-away camp where we all got to nest back to front in spoon position while the counselor read us ghost stories. And, speaking in the past tense, of course, I have a lovely memory of my departed ex-husband at the very beginning of our romance. We had this one amazing full-body hug before we started to touch each other sexually. We stood in the doorway holding each other and breathing for what seemed like hours (it was probably three minutes). He was out of town, and it was a month before we saw each other again, but that hug was a bond between us— sort of a physical and spiritual promise of things to come— a connection even though we were living far apart."

Tony jumps into the conversation, still halting and questioning herself: "I guess you could say I'm turned on by almost anything to do with hair? You can stroke mine or yank it." She grasps a piece of her black curly hair and gives it a hefty tug. "Once I had a group massage where we could ask for anything we wanted? I asked for people to massage me with their hair. So there I was with five people kneeling over me stroking me with their head hair, except one fellow was bald, so he used his beard. The guy I used to live with—he got jumpy if I got anywhere near his head. I used to run my hands through his hair but he didn't like it so that's when I got Emily, my cat."

As Faith begins to talk, a beatific smile spreads over her face. "I'm especially sensitive right behind the ears. So much so that I can hardly stand to be touched there. But I can last forever with a partner sucking my earlobes, blowing gently in my ears, licking them. I even got off at the doctor's once having the wax swooshed out."

From the top of their heads to their popsicle toes, women can find pleasure, orgasm, ecstasy when any of these is stimulated. What are the kinds of touch that are most evocative? I challenge the women who have already mentioned hands and mouths and vibrators and feather dusters to elaborate.

"The hand! Warm and slow and tender!" cries out Mary-Jo. There are nods and smiles around the room. "A long, leisurely all-over massaging and stroking. I had a lover once who used to trace my entire body with his fingertips, so lightly, so soft. Break-your-heart tender. I melted from the inside out. He wasn't any good at doing dishes, though, so the relationship never worked out."

Rachael adds, "Well, I agree about hands. But it depends on where I'm being touched. If it's directly on my genitals or breasts, firmness is important to me, to break the tension in the rest of my body. I just don't like to be tickled there. And I can't stand anything that feels tentative. If you're going to move in where I'm most vulnerable, don't diddle around asking questions. I want a hand that's intelligent, that knows where it's going and what it's doing. And I want it to stay with me when I start to move around."

"Right," grimaces Iris. "I hate it when my husband starts to space out and twiddle my nipples like radio dials."

"Or play doorbell with them. Yuck!" adds Rita.

Body Image, Respect, and Trust

At this point, the group falls into general conversation about being taken seriously and treated respectfully.

"Do you think respect has anything to do with body image?" asks Rachael from beside the box of tissues. "When I first got married, I was a size 6—really nervous and neurotic, anorectic almost. And frankly, I didn't have all that much interest in sex, I mean a real appetite for it, like ready to *kill* to get it. Of course I pretended to because I liked to see him turned on, I mean, in those days that was a turn-on itself. Then I guess I started to relax, because before you knew it I'd put on twenty-five pounds.

"Now a funny thing happened, well, it's tragic, really, not funny at all. As soon as I started to gain the weight, I could begin to feel my body—the roundness and curves—and I began to feel incredibly sexy and lush, like I *wanted* him. But you know what happened? He refused to touch me anymore. I'd gotten too big for him, he said. He called me awful names like Fatso and Chops. That just made me want to binge out on pecan pie and ice cream. So once I began to feel sexy, I didn't get any respect, and I didn't get any sex either."

"How do I get respect for my body?" Iris responds. "I wear makeup. I know that makes me sound like a throwback to June Cleaver, but I don't wear it to hide who I am, I wear it to accentuate certain parts of me. It happens in nature all the time. Look at birds and animals and plants, the kind of markings they have. I like to accentuate my eyes. That's the part I want people to see. And in bed, I want my husband to look at me, look me in the eyes and notice me."

"Body image and respect," breaks in Mary-Jo. "Try this one: When I was in college, I learned how to do belly dancing. For a couple of years afterward, I made pocket money by delivering belly-grams, where you put on a bangly costume and deliver a message to someone by doing a little

115

shimmy in the doorway. Mostly it was greetings to rich businessmen, and once I had to rise out of a cake at a bachelor's party. But I remember one poor sixteen-year-old boy whose mother bought him a coming-of-age belly-gram as a joke. When I showed up at the door, he was hanging out with his friends listening to records, and I had to chase him from room to room to deliver the shimmy with his message. He kept covering his head with his hands. He was mortified and so was I. That's when I decided the pocket money just wasn't worth the effort."

Tony has been listening to Mary-Jo with rapt attention. "That's amazing?" she affirms with her ever-present question mark. "The only thing I ever did for pocket money was make caramel apples?"

Iris observes that in terms of body image there's sometimes a thin line between being grandiosely pleasured and being treated like a sex object. "I know I don't like him playing doorbell with my boozies, but sometimes it's hard for me to know when he's just messing around like that or when he's actually adoring my body." She laughs.

"For me, the difference is with the intent," says Rachael.

"I think it's the feeling and energy," says Faith. "If your lover has your best interest at heart, the energy is always directed toward how you're responding, so there's built-in feedback there. I always pick up how someone feels about me. When there's love, I feel it through the hands. And well, that's an orgasm right there. That's sexual ecstasy."

"It's all a trust exercise . . ." intones Mary-Jo, lying back on the carpet and doing leg lifts.

"Speaking of trust exercises," Rita bursts in, "let's talk about kissing."

"I like it!" says Iris.

"I'm actually a little scared of it," says Mary-Jo, stopping her leg lifts and propping herself up on one elbow. "Mouth-to-mouth kissing or mouth-to-anything-else is a real risk for me. It represents my letting go of all sorts of emotional stuff like: Will I get herpes? Will God strike me dead? Will my partner bite me? Will I get AIDS? So already if I'm kissing someone, I've decided to be open and can relate to this person pretty wholly."

"For me kissing is a sign of commitment, a sign of intimacy," Rita adds. "I find my lover's mouth so much more intimate than her hand. She doesn't go through her day touching other people with her mouth. She saves that for me."

Faith says, "Kissing becomes spiritual for me. Maybe it's because I get so high on it. I zone out to another sphere. I can remember once kissing the whole evening long. It felt like flying through time and space, and all the time we were surrounded by a golden aura."

Mary-Jo raises her eyebrows and mumbles, "Oh sure, I guess that's how you do it as long as you're some kind of saint."

"Well, OK," Faith responds. "Kissing can be pretty carnal, too. And to tell the truth I can be very turned on by nipping and nibbling—even a little gentle gnawing is nice. Nibbling my earlobes means an immediate orgasm for me. Once I had a partner who bit me gently all over my body, taking little nips at each muscle. It was like a massage from a wild animal—a friendly wild animal, of course— amazingly exciting."

Mary-Jo wrinkles her nose and adds, "I can't stand really hard kissing, though, the kind where it gets down to your teeth. And biting will stop me anytime. Frankly, I don't want my partner to act as if he's making a meal out of me. He should have dinner before we have sex."

"Does anybody else get off on roughness?" queries Tony suddenly, looking embarrassed and speaking with the usual question marks after her statements. "Sometimes when I'm surprised or shocked, it wakes me up and gets my blood flowing? I'm talking about a little squeezing and pinching? Or having my back scratched with fingernails. That's an orgasm for sure."

Rachael breaks in. "The first person I was ever madly in

love with put me across his knees and smacked me a couple of times right up under the buttocks. *Thwack!* It wasn't a power thing or abusive or anything like that. It was like a bolt of pure pleasure. I think it worked only because I was in love and feeling very good and sure about myself. It was electrifying."

"Speaking of electricity," asks Rita, "that reminds me . . . anybody have any good vibrator stories?"

"You mean beyond the genitals? A vibrator can be very tantalizing all over the body," offers Iris. "Sometimes I'll use it just lightly on the side of my neck, like butterfly wings. Or very gently between my breasts."

"Well, right now, my Hitachi Wand happens to be my significant other," drawls Rachael, "so I'm feeling very close to her. But I can tell you it didn't feel so good when Dearly Departed Hal would whip out the old Hitachi and start running it up and down my thighs like a Tonka Toy."

"The key word is *control*, sweetie," interjects Mary-Jo. "He didn't have to treat you like a plaything. You should have told him that when it's your body, *you* get to control the machinery."

"Otherwise it's nothing but a macho power trip," agrees Iris. "I don't have anything against extraordinary stimulation. In fact I can remember being tied down once with my nylons and having a dildo inside me while my whole body was worked over by a vibrator. My *God*, I thought I'd *die*," she groans. Iris is gesticulating so broadly that she slides off her pillows and ends up on the carpet on her back, laughing and hugging herself.

As she crawls back onto her pillows and is rearranging her poncho around her, she comments in a less exercised tone, "You know, dress-up and fantasy and all that intense stimulation are fine, because they're conscious. But I think a lot of couples get into torturing each other without any consent. It's sort of a built-in part of the relationship that plays itself out in bed, too. S/M without any wittiness or fun."

"Sometimes," says Rita, "my lover and I will both use vibrators on ourselves, just to break down barriers, get us into our feelings, not necessarily even to be orgasmic."

"The man I was with—he would never let me use one," complains Tony.

Iris retorts, "Some men are threatened by sex toys. They have more rigid rules than we do about what it means to be a sexual person."

Seeking the Meanings Behind Touch

As I listen to this group of women talk about various kinds of extragenital touch, I begin to hear between the lines. There is a growing awareness that where the touch occurs on the body is not as important as how the touch is perceived and that quality, not quantity, is the secret ingredient. There is an awareness, too, that the feeling behind the touch is as important as the touch itself, that flooding the senses, as Iris puts it, does not exist in a vacuum. The tenderest fingers, the most vibrant vibrator, the slitheriest silk, may convey nothing without a constellation of other factors that give them meaning and connection. Setting, mood, love, commitment, time, and appropriateness are some of those factors.

My speculations are corroborated when I ask the women if there are certain conditions that affect their ability to respond sexually and fully to the various kinds of extragenital stimulation.

Mary-Jo says, "It depends entirely on whether I feel ready—not exhausted, but ready and turned on. Anywhere I'm touched is exactly the right place if I'm up for it."

"My skin is extremely sensual during my menstrual cycle," states Iris. "And when I was pregnant and nursing, I felt like a volcano, ready to erupt at any stimulus." Her

119

body seems to flow onto her tower of pillows, more like an earth mother now than a queen.

"Caring is the key for me," says Rachael. "Then body stroking head to toe. Breast stroking and kissing and stroking inside my thighs."

Rita says that orgasm is often a precondition for extragenital sensitivity: "After one or two orgasms, I feel as if I'm wired for flight. My lover can touch any part of me and I'll go off like a two-dollar pistol—my arms, hands, face, it doesn't matter where. My abdomen is especially sensitive right after orgasm."

Tony mentions no particular conditions: "Just the stimulation itself—and of course, feeling turned on by it?"

Faith reflects: "It makes a huge difference who my partner is. There are some people with whom any sexual interaction is orgasmic, and others, well, let's face it, I'm just not that turned on by everybody. Also, it makes a difference if I'm being an active partner. If I'm reaching out and doing the touching as well as just being a receiver, I get much more excited and energized."

The nods all around the room spark some banter about how good it feels to take care of a partner as long as your partner is also taking care of you. We spend a few minutes passing the women-who-love-too-much argument back and forth. Rita puts it to rest with the comment: "When I feel like reaching out it's because I'm feeling excited and loving. It's a natural reaction. That doesn't mean every time my heart goes pitter-pat I'm codependent."

Tony breaks into the general talk. Her statements have begun to lose their question marks at last: "But you have to watch out for being consumed with pleasing someone else. Because when I tried it, it certainly backfired. I ended up spending all this energy on him and he didn't give back to me. He ended up hating it and treating me like scuz."

This group of women who love sex has begun to enumerate not only what it is they love about their extragenital sexual encounters, but the virtues and flaws of their partners.

"Well, if we're talking about wonderful relationships," begins Mary-Jo, examining the soles of her pink running shoes. "when the going gets tough, the tough get out there and go shopping. And relationship shopping is exactly where I'm at. I can tell you what I love about sex, but at this point, I can't tell you who I love it with."

"I'll second some of that," says Rachael. "I would like the perfect person to materialize—pouf! But if he did, would I be able to recognize him? Until I'm sure, I'll stay home and get to know who *I* am."

Rita puts the conversation into perspective by saying, "I feel blessed because I love my partner and we are totally committed to living together long-term—and that's what makes all the difference for me. Sex is only a part of it. Being physical is only part of it. You can talk all you want about this kind of touch and that kind of thrill, but what it all shakes down to for me is that we're in the same place on the same journey together."

Iris clears her throat and settles into her pillows. It is evident she has a story she's ready to tell.

"I've been with the same man almost all my adult life. He's far from perfect, and we're far from perfect together. But I made up my mind about something years ago when I was going through sort of a three-year itch. I decided I could break our marriage apart by finding other lovers who could just maybe collectively, if they all worked hard together at the same time, meet all of my needs for skin contact. Or I could push the boundaries of the relationship I had and see how far they could bend. That was when I decided I had to be totally open with my husband about where I was at sexually—to have done less would have been to deny him, not to mention myself. And I asked that he do the same for me. So we ended up doing some pretty outrageous things together."

I ask Iris if there is a particularly outrageous experience she would care to tell us about.

She licks her lips and smiles. "The one that's coming to mind—maybe it's more *in*-rageous. It's when we were opening up to each other and there was nothing we did that didn't affect me inside as well as outside, you know. And when we played, it was that kind of psychobiological role playing that goes really deep."

She begins her story:

It began one weekend morning before we had kids. We were taking a shower together. I was starved for touch and we were soaping each other's backs. We'd just discovered peppermint soap—Dr. Bronner's—I remember the smell, the tingling. We were sliding around on each other's skin and the morning sun was shining into the shower through the hanging plants and the water sparkled on our bodies as we splashed.

Suddenly the scene shifted into something erotic and primitive. We weren't a married couple in a New York City shower stall anymore, we were in a jungle waterfall, cavorting among vines and rocks. We became wild animals, and we began to growl and paw each other's bodies. I grabbed him and started to lick him all over, starting with the very bottom of his backbone and moving up his spine. He called me his tiger woman and he was my hot, supple tiger—my mate.

We got out of the shower and shook the water out of our hair and rolled ourselves dry on our big shaggy towels. Then we worked our way all around the house licking each other.

As we landed on different pieces of furniture, we moved around in time and space. You know, first it's the bed under the covers and suddenly it's the cave, nesting with animal skins, snorting and grunting and gnawing at each other's pelts. And then next he's my cute guy again on the sofa, rubbing his beard against my belly. Then he's down on the rug—a wild man with many looks, many personae. As this is happening, it's dredging up all sides of me—sensual, tough, hungry, loud. Proud. All my animal tendencies, all my trashiness, too. There were no boundaries. We were inside each other's consciousness and bodies. There wasn't an inch of each other that we didn't explore—inside or out.

As Iris talks, she is hugging her knees and rocking on her pillows. Her eyes are focused inward as if this is the first time she has opened this particular window on herself.

We were breathing fire that day. He was breathing a wild fragrance, something I've never smelled before. His body was strong and gamy. We were touching everywhere, but what we were doing was much, much more than touch. We were totally synchronous, not only our bodies—it was psychological and emotional. We were dealing with archetypes here—the animus/anima—Jung said it. And we were gender hopping. It wasn't just the woman in me meeting the man in him. It's that the man in me had found the woman in him. I mean, at that moment, if he were a woman, he would have been me. We became mirrors for each other, infinite regressive mirrors. Powerful, reflective. It was as if I was making love to myself— and making love to myself as a man.

I felt so filled with power—so elemental—that I was ready to let go forever. I really felt maybe this time I wasn't coming back.

She pauses here, allowing the complexity of her remembered experience to move through her. Tony leans forward and asks, "Didn't you worry about fusion?"

"Not at that very moment, I didn't. I have this theory that as a very strong woman who's always on, I secretly long for escape, to let myself be dissolved, just out of relief of not having to be myself for a while. As a woman, I'm programmed to submit. At some level I guess I need to, it's genetic—and what's great sex about if it's not about that? I depend on it. I feel cheated if I don't get to that state.

"Other times, sure, I've had my concerns—fears that I could become completely overwhelmed by the flood of sensation, by the submitting that's a part of such strong sex. It's hard not to crumble and give over to the extreme sense of his person—to me he's kind of a walking archetype. I've had to work to maintain a healthy sense of my own self, so I'm not falling apart if I don't get that sort of attention all the time, so it doesn't become a fulcrum for my self-esteem."

Iris closes her eyes and breathes deeply. Then, as if by some inner command, her shoulders relax and her arms relinquish the knees they have been hugging. Her whole being radiates warmth as she opens up and looks at each woman in the room to indicate that she has finished.

Faith meets her gaze. "What you said really touches me. Especially because I had that somewhat similar experience I mentioned earlier. Not so soulful, but very wild feeling all the same. I always felt just a little embarrassed about liking it so much, but hearing you talk makes it seem OK to just enjoy it." She laughs as if she is delighted with the gift that Iris has given her.

Adventures beyond the jade gate. Once again, as I listen to stories of women who love sex, the physical becomes the emotional. Sex becomes the body–mind–spirit connection. No matter where women touch or are touched, it is most often what's behind the touch that counts. The pleasure, the orgasm, the ecstasy, are induced not so much by the actual stimulation as by how women think and feel about it and what it all means to them.

Faith continues the dialogue that has been punctuated by Iris's story. "Now I'd like to change the subject. I'd like to hear more about the safe-sex aspects of extragenital touching."

Adventures Beyond the Jade Gate

It so happens that just at the month this group is meeting I am also beginning work on a book about safe sex for women. The message of the book is that "just say no" is a nonanswer to the AIDS crisis; there are safe and positive alternatives to intercourse in this age of sexually transmitted diseases. Faith's question gives me a chance to launch into my essay on *outercourse*—the necessity of discovering pleasures beyond the genitals.

A woman's jade gate may be an avenue for pleasure, but it is also an avenue for organisms that carry infection, from herpes and chlamydia to the AIDS virus. Women can learn a great deal from the gay male community, which has become only too painfully aware of the lethal consequences of penile penetration (the fragile mucous membranes of both anus and vagina are alive with capillaries that are easily ruptured, and HIV is borne by both semen and blood). A great many gay men are now actively pursuing the erotic possibilities of touch that is safe and also "hot and horny." Their rallying cry is *"On* me, not *in* me!"

The facts are that extragenital adventures feel good, and they keep both women and men clear of HIV and other dangers transmitted by penetration of the penis into the vagina or, for that matter, into the anus or the mouth.

Mary-Jo and Rachael both have the same question: Is extragenital orgasm normal? "Let's face it," they agree. "The women in this room are not your average American consumers of sexual stimulation. I mean, how many other women out there are going to be having experiences like us? Maybe we're some kind of freaks or something."

Iris rises from her pillows in self-defense. "Are you saying I'm not supposed to believe what my own body tells me? So maybe we're the only women in the country who can come off to nongenital touch. Or maybe every woman in the universe can if she just finds out it's an OK thing to do. I don't know the answer to this. But I do know we've been telling the truth today. And our truths are common to all sexual relationships that are balanced ones. We know

125

what feels good. We go after it. We feel better about ourselves as a result. We may not be normal in the sense of
usual, but I think we're normal in the sense of healthy. And
I know our stories can inspire women whether they're Jane
Q. Housewife or Ms. Flipping Marvel."

"I agree with you," says Faith. "In my bioenergetic therapy practice I see so many women who say they're sexually
dysfunctional. Some of them have physical problems, like
this one woman who's quadriplegic. She has no feeling in
her pelvis. What does genital sex do for her? I'm working
with her so that she can begin to feel some pleasure again—
to develop the potential for pleasure that she does have—
on her arms and shoulders."

Iris picks up on Faith's comments. "I also see women in
therapy who say they're dysfunctional. Sometimes their
only dysfunction is that they don't accept that what they're
doing and feeling *is* sexual. And sometimes it's that they're
terribly cut off from their genitals by the terrible things
that have happened to them. If these women could engage
their whole bodies, they wouldn't have to blank out the
experience of sex."

"OK, I get it," says Rachael. "We here in this room are
just as normal as anybody else. Or maybe we're no more
abnormal than anybody else. Because probably most
women are abnormal if you believe all the messages out
there about what normal sex is." The penny has just
dropped for Rachael. She has just understood the homing
site theory of sexual normality.

"Right," responds Iris. "But I think we have to take care
that these extragenital orgasms we're talking about aren't
somehow taken as a new norm, a new goal. That would
just leave some women feeling worse because they don't
come to orgasm every time they brush their hair."

There is an appreciative silence. I ask the women if they
have anything further they want to discuss about extragenital sex before we disband.

Rita says, "This has been really powerful for me. I'm so

happy to find other women who will talk about this. So much of women's potential is discounted in the world—and here we stood up to be counted." Rita glows as she looks into the eyes of the other women in the room. "Thanks," she says.

Tony is the last to speak. She looks out onto the pond where the muskrat has finished lunch and has resumed swimming with swags of greenery from bank to island. "Things look really different out on the pond now. I look out there and I see a muskrat. A glossy little gray muskrat swimming back and forth with grass in her mouth. It seems amazing that just a couple of hours ago I could have mistaken her for an alligator." There is no hint of a question mark at the ends of her sentences.

Tony may well be amazed at what she has learned from Myrtle Muskrat. Perhaps it is Myrtle who has delivered the most eloquent message of the afternoon: Things are not always what they seem to be at first glance. Women's sexual response is too complex for that, too intricately connected with feelings, meanings, memory, and acts of defiance and courage. Many of our sources of sexual energy lie underground, perhaps in a warren of soft caves such as Myrtle Muskrat has dug beneath the pond bank to keep her babies safe from predators.

Even women who love sex may not be fully aware of those underground riches until they are directly asked about them. The stories of Iris and company open up new possibilities for sexual adventure, or for validating adventures women may already be having. If, as Mae West suggests, too much of a good thing can be wonderful, imagine what can happen if we keep expanding our definitions of what a good thing is.

5

Dr. Suzanne

Thinking Off and Other Thoughts on Sexual Imagination

Only through each woman's discovery of "her own interior wavelength"—her exploration of what it is that she herself, separate from her programming, thinks is erotic—can an integrated self, which is a possible and honorable goal, be approached.

—*Robin Morgan*

ORGASM WITHOUT TOUCH. Women who love sex say it's a possibility. Whether it is a solo treat or experienced in the presence of a partner, they say it feels like a gift from the Good Witch of the North, a magnificent event like being blown out of Kansas and into the Land of Oz. The clinical label is spontaneous orgasm, but Dr. Suzanne Adesta, a woman who particularly loves this aspect of sex, has offered up a more graphic name. "Doing it without hands?" she says. "I do it all the time. I call it *thinking off.*"

Dr. Suzanne is a sociology professor in a small-town college, the kind of community where you still don't need to lock your door. A single mother, a yoga enthusiast, an advo-

128

cate for women's rights, she has few secrets from her students and colleagues. But there is something they don't know about her. She is uniquely skilled at coming to orgasm without touching herself physically and is one of twenty women who have volunteered to have these kinds of skills documented in a laboratory setting.

Let me back up. During the summer of 1987 I was privileged to coauthor a how-to book on safe sex with Dr. Beverly Whipple, research scientist of G-spot fame.[1] Beverly had just acquired a new computer setup for her laboratory at Rutgers University in Newark, New Jersey, which was now equipped for impressively high-tech measurements of the human condition, including women's sexual response. In the course of collaborating on *Safe Encounters*,[2] she became fascinated that so many of the women I had interviewed for my dissertation had reported being able to come to orgasm without touch. At first she was tuning into the safe-sex ramifications inherent here—no partner, no problem. No *hands*, clearly no problem.

But important as women's ability for orgasm without touch might be as a technique for safe sex, we could see that the implications went far beyond avoidance of physical diseases. To take seriously the fact that women can generate sexual satisfaction just by thinking about it challenges the myth—still amazingly current on the cusp of the twenty-first century—that a woman needs a man to give her orgasms or else she turns into a cranky, unfulfilled shrew. It challenges the most sacred tenet of sex research: the notion that sexual pleasure is centered in the genitals and depends on physical stimulation. It also challenges the norms of politically correct feminism with its focus on the violent and destructive aspects of sex and its virtual denial of positive possibilities. If women are able to experience this degree of delight through playing with their own imaginations, it gives them the choice to experience sex without being victims of an invasive partner.

Searching the literature, I had found the references on

129

spontaneous orgasm to be almost negligible. For instance, the Kinsey interviews reported that only 2% of their sample of women experienced orgasm on "fantasy alone."[3] Hite found less than 1%.[4] Masters and Johnson reported that not a single one of their research subjects was able to experience fantasy-stimulated orgasm in the laboratory.[5] Yet of my original sample of women who love sex, a whopping 64% had said yes in answer to the question, Have you ever come to orgasm without any kind of touch? In the years before and after I interviewed this research sample, other women stepped forth to offer a wide variety of anecdotal information.

Clearly, there was an irreconcilable discrepancy between the literature and the reports of these women who love sex. What could we do to explore it? How could we validate the stories of the women? Ever the scientist, Dr. Bev turned to me and said, "I'll bet we can quantify your research in the lab."

"Why not?" I replied. Even though I had been outspoken against most quantitative sex research because it seemed to limit and codify the meanings of sex rather than expand them, I felt this collaboration might be an adventure. For one thing, participating in such a lab study might shake loose some of my own prejudices. More importantly, it could further the cause of women. I knew that even as I spoke there were women in cities, towns, and hamlets all over the world happily thinking themselves onward and upward, but I also knew that to many people, among them sexologists, this ability seemed about as credible as a sighting of killer bees over Nome, Alaska. But numbers talk. And in this instance, I felt computer-recorded data could help doubters believe that women really can do what they say they can do. Beverly and her collaborator, Dr. Barry Komisaruk, had already devised much of the methodology we would need.[6] All we had to do now was find the women.

Thinking Off and Other Thoughts on Sexual Imagination
Setting the Stage for Laboratory Research

In my dissertation days, finding women to interview behind closed doors about their peak sexual experiences had been both simple and serendipitous. But locating women who are willing to travel to a steaming city on a Thursday or Friday afternoon in the middle of summer to come off to their erotic fantasies while hooked up to monitors that measure their physiologic responses turns out to be a whole other ball of wax.

Eventually, through colleagues in the sex field, we manage to luck into a network of women who are not only eager to lend their bodies and minds to science, but also to recommend their friends. Suzanne is a very well-recommended friend. Articulate and messianic about getting the word out to other women, she is walking proof that it is possible to learn extraordinary control over the orgasmic process. "Just tell me which chakra you'd like to measure," she announces as she settles onto the decorative pillows with which we've softened the hospital bed and is being hooked up to monitors. "I can orgasm up and down all the energy centers. I don't know how much time you've got, but I won't have any problem keeping things going all afternoon."

Patently, Suzanne feels more comfortable at this moment of research than I. It isn't that I am nervous about witnessing her thinking-woman's calisthenics. In fact I am wildly curious and quite confident she can do her thing as stated. But will I be able to do mine? After all, she's been orgasming up and down her chakras for years, but this is my very first whack at bona fide laboratory research. Even though she is not the first subject whose responses we are measuring, I still have some performance anxiety about the mechanics of it all. I have bought a white doctor's coat on the trip down to Rutgers to help me get into role, but how much is that really going to help?

Suzanne is dressed in a pink cotton skirt and print blouse

131

and looks like a well-scrubbed sorority housemother. I slide into a chair beside her bed and explain the sequence of the study we are about to do:

There are three ten-minute segments, with five-minute resting periods between each segment. With an additional resting period at the beginning and end, the experimental part of the study will take about an hour.

Her job, I inform her, will be contained in these three segments. First, she will listen to a ten-minute guided imagery tape,[7] allowing herself—if possible—to come to orgasm *without touch*. Second, she will stimulate herself genitally for ten minutes, bringing herself—if possible—to orgasm *with touch*. In the final ten minutes, she will use her own internal imagery to bring herself—if possible—to orgasm, *no touching*. I indicate that I will be interrupting her throughout the sequences to take measurements.

"No problem," she says with a big smile. "What do all those machines do?" She gesticulates in my direction. So many wires crisscross my space that despite the white lab coat I feel like Lucille Ball about to launch into a telephone operator routine.

At my elbow are a tape recorder loaded with the guided imagery tape I have recorded earlier, a split-screen monitor that manifests four sets of measurements second by second at one-minute intervals, an intercom for communicating with Beverly sitting at the computer in the next room, and a spare vibrator in case it is needed for the genital part of the study.

"And what about me," she asks. "What am I wired up for here?"

Suzanne has a blood pressure cuff strapped around her left calf and a pulse monitor Velcroed to her big toe.[8] These will record automatically, I explain, vastly relieved that I don't have to fuss with them.

"Let's demonstrate the pressure gauge," I say, showing her the Lucite and chrome instrument on the table by her left hand.[9] I ask her to place a fingertip on the point of a

132

small cone at the base of the instrument while I activate the gauge that slides along the top, providing increasing amounts of pressure.

"Ow!"

"Oops," I say, releasing the pressure. "Well, that's how it works. When you first feel something, please say 'now,' and just as it becomes painful, say 'stop.' Then I'll stop the gauge.

"This is how we're going to measure pain thresholds on each one of the fingers on your left hand. We'll repeat this process at least ten times, once during each of the resting periods and then every five minutes or each time you come to orgasm."

"You'll have to keep me posted," she says. "What's in that box? Buried treasure?"

Balanced on my knees is a foot-long plastic container of nylon filaments, each minutely calibrated in graduated thicknesses from the size of a small dowel to the delicacy of a hair.[10]

"After each set of finger measurements, I'm going to brush the back of your hand with one or more of these fibers to measure your ability to distinguish skin sensation."

"And what's that thing?" She waves her free hand at a futuristic ophthalmic device on a dolly over the bed.

"That's the pupilometer.[11] Its purpose is to detect enlargement in your pupil diameter. It's the most sophisticated measure we have of orgasmic response."

"It looks like it belongs on 'Star Trek,' " she remarks.

"Well, you're going to become very familiar with it. We'll be using this each time we do the finger-pain measurements and the tests for skin sensation." To practice using the pupilometer I ask her to sit upright, place her chin just so in the chin rest, and stare without blinking through the eyepieces at an X marked on the wall. I indicate the TV screen across the room, where her pupil diameter materializes like

133

a harvest moon. The VCR underneath is recording it for posterity.

"Let's get started," she says when we finish the test run. I notice that her eyes are beginning to glaze a little.

"OK, we're ready," I announce to Beverly over the intercom. Almost instantly the amber monitor at my elbow jumps into motion. The first minute of our study begins to pulse with the recorded data of Dr. Suzanne.

Witnessing the Mind–Body Connection

The opening moments of the study are a so-called resting period, one of five control periods with which we will compare the experimental pieces of the study. During the initial run of measurements I ask Suzanne how she discovered her ability for thinking off.

"Ow!" she says as the pressure gauge catches her finger by surprise again. "I've been doing it since I was a little girl. My grandmother lived with us. She was a pretty fierce lady, kind of a self-styled Calvinist, you know, work yourself to the bone, but never, ever have any fun. Well, she told me never, ever to touch myself Down There. And I obeyed her. Everyone obeyed Granny. It was one of the laws of nature. But I found out I could daydream. In my head, I could do whatever I wanted, and Granny couldn't do a thing about it. And then I discovered something wonderful in the school playground. One of those wooden swings with long, long ropes hanging from a tree. Every time the swing went up—Whoosh! I'd come off. And then down—Aaaahh! Of course I didn't know what it was called then, but I sure used to spend a lot of time on that swing when I was a kid."

Suzanne's reflection makes me marvel at how inventive women can be. In their sexuality, as in other aspects of life, some women seem to possess the gift of using oppression as a springboard to enhance their lives rather than letting it knuckle them under to a pleasureless existence. Betty Jane—B.J.—is another volunteer for this study and another case in point. It wasn't a disapproving granny but a foul-breathed, panty-snatching alcoholic uncle who precipitated her penchant for fantasy orgasms: "I hated him so much. I learned to dissociate when I was young. It probably never would have occurred to me to develop it into the sexual arena if I hadn't needed so much to feel perfectly hidden and safe." B.J. confided this to me, as easily as if she were saying, "Well, after all, when life hands you a lemon . . ."

Oppression is not the only reason women learn about spontaneous orgasm, of course. As I reflect on Suzanne's and B.J.'s talent for defensive thinking off, I also remember many women speaking of spontaneous delights first discovered through sheer serendipity—during dreamy childhood summer days when fantasy was encouraged. Or as an adult jogging along the San Francisco waterfront breathing in the invigorating air and expansive images. Or lolling around on pillows listening to music. Or sitting beside a lover in a movie theater watching the sex scenes.

The first measurements completed, it is time for the guided imagery tape (a complete transcription starts on p. 257). This is ten minutes of permission for Suzanne to breathe fully and to follow the rhythm of her breathing into any kind of sexual imagery and satisfaction she desires. The tape invites listeners to be exquisitely aware of their sexual imaginations and to allow their responses to flow, but it does not mention body parts or explicit genital actions. Suzanne finds listening to the tape to be intensely erotic. As advertised, her energy begins to move and build to the release of orgasm.

There is no motion I can discern from her body except her breathing, which deepens to quiet moans. I can see tears gathering at the edges of her eyelids. The amber monitor shows her blood pressure steadily rising and her pulse rate beginning to spike.

Her orgasm is long and graceful. It becomes a presence in the room. An awesome, almost holy being, as if we are both being blessed by the flow of energy. I, too, am moved to tears. As gently as I can, I interrupt Suzanne to take the required measurements, suggesting that she keep her energy focused on her internal images and let me do the work.

"OK, Coach," she moans without missing a beat.

I place her left forefinger on the Lucite cone, and the pressure gauge begins to bore into Suzanne's fingertip past the point where she has routinely said "ow," past the last marker, and finally off the scale. In the midst of orgasm, she apparently feels no pain. This happens with each finger.

"Did you feel anything?" I ask her.

"Whunh?" she responds, still in *status orgasmus*.

During the resting measurements of her pain thresholds, Suzanne has been vocal as she feels the pressure gauge revving up. In midorgasm, however, she registers dramatically little pain. She seems barely aware that she has nerve endings.

Yet seconds later, when I flick the back of her hand with a hair-thin nylon filament, she responds immediately: "Sure, I can feel that." Her tone conveys: "Why are you asking such a dumb question? Of course I have sensation there. Doesn't everybody?"

At this point during Suzanne's orgasm without touch, we are replicating a phenomenon that the Whipple and Komisaruk studies have reported in earlier research on orgasms from genital self-stimulation: Orgasm has a pain-blocking effect.[12] We are also replicating a corollary discovery: Even with the pain-blocking effect of orgasm, there remains an acute ability to perceive skin sensation. During her orgasm without touch, Suzanne reacts immediately to the slightest whisper of the von Frey fiber brushing the back of her hand.

It is pupilometer time. Time to cajole her into sitting up to relate to the sophisticated measuring device suspended over the bed. This is not a simple operation. Suzanne is prone in a trancelike state, almost oblivious to outside influence. As my orders filter through, she has to figure out a way to retain her orgasm while rising into a ramrod position, chin and forehead clamped just so against cold black metal. Then, still retaining the orgasm, she has to stare through the eyepieces, locate the X on the wall before her, and focus steadfastly on it until Beverly's voice over the intercom crackles and whines, "OK. I got it on the computer. You can relax now." The pupilometer turns out to be a devilish distraction for some of the twenty volunteers for this project but not for Dr. Suzanne. "Oh, God," she pants as she lurches upright to stare unblinkingly at the X on the wall. "This thing turns me on."

During the next resting period I ask Suzanne to describe what she has just experienced as a result of listening to the tape. The members of our research team are curious to know what images women conjure up as they think off. Our colleague, Barry, hypothesizes that some kind of genital stimulation will invariably be part of the imagery.

Suzanne surprises us.

"I saw myself floating in bright sunshine," she begins, her eyes still damp and dreamy. "Then there was an even brighter light, and I was floating with the Great Spirit— the Goddess. And all the light entered my being. And I could feel it moving through every part of my body until it reached my heart. I had this insight that every culture has its name for essence and that the name for mine was Heart. I could feel tears starting, and then my heart just sort of opened like a flower. And the energy started to move. I felt so loved. I really wanted to stay there forever. I was sorry when the tape was over. Did you get the measurements you needed?"

I assure Suzanne that everything is going just fine.

During the ten-minute sequence of genital self-stimulation, Suzanne begins by reaching her right hand down to her clitoris. Her orgasms are almost immediate, with more obvious muscle tension than the guided imagery orgasms and with much more sound: A lusty "Mmmmmmmmmmmmm! Ooooooooooooh! Ayeeeahhhh!" replace the breathy moans from the guided imagery sequence. The amber monitor spikes higher. The finger measurements, however, record a similar nonawareness of pain, and the von Frey fibers produce a similar acute awareness of tactile sensation from the lightest touch. From my vantage point beside Suzanne and the other women who volunteered for the study, a pattern begins to emerge even before we analyze the computer data. Orgasms from imagery, like the genital orgasms in former studies from this laboratory, apparently induce analgesia without reducing a woman's receptivity to pleasurable touch.

I find myself wondering about orgasm and the diminution of pain. Does a woman's orgasm really block pain as the Whipple–Komisaruk studies have suggested? Or does sexual arousal and orgasm actually expand a woman's ability to tolerate everything? I am remembering Maya's conversation with a woman who had detailed the excruciating pleasure of being whacked with a leather paddle on her buttocks until she came to orgasm: "The further out there I am with arousal," she had told Maya, "the more the pain changes its form and doesn't feel like pain anymore. It feels like another state of sensation where I'm pushing my tolerance boundaries and begging for more."

After five intensive minutes of clitoral stimulation, Suzanne asks, "Would you like me to switch to a vibrator now to see if there's any difference in the data?" She reaches to the bedside table and plucks a Hitachi Wand from her velour bag. Almost as soon as she plugs it in she begins to orgasm again.

I notice that a portion of the amber monitor at my elbow has suddenly gone blank, indicating what looks to me like brain death. I quickly check to see if Suzanne's vital signs are showing. She is arched in orgasm, alternately panting, grunting, and asking, "Is this giving you what you want?" The monitor's problem is not with Suzanne, but with the blood pressure cuff. It has blown its Velcro tab, and because I am too trapped by wires to reach Suzanne's left calf to reattach it myself, I hiss a Mayday message into the intercom so that Beverly can creep discretely into the room and make repairs.

Everything else during the genital part of the study goes without a glitch. The numbers record smoothly, and Suzanne is patently enjoying herself. It seems she is just beginning to hit her stride.

Has she had any images during the genital orgasms? I ask her during the next resting period.

"The images kind of came and went," she replies. "First I was in a bar in Sao Paulo ogling this gorgeous male dancer. Then I was in a beach house with my husband and he was bringing me breakfast on a tray with wild roses and nuzzling me all over my body. Then we were joined by three women and I was lying back on the pillows sucking on mango slices and watching while they sweetly ravished him and each other with fingers and mouths. I was letting myself feel what each of them was feeling. I think that must have been when the blood pressure cuff blew."

This kind of graphically erotic storytelling was typical of the fantasies of some of the other women in the study. Each had her own unique story line, of course, ranging from trysting with a new love on a brass bed to a Red-Riding-Hood escapade with a wolf who lavished his victims with oral sex. One of the women, however, had a drastically different take on the notion of sexual fantasy: "For me sexual imagery is not so much about thinking *off* as about thinking *in*. I go totally inside. I empty my mind. It's a spiritual space. Quiet and light. The image is always a place where I can take care of my self. Sometimes my orgasms are very subtle and sometimes they're major explosions. What makes them feel so good is they're always an expression of self-nourishment."

*　　*　　*

139

During the final sequence of the study, I direct Suzanne to use her own imagination as the sole stimulation to bring herself to orgasm. No guided imagery, no touching. I watch and wait and eye the monitor.

She lies perfectly still, yet the quality of her sexual response shows still another aspect of orgasmic possibility. At one point, at the apex of release, her energy seems to disappear for about a minute into some kind of limbo, and on the amber screen there is a concomitant drop of heart rate and blood pressure, as if her vital signs are hovering there, waiting for Suzanne to reappear.

I ask her where she has been. Her voice is deep and slow. Her eyes are closed and she speaks with great feeling in sentences of few words: "Moving. With Tony. A long time ago. On a boat."

"Where are you now?" I ask. It is evident to me that she has been, and still is, in a state of orgasm despite the drop on the monitor.

"I'm in my throat." She is whispering hoarsely. "I'm orgasming in my throat chakra . . ."

Much as the researcher in me would like to learn every detail about this extraordinary unfolding, I feel it would be a breach of privacy to ask more questions. It seems intrusive even to observe. I quiet my energy and witness her as smoothly as I can. Her body is still, yet with each exhaled breath, spaced long moments apart, energy seems to be undulating along the length of it in waves.

In the last minute of the sequence, I interrupt Dr. Suzanne to measure her pain thresholds and pupil size. On the TV monitor across the room I can see a definitive sign of vast arousal; her pupil balloons up big as a basketball.

Thinking Off and Other Thoughts on Sexual Imagination
Owning the Power of Sexual Imagination

When the experimental part of our study is over, Beverly enters the room and the three of us sit down to debrief. As Beverly explains, Suzanne is no longer a "naive" subject, that is, we no longer have to keep details about our hypotheses from her. This is a time we can all relax and ask each other anything we want. We begin by questioning Suzanne about her chakra orgasms.

"During the genital part, I was definitely orgasming in my pelvis. I could feel the contractions—vaginal ones at first and then uterine ones when I used the vibrator. I guess those are what you'd call my 'normal' orgasms, where I tense up and let it all go.

"During the guided imagery, the release was in my heart chakra. My whole chest got warmer and warmer, and then it simply opened up. It was basically all above the waist. I felt immensely sacred, loving feelings flow from my chest and out through my arms and fingertips. That's probably why I was so unaware of you taking the pain measurements." As a matter of interest, we inform her that the women who had preceded her in this study also had dramatically lessened perceptions of pain during the guided imagery, even though they could not so precisely chart the flow of their orgasms.

Beverly asks, "What happened during the third part of the study when you provided your own stimulation through imagery?"

"Now that was another interesting one." Suzanne laughs. "The orgasm was up in my throat. I was feeling so in love with Tony on a boat trip we took. Did you ever get so filled up with emotion that you couldn't talk? As if you'd unplugged your head and were living on pure love? Well, that's what was happening. It was all in my throat. And in my eyes. Finally I felt it behind my sinuses and eyes."

"What *was* it you felt?" we ask in unison, like the Doobie sisters.

"I felt beauty and grace. I felt a marshaling of all my forces. An opening and moving of all my energy. I guess you could say I felt like a landslide about to happen."

And then, as our data obligingly documented, Suzanne happened.

Suzanne has questions for us.

"I can feel myself thinking off, so I know it occurs," she says. "But how? Is there a scientific explanation for what happens physiologically?"

Beverly admits that the study in which we are now engaged is so far the only laboratory test. (As a result of that study, it is now, for the very first time, a quantified fact that women can come to orgasm at will just by thinking about it with no physical stimulation of the genitals or any other part of the body. Thanks to Dr. Suzanne and her cohorts, we were able to document proof-positive signs of orgasms without touch: increased heart rate, systolic blood pressure, pupil diameter, and also tolerance of pain combined with acute awareness of skin sensation.)[13]

"Otherwise," we say, "we can't give you scientific data to answer your question."

We point out that sexual science and scholarship have shown little interest in women's spontaneous responses of orgasm, reminding her of the negligible percentages reported by both Kinsey and Hite in their comprehensive surveys of women's sexual behavior. We remind her, too, that aside from our study, researchers have had zero success in trying to measure spontaneous orgasm in a laboratory setting—obviously they weren't lucky enough to have met Dr. Suzanne and her friends.

"But there's plenty of data about spontaneous orgasm for men, isn't there?" she queries. "I mean, isn't it supposed to be normal, even expected, especially for young men?

Poor things. Especially in places where they get caught, like math class and the back seats of cars."

"Yes," I answer. "And we can giggle about this, but sometimes it isn't funny at all. Sometimes thinking off for men is spelled Premature Ejaculation." We remind Suzanne that the clinical literature is full of accounts of this dreaded dysfunction, which (in the literature) means that a man is unable to satisfy his female partner because he ejaculates "spontaneously" and loses his erection before enough penis–vulva contact is made for the woman to come to orgasm. I add that it's also well known that men have spontaneous sexual experiences during sleep. Starting at puberty they routinely have spontaneous ejaculations, a.k.a. nocturnal emissions or wet dreams.

"Well, it shouldn't take laboratory research to prove *that*," she laughs. "My son is fifteen and whenever I do the laundry it's pretty obvious from his sheets and pajama bottoms what's happening for him at night."

"Right," I agree. "Women don't produce telltale evidence like that. There's actually research that supports the notion that nocturnal orgasms are rare for women because they're a result of hormones—*male* hormones." I cite research that speculates that it is high androgen levels that trigger wet dreams.[14]

"What does the research say about sleeping *women?*" queries Suzanne.

"Not much." Again I cite what literature there is. Sexologists have conceded that during sleep, female paraplegics can experience orgasm. But according to them, these are not grade-A certified orgasms. They are only phantom orgasms, "purely cerebral event[s], with no genitopelvic concomitants."[15]

"It's the same boring fact." Suzanne snorts, leaning back against the pupilometer dolly. "Sexual science assumes that men are the star performers."

I agree with her wholeheartedly. The research, or lack of it, leads readers to imagine yet another physiologic inequality between women and men: "What the literature seems to want us to conclude is that men can have orgasms spontaneously and women can't unless we have spinal cord injuries. And those orgasms aren't real orgasms anyway, we are only *imagining* the sensations."

"As if imagination isn't crucial!" whoops Suzanne. "As if it isn't a crucial factor in the perception of *all* sexual sensation!"

Despite the spotty scientific data, there is plenty of anecdotal evidence of happily spontaneous orgasm from women who love sex. These women include Dr. Suzanne and others who opted for laboratory research. They include the 64% of the women from my dissertation interviews and a variety of other women over the years. Granted, these women are hardly a cross section of urban and rural America, any more than were Maya on her mountaintop discussing sexual ecstasy or Iris and company discussing extragenital stimulation. But they can give us valuable insight into the possibilities, both sleeping and awake.

Many women who love sex report experiencing orgasms in their sleep, androgen levels notwithstanding. Some say this has occurred only once or twice in their lives. Others speak of some regularity: "Every few months." "In clusters when I'm turned on to life." "Sometimes just before my period." Says Sandra, mother of four, innkeeper, and professional baker whose life is filled with busyness and warmth: "There are cycles when sleeping seems more exciting than being awake—more alive, more tuned in. There's a lot of psychic movement I don't feel any control over and opening up sexually is a part of it. Sometimes there are dreams involved, but mostly there's no content, just a feeling."

Author Judy Grahn writes of her sleep orgasms, corroborating the "scientific" notion of no genitopelvic concomitants and stressing the pleasure she felt: "I have on occasion been awakened by an orgasm in my sleep, accompanied by an erotic dream. And when I reached down to my vulva to continue the pleasant sensations and possibly encourage a second helping, I have found that my clitoris is quietly tucked into her vulval bed, not hot, not swollen, not sensitive, not even awake. The orgasm had not happened in my clitoris, or anywhere in my body. It had taken place in my mind."[16]

Other women report using their minds to think off when they are wide awake, and some are able to exercise a fair amount of control. Maybe they don't all play in Dr. Suzanne's league, but they are control pitchers nonetheless, using meditation and guided imagery: "I make up elaborate fantasies to amuse myself." "I create an atmosphere by putting myself there with my mind." Other women simply let nature take its course: "I have no idea how I get there," remarks Carol, who lives on a farm and trains horses for a living. "Sometimes it's just as I'm waking up or when I see a certain kind of movie."

Everyone seems to want to know *what* women think about when they're thinking off. I was once asked by an interviewer on national television: "Do they think about their *husbands?*"

Yes, they think about their husbands. They also think about other women's husbands. They think about their boyfriends, girlfriends, lovers, movie stars, and the luscious hunk fixing the hole in the road outside the office window. They think about snatches of music and how the light plays through the leaves on a spring morning. Like Suzanne, they think about everything from group sex to the arms of the Goddess. In short, they think about whatever turns them on.

And sometimes, paradoxically, they think about what turns them off. Women have the capacity to be orgasmic to fantasies of putdowns, whipping, hitting, biting, and chains around their necks. They can learn to switch thoughts around inside their brains until even the things that turn them off turn them on. I remember Betsy, a colleague in the sex field, whose most surefire erotic fantasies include being bound by black leather thongs and being led around by a studded dog leash. And there are women who use terrifying memories of rape and abuse to excite themselves to orgasm.

Some women who love sex say they can think off even when stimulation is not particularly exciting or overtly erotic: "I was at my desk writing about intense emotional feelings," says Moira, a family therapist interning at a substance abuse clinic. "I felt myself becoming extremely sexual, and I let myself let go." Michelle tells me she is a nature lover: "Just lying in the sun does it for me. Letting the warmth wash over every inch of my skin, I feel as if I'm melting and becoming part of the universe."

Still other women mention using no-touch techniques with a partner: reading a love letter, listening to a phone call, making eyes across a crowded room. "It's like getting a psychic massage," says Jess, one of the women in the original interviews. "I don't even need to be touching him. When he's nearby, I *feel* different, my body feels tingly. Full of love vibrations."

Arlene, a physical therapist, has experimented extensively with such psychic massage. She speaks of herself as an "assistant," a "channel" ("and of course a magnificent lover!"), able to orchestrate in her partner a kind of organized excitement redolent of Dr. Suzanne demonstrating how she can call forth orgasm in each of her chakras. "It's altruistic, but it's powerful," Arlene tells me as she talks about stroking her lover's aura to invoke orgasm and ecstasy: "I pass my hands over her, slowly, slowly, never touching, just a couple of inches above her flesh. She gets incredibly excited and she comes, sometimes many times. The places of most energy seem to be her pelvis and her throat and her heart area. Mostly we make love with our bodies, but sometimes it's wonderful to get our auras together and let them play."

From years of listening to stories like these, I have come to believe that thinking off is much more common than is reported in the sexuality literature. I indulge myself by speculating for a moment with Dr. Suzanne as we continue to debrief in the lab. She has risen from her perch on the bed and is now standing up and fondling the black plastic of the pupilometer.

"Let's say that women are born with the capacity for a very great deal of sexual imagination and that over the centuries we've had to go underground."

"Or be punished as sexual witches." Suzanne is exactly on my wavelength. "So we've had to keep this capacity a secret. Shrouded from light. In the collective inner sanctum of our sexual consciousness."

"And let's say that this thinking-woman's secret is a source of power," I continue, warming to the subject. "Satisfaction without touch is a way to contact sexual energy without being defined by a partner, even when the experience may be in the presence of a partner. It's a way to invoke the spiritual energy that connects body, mind, and emotions. This is something women can do at any time in any place, because it's all in our heads. Or all in our chakras." I nod at Suzanne. "It's so private that it can feel like a kind of parthenogenesis. The flow of power stays with the woman from beginning to end."

"That certainly describes my experience," says Suzanne. "My sexual feelings belong wholly to me. They conceive themselves in my brain, they gestate in my senses. They get birthed through my body; I feel like lover and loved. Nurturer and nurtured. Mother and child . . . literally born again."

For some women, such parthenogenesis can feel momentarily disorienting and scary. But Suzanne says she finds it exhilarating: "A spiritual oneness, like walking in the woods on an autumn afternoon or singing or being in the presence of an incredibly tender painting. It's as if I've joined the stream of life."

Suzanne and these other women are talking about becoming their own lovers. "Getting off on myself in this way," says Suzanne, "makes me realize what a powerful person I am. All I have to do is think about it, and then *shazam!* It's some-

147

thing nobody can take away from me. Even if I end up in a Catholic nursing home like my grandmother, I'll have my secret weapon. And they'll never know!"

"And clearly," I add, "the ability to think off opens up a whole new level of safe-sex possibilities. *Shazam!* Pleasure without risk."

Gaining Control of Society's Images and Our Own

Shazam! It's an accepted fact that the brain is the most important sex organ, but little is known about how imagination impacts on women's desire, taste, and actions. Even when imagination does not involve orgasm as in thinking off, gender-based myths still abound. Nancy Friday's books have done much to dispel the myth that women don't have sexual fantasies,[17] but there is still a belief, backed up by respected sex researchers, that women are not aroused by sexual imagery to the extent that men are.[18]

One reason for women's apparent lack of interest may be that most of what has been labeled *sexual imagery* belongs to the realm of *man*—to the "adult" bookstore, the X-rated movie house, the dirty joke, and most recently the 900-number dial-a-date phone lines on the late-night sex channel. It's true, women don't generally find pleasure jerking off in the back seats of X-rated movies. And they don't generally have money for TV dial-a-dates, even if they had the inclination to use them.

What do women do instead? Some women go on about their business, paying no attention to this caliber of sexual imagery. Others actively fight it. They get together and form organizations like WAP—Women Against Pornography. To a visiting Martian witnessing these phenomena for the first time without understanding the reasons for them, it may look as if women are below ground zero in the sexual imagination department. Unless the Martian subscribes to publications like *On Our Backs* or rents an erotic video by a woman director from Femme or Tigris productions, it might be reasonable to conclude that women of the '90s do not possess sexual imaginations at all.

But women do. There is Dr. Suzanne, and there are the other women who blew the blood pressure cuffs off during our laboratory trials. There are the 64% of women in my original interviews who said they were able to come to orgasm without touch. There are the writers, artists, photographers, and reporters of women's erotica, women like Jane Rule, Betty Dodson, Tee Corinne, Susie Bright, and Nancy Friday.[19] There are the producers of feminist erotic films who show the whole, complex spectrum of pleasure, orgasm, and ecstasy for women and show it with grace and often with humor.[20] There is the Kensington Ladies Erotica Society—seven merry California housewives who got together and wrote their fantasies into two best-sellers.[21] For that matter, there is Saint Teresa of Avila, whose imagined visitations by "the flaming arrow of God" kept her for years in a transcendent *status orgasmus* in the confines of her cloistered cell during the Counter-Reformation. These women are living and historical proof that women can and do have very active sexual imaginations and that sexual imagery is everywhere, not confined only to specific body parts and specific actions.

Also proof of the activity of women's imaginations are clients like Alice in Chapter 2 who have problems with sexual dysfunction (more accurately, with sexual relationship). In their case, they are imagining the worst of sex and not the best. They are imagining the worst because that is their image of sex, what they know from experience. In their case, sexual imagination negates their sexual responses even in a potentially positive encounter, negates their ability to assert themselves, to trust, to enjoy their senses, to lubricate, to tumesce, to let go. And for as long as they continue to imagine the worst, sex cannot feel good to them, for pleasure, orgasm, and ecstasy do not thrive in a climate of fear and anxiety.

Suzanne has been pacing around the lab during my monologue, stretching her body like a cat. "I have so many questions," she says. "How can an image be wildly erotic to one woman and a total turnoff to another? Where do sexual images come from and where do they go? There must be filters we use to translate what's out there—the erotica, the pornography, the deodorant ads, and all that stuff. What are they?"

There are no lab-tested answers to these questions, but I have some clinical guesses. The basic guess is that the effect of imagery varies, depending to a large extent on the eye of the beholder. The exact sexual response to a given stimulus of sexual imagery is both individual and unpredictable. Working with this material over the years has led me to envision a model.[22] "I'll bet this model fits what happened for you just now while we were measuring your responses," I say to Suzanne.

Picture two classes of imagery. One is *internal imagery:* self-generated images such as sexual fantasies, visitations by the Goddess, trips with a lover, whatever is going on inside you. The second is *external imagery:* images that are generated from the outside such as magazines, videos, a beautiful body walking down the street, or a tape you just listened to.

When women process any kind of sexual image, I believe there is a constant flux between the internal images and the external ones. This flux is similar to the process of breathing. Breathing in and breathing out exist in a fluctuating balance—each is a distinct entity, yet they're both dependent on each other to keep the cycle going. But instead of exchanging oxygen and carbon dioxide, there is an exchange of images, a continuous process of introjection and projection.

"For instance," I say to Suzanne, "when you listened to the tape in the first part of the study, you 'breathed in' or introjected images from outside yourself—external imagery. Then, to keep the cycle going, you 'breathed' those images out, meaning that you projected your own internal images onto what you were hearing on the tape. You repeated this process again and again, letting the words on the tape enter your consciousness, then projecting your own internal images onto the tape. You kept on like this for ten minutes, introjecting and projecting. As if you were breathing those images—in and out."

As I am talking, I am sketching a diagram for Suzanne: "Graphically, this process can be expressed like this, especially if you can imagine the diagram as a mobile that is alive and pulsating with energy flow and exchange."

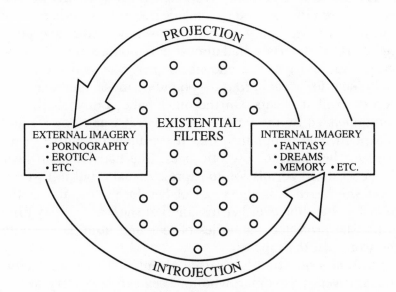

**EXTERNAL AND INTERNAL SEXUAL IMAGERY
(PORNOGRAPHY AND EROTICA, FANTASY, DREAMS
AND MEMORY): THE PROCESS OF PROJECTION
AND INTROJECTION**

"So," says Suzanne, "this is how that tape was triggering all those memories and fantasies for me."

"Exactly. It was an open-ended, nonexplicit bunch of suggested images. It was designed to let you fill in all the blanks. Whether or not you were consciously thinking about it, you were constantly personalizing and enhancing everything you were hearing. Tailoring it to fit yourself. The more you turned on, the more you enhanced and the more you projected. Your cycle of projection and introjection gathered more and more positive momentum. This is a classic example of what you call the process of *thinking off*."

Suzanne giggles, remembering how well engaged she had become in her continuum of pleasure, orgasm, and ecstasy, all from the energy exchange triggered by the tape. "Were all the women in the study turned on by the tape?" she asks.

"Not so far," I respond. Although several of the women were aroused by the tape to some degree at least, others were not. For instance, Mary, who works in a bookstore specializing in erotic materials, had almost dozed off because the tape wasn't hot and physical enough for her. She said she needs excitement for sexual arousal—pounding music and an explosion of explicit events. On the other hand, Lillian had been quite offended by the tape, even though it was so gentle and unexplicit. She complained that it stimulated negative memories for her instead of erotic ones. She had failed to hear the generalized permission to express sexual arousal. Instead, what she heard was the voice of her forbidding uncle, the minister, standing over her hissing that she was "a dirty little girl." She projected memories of fear and humiliation onto the words on the tape.

Suzanne's question has raised an interesting point about sexual diversity. Women who love sex can have very different responses to the same sexual image, whether it is a tape, a movie, a book, a body, or whatever. How can Suzanne and these other women all love sex and yet have such different reactions to the same sexual image?

I refer to the diagram. "Look at the variety of effects sexual imagery has on women. Start with internal imagery—memories, fantasies, dreams."

152

Thinking Off and Other Thoughts on Sexual Imagination

"You mean the kind that moves us all to think off in the lab and moves women to form groups and write best-selling books like the Kensington Ladies!" Suzanne laughs.

"Also the kind that moves other women to turn off," I reply. "The kind that brings up awful memories. The kind that shames and terrifies."

As an aware woman and a sociology professor, Suzanne knows that not all internal sexual imagery is positive or has a positive effect. It can include the negativity that has osmosed into women's brains from hissing uncles, from controlling partners and families, and from the culture—religious proscriptions, skewed messages, experiences of abuse, shattered self-esteem. Most women in this culture can't help but have at least some negative images. In fact, women who love sex and feel at home with their sexual performance may report the very kinds of memories, fantasies, and dreams routinely reported by clients with sexual complaints. *But their response is different.* My sense is that women who love sex have learned to minimize some of the effects of the negativity so that sexual stimulation gives them positive energy instead of taking energy away.[23]

I point to the diagram again: "Now, look at external sexual imagery. Most of the women who have talked with me about their peak sexual experiences say that at some point in their lives they've used erotic pictures, stories, or movies to turn themselves on or enhance their pleasure. Eighty-six percent of my original interview sample stated that this was true for them."

"But women aren't always able to choose the sexual images that affect them," Suzanne interjects. "There's all sorts of yuk flying around out there that's part of our lives whether we like it or not."

She is referring to the images that assault women daily, that become gauges of women's worth and self-worth. These images range from violence, incest, rape, and sexism to the ads that use women's bodies to sell products and, as Jean Kilbourne says, "kill us softly."[24]

153

And she is referring to pornography and erotica. Women who love sex generally characterize pornography as power sex, violence, and objectification—not taking women seriously. They say that the pornographic view of sex is narrow and man pleasing, or more specifically, penis pleasing.

"Erotica," says Suzanne, "feels different from straight porn. It's softer, full of feelings. I don't feel assaulted by it. It's not only about pleasing men. I can enter into it and choose the quality of my experience. Besides, it's high-hearted. It's fun. It's the kind of stuff Gloria Steinem says is OK for you to have on your bedside table even if you're a feminist."

As Suzanne and I talk about the distinctions between pornography and erotica, she mentions the magic word: *subjectivity.*

"If anyone tries to tell you there are any objective definitions," I say, "they're making a totally subjective statement. Sexual imagery is an emotional topic. How can there be objectivity?"

"Legal precedents, yes," agrees Suzanne, "but not objective definitions. So what about the filters for all these sexual images. What does your model say they are?"

"We've been talking about them. Your life is an existential filter. Sex is an integral part of your life, so everything that goes on affects your sexual response to images. Your emotions, your expectations, your needs, how your life is scripted. All your experience, past, present, and future. And your fantasies, your dreams, your memories."

"Memories," muses Suzanne. "Memories color all of those filters. And it's not only what I can remember with my head—first this happened and then that happened. My memories come from my body, too, as if my body has a life of its own. I have different sets of memories for every chakra. And they can reach a very spiritual plane, like what happened during the tape when I met the Goddess. When you mix sexual response and memory, it is extremely connecting. Memories are in the past but they're in the future, too. You might almost say memories of things to come!"

Thinking Off and Other Thoughts on Sexual Imagination

"Your senses are filters, all of them," I continue, appreciating her pun. "They're indicators of pleasure and pain unless you've numbed them out somewhere along the way or lost them through accident or disease."

"My sense of smell is a powerful filter for me. Wonderful pleasures come through it—even here." Suzanne sniffs the basement air of the laboratory and smiles. "Other senses work for me, too. There are times in my life when *everything* registers as sexual. I can get ecstatic just looking at my cat sunning herself in the kitchen window."

"Right, and pain and turnoff come through those sensory filters, too. When you're crouched over the carpet scraping up Kitty's hair ball with a kitchen knife is probably not the moment for your husband to come on all romantic. Your mind simply isn't with it."

"And there must be situations where *no* image evokes a sexual response," she counters.

"Serious illness can do it for women. Your imagination is wholly involved in the minute-by-minute business of getting well."

"Or when a woman's been abused or hurt, she just closes off."

"So then, if she wants to open up again, she needs to find some imagery that will help her feel powerful and in control."

"Facts are wonderful images," muses Suzanne, shifting into helpful mode. "Knowledge is power, and for women to understand how sex works can be a powerful aphrodisiac."

"A positive partner experience is another great image," I add from my perspective as therapist. This is something a woman can plug into her memory, especially when it's within an ongoing relationship. Aside from the limitless potential for pleasure in bed, a positive partner can become a significant touchstone in a woman's journey to sexual healing. In Chapter 2, Alice's transformation was greatly enhanced by the concurrent transformation of her husband, Frank.

The last thing an abused woman needs, we agree, are

sexual images that abuse her more. We recite a litany of those images, from centerfold pullouts to the now historic cover of *Hustler* Magazine that depicts a spike-heeled, net-stockinged woman being forced through a meat grinder to emerge as pieces of hamburger.

It doesn't take a great deal of imagination to understand that women might be sexually turned on by images that enhance their lives and turned off by images that put them down and grind them up. Yet it's not always this simple. If sex is a social construction, sexual imagery is a social construction, too. Women are bombarded in this culture with images that say "sexy" means being weak, compliant, other-directed, even bound, trapped, scared, and hurt. For some women, meatgrinder images are a turn-*on* to sexual arousal and even orgasm.

I tell Suzanne about Clara, a colleague I interviewed about sexual imagery. Clara describes herself as a staunch feminist. I know that her daily life is filled with well-deserved self-esteem, but when I asked her what was her surest fantasy route to orgasm, this is what she replied: "I have a memory of being eight years old. I'm sitting on the stairs and my mother is being held down on the dining room table by my stepfather and raped by poker-playing buddies."

This was the memory she routinely used to turn herself on, and yet when she talked with me about it, she was shaking and unable to meet my eyes.

"She must have felt so scared and betrayed," responds Suzanne. "She must still feel that way. What I don't understand is how do some women—even women like that who call themselves card-carrying feminists—how do these women become aroused and even orgasmic by imagery that hurts so much?"

Suzanne has raised a crucial question: What is the process by which some healthy, high-functioning women continually, even ritually, derive sexual pleasure from pain?

I answer by pointing to the diagram of projection and introjection. "When pain is what we see and hear around us,

156

then that's where our projected sexual images come from. It's all part of the process to breathe them in until they finally become our own—our own internalized images."

Transforming Pain

"How do women change the process?" asks Suzanne. "What choices do we have?"

"I think we have a number of choices, that is, other than to knuckle under to the pain or alter the entire social construction of sex. One choice is a negative one or one that's perceived as negative because it's angry, and nice women are not supposed to be angry. It's to stomp out of the X-rated movie. Scream and yell and march against images that hurt. Get into therapy and try to unload the memory of your mother being gang-raped."

"You mean short-circuit the imagery process," says Suzanne.

Such short circuiting prevents internalizing any sexual images at all. It is a time-honored choice and one that gives some validity to the myths that women aren't turned on by sexual imagery and don't have sexual fantasies.

A second choice is to create our own images, like the Kensington Ladies or the women at Femme or Tigris. This is positive, proactive, sexy, and it threatens the establishment, from the lawmakers to the sensitive New Age guys who want to be our partners. This can be scary, of course, because it brings on their wrath.

"Don't we have a First Amendment right to publish whatever we want?" Suzanne asks.

"Sure we do, but the establishment has the money and the power to put you out of business while you're trying to assert that right," I answer, thinking of the struggles the women filmmakers are going through as they try to maintain their ability to produce high-quality work.[25]

Another choice for women is less noticeable, but I think it is equally time honored. It packs just as much social consequence as the other choices, maybe even more. This is the choice to change the perception of sexual pain. To take in the external images that give pain and to quietly transform them into internal images that give pleasure. That is, to use pain as the stimulation for sexual arousal rather than for defensive withdrawal and use the adrenaline triggered by anxiety to enhance sexual excitement.

This, I explain, is how my colleague Clara is able to sit again and again on the childhood stairs of her imagination and invoke as sexual stimulation the terrible scene between the banisters.

"If you think about it," says Suzanne, "this ability to transform pain into pleasure is a brilliant mutation. An abused little girl steps into a phone booth. She can emerge as Wonder Woman brandishing a magic bracelet."

With Dr. Suzanne, the sociology expert, I agree that this ability is one that women have developed in order to survive a social order that is often at war with us or at any rate punitive about our enjoying sexual pleasures.

And I admit to her that it's still not the whole solution. We have a phrase in Boston, where I grew up, a phrase born out of a deprivation economy and the rocky New England soil: *Use it up, wear it out, make it do, or do without.* This is essentially what some of the women who love sex are doing with disempowering sexual imagery. In order to experience sexual pleasure, they are making do with hand-me-down images. But like the threadbare Bostonian clothes I grew up with, those images take a toll on a woman's self-esteem.

As I reflect on Suzanne and each of the other twenty women who volunteered for the laboratory study, noting their increased pain thresholds during their thinking-off orgasms, watching their pupils pulse and balloon on the TV across the room, witnessing dramatic jumps in blood pressure and heart rate on the split-screen monitor, I am struck with awe. Their orgasms on command are astounding in themselves. But I know the histories of these women. These are not all women who have had easy lives. Some of them have suffered major losses and setbacks, including incest and rape. I marvel at the core of health or determination that has moved them through their personal turmoil to such a powerful and seemingly centered sense of their own pleasure.

I am also suffused with a warm sense of camaraderie, for instance, the kind you develop after traveling all night on a bus to Washington singing freedom songs. We are in this thing together. Nobody has ever measured the phenomenon of thinking off before. We are a first. Maybe this study can help other women, women who are unable to touch themselves for pleasure because they are physically injured or because they've been abused or because they are brainwashed to believe that touching themselves is sick or sinful. Maybe deepening our understanding of how women think their way in and out of pleasure will spark a change in the system that perpetrates pain.

It is grossly inaccurate for researchers to imply that women do not have vivid sexual imaginations. They do, and women who love sex are possessed with particularly vivid ones, however they choose to use them. They may invoke them to escape pain or turn pain into pleasure, to enhance physical sensation, or, like Dr. Suzanne and lordy knows how many others, to think off without touching themselves at all.

It heartens me to know that every time a woman drifts into her imagination for the sake of sexual pleasure that is one moment in which she is beating the system. In that moment there is a possibility of enhancing her relationship with her self. Of connectedness and personal power, enjoyment and release of energy. *Shazam!* A secret weapon to help her transform the quality of her life.

6
Molly

Sexual Nurturing—
The Dance
of Give and Take

Once again, Aphrodite,
I have run to you fluttering
Like a little girl to her mother.
                              —Sappho

WOMEN WHO LOVE sex say they crave cuddling and holding
because it may be the only time in their adult lives they
ever feel fully given to. They delight in the closeness and
concern, the eye contact, the whispered jokes, the patting,
the plumping of pillows. They delight in their own sexual
generosities, too. They enjoy exercising their empathy muscles by moving to a partner's rhythms, attending to a partner's places of pleasure, indulging a partner's steaming
appetites.

Molly introduced herself to me as a woman who especially loves these nurturing aspects of sexual relationship.
A wide and comfortable being with a habit of running her
hand through her flaming red hair, she exudes vitality from

the vibrant colors she wears to the earthiness of her laugh. "I love to cook, I love to eat, I love to make love," she announced. "I love to be warm and make other people feel warm. I think I must have been a wood-burning stove in a former life."

A wood-burning stove does not seem farfetched, for Molly has a remarkable capacity to radiate both warmth and light. I met her at a conference in Minneapolis where we were both presenters on a panel. When she first walked into the room, I noticed that people turned their faces toward her, gravitated to her. When she listened, she listened from her heart; when she looked at me, she seemed to touch my core. As I got to know her better, I realized that putting out energy for other people actually seems to renew her own. Her ability to refuel herself is a crucial one to her as mother of two teenagers and director of a women's center.

Molly's message on the panel was about women taking care of themselves—a down-to-earth message and at the same time expansive and empowering. I was in the process of reassessing the interviews of easily orgasmic women, and because so many had said that nurturing was an essential ingredient of their peak sexual experiences, Molly seemed like an ideal person to consult. We met for dinner that evening to discuss some ideas. A couple of months later she came for an East Coast visit and we had a chance to spend several hours discussing what sexual nurturing is and what it means to women.

"I think it means knowing how to get under someone else's skin while still staying zipped inside your own," she tells me when we settle in to talk. "I see sexual nurturing as a dance between two people. A complex, weaving dance of give and take."

Here, again, is sexuality being described as an enlightened dance. Molly spreads her arms wide and moves her whole being as she talks. Here, again, is body language being used to convey the ideas. Like Maya's choreographic

161

concept of pleasure, orgasm, and ecstasy, Molly's dance of sexual nurturing extends well beyond the body. It includes how women relate to their partners, their meeting of minds and exchanges of wishes and dreams. As I watch the arcs and swirls she describes, I can see that the dance is round and mobile, full of feeling, quite a different view of sexual relationship than the "scientific" one that narrows sex to a genital act, measurable and stereotypical.

Molly elaborates on her idea of sexual nurturing: "It's a dance of TLC. Tenderness. Loving and being loved. Caring and being cared for."

She underscores that it begins with a solid, connected, empathic sense of self. "Otherwise," she says, "you end up feeling like a concubine with bound feet, and then you can't dance at all!" Molly flexes her red high-top sneakers as if in sisterhood with generations of hobbled Chinese wives. "The art of nurturing in bed means you have to honor your own needs as solidly as your partner's."

Molly mentions another factor that strikes her as vital to sexual nurturing. That factor is memory. "I don't come into this experience as a virgin." She laughs. "I come in with a history." Like many women who love sex, she agrees that a number of lovemaking behaviors open up direct pathways to past experiences, even to childhood. Touching, snuggling, all sorts of minute attentions to body and soul, can evoke scenes of earlier comfort, when summer days seemed to last forever and somebody else did the cooking: "You want to know what sexual bliss feels like? It's letting myself trust, like an infant."

Trusting like an infant may be all well and good if a woman has a trustworthy partner—and if she can keep the experience in perspective. All too often I see women in therapy who are conditioned to believe that sexual bliss stems from the helplessness of infancy rather than from the nurturing they should have been receiving then. I am thinking of Sylvia, a recovering alcoholic, who was working hard in therapy to recover her crumbling self-esteem: "Nobody

162

took care of me when I was a kid," she told me. "Everything I have I got for myself. Do you know that all my life I've had the fantasy of somebody taking care of me in bed? And as long as I was a flopping-around drunk I got that. At least I thought I got that. I just zoned out and let myself be done to. The sex felt wonderful, at least till the hangover the next morning. When I quit drinking, I found out that kind of sex was just the same old slam bang stuff. Nobody was taking care of me. They were just using me."

A problem for Sylvia and other women who yearn for sexual nurturing is how to reclaim innocent feelings of being cared for without having to be in a state of helplessness in their adult lives. Even when sex is genuinely close and loving, many women, including Molly as it turns out, find that tenderness in the bedroom can trigger memories that are confusing and sometimes downright frightening, painful, filled with shame and panic. Women who love sex include women who are survivors of rape or of violent childhoods where cuddling and holding was abuse, not nurture. They also include women who were brainwashed by their straightlaced families to believe that pleasure is a sin and that any attempt at self-pleasure would surely bring on the wrath of God or the neighbors, depending on the family priorities.

I admit to Molly that these are the women I can most easily identify with myself. In my fearful Boston household, even thumb sucking fell into the category of sin. When I was a baby, my wrists were tied to the sides of my crib with white yarn to prevent me from exercising my most primal instinct to self-nurture. I think this was a starting point for my lifelong spaciness in taking care of myself; I still sometimes have to leave notes around the house to remind myself to do simple acts of self-caring, like eating lunch.

But as negatively charged as memories like these can be, most of the women who love sex agree with Molly: Ultimately, memory enhances and enlarges what is going on during their experiences of sexual pleasure, orgasm, and ecstasy. It is the evocative quality of nurturing that makes it so touching to body and mind, heart and soul; that makes it possible for women to feel a connection with themselves and with their partners that transcends the bounds of time past and time future.

"Sometimes," Molly points out, "the special connections come because you have to struggle so hard. I had to ask myself, Why don't I automatically feel wonderful when my honey is being attentive and dear? I never did come up with the answer till I had this amazing dream. I was in a big meadow, and I was wrestling with the Angel of Sweetness. Honest!" Molly laughs slightly and clears her throat. "That dream made me understand how intense the past can be—*my* past can be. How difficult it was for me to trust kindness or any other good feelings. How I would actually try to wrestle them into the ground."

She tells me how she has consciously trained herself in techniques to allow positive emotions to flow. She reaches into her backpack and hands me a sheet of lined paper on which she has written a fragment from the poet Ntozake Shange: "This is a piece about nurturing that has affected me for twelve years, since I first came across it. Sometimes I read it over just to keep on track."

I ask her to read it out loud:

Fill a glass that sparkles in sunlight with pure spring water. Place one sprig of fresh mint in the water, and a mouthful of honey. Take your middle finger gently round the curve of your lips as you imagine your beloved might. Kiss the edges of the fingers. Take a breath so deep your groin senses it. Hold your breath while envisioning your beloved's face. Release the breath still picturing your beloved. Then with the kissed finger, make a circle round the rim of the glass 12 times, each time repeating your beloved's name. Each time seeing your beloved filled with joy. Close your eyes. Let your beloved fill your heart. Bring

Sexual Nurturing—The Dance of Give and Take

the glass to your lips. Drink the gladness that shall be yours.[1]

As Molly reads this passage, it is abundantly clear that the language of sexual nurturing is sensuous, poetic, and mystical; surely, it is not the objective language of science. How is it possible to count or measure just how much gladness a woman can drink? Or to document definitively how good or scary or difficult it feels to give a mouthful of honey or to receive joy? Laboratory experiments that might shed light on the role of nurturing in the whole scope of sexual behavior fall sadly short. For instance, when the expert in animal behavior showed us as sexology students how he had cleverly created sexual dysfunction in the macaque monkey troupe by disrupting the social order, he was focused on one aspect of sexual function and one aspect only: the ability of the male monkeys to copulate successfully with the females. He was not looking at the nurturing aspects of sexual behavior, even though these were directly affected in the monkey troupe by the induced slovenliness in grooming habits. Remember, that kind of sex research is concerned with genitals, not with feelings.

If we stop to listen to women, however, anecdotal evidence can give a great deal of insight about the role of nurturing in sexual desire, arousal, and satisfaction. When I ask Molly to describe an incident to illustrate her statements about the dance of give and take, she softens and flashes her wide smile. "I'll tell you about how my partner and I got together," she says. The scene she describes occurred more than ten years ago, but as Molly relates the story the details seem as clear as yesterday.

I'd finally walked out of a nowhere marriage with a pothead—the father of my girls. He wasn't the kind who beats everybody up. Just the kind you can't have a conversation with after he has his first joint. Or any kind of

165

exchange about feelings. No sex for the last four years. It seemed like forty.

I was ready to fall in love—and Kate and I had been friendly for a few months. Well, more than friendly. We were wildly attracted to each other—I'm not sure why. She was so different from me. I was just a feisty Jewish kid from Milwaukee and really unclear about what I wanted. She was an out-front lesbian and a whole lot of nationalities all at once—part African, part Spanish, part Cherokee. She seemed to know everything I wanted to know.

The girls were off at their grandmom's for the weekend. Kate had this little cabin up by the lake that she used as a summer place, and she asked me up for a couple of days of escape before the winter holidays began.

Molly maneuvers her chair so that it is closer to mine and speeds up her story as if the images are coming almost faster than she can speak:

It must have been below zero when I got there. The snow squeaked under your heels, and the hairs in your nostrils—you could almost hear them tinkling against each other like little wind chimes. Her cabin had one of those old black and silver pot-bellied stoves that pumped out so much heat you had to keep rotating so your pants wouldn't melt off your butt. We joked that maybe that stove had been a great-aunt of mine.

When I walked in from the snow, she had candles on the table and soup on the stove. Such good smells. Such comfort. I could hardly take it all in. All those years of tension and keeping things together for everybody else, I just put my hand over my mouth and couldn't say anything, not even hello.

Kate just reached out and led me over to the mattress on the floor and asked, "How'd you like it if I gave you a massage?"

166

Sexual Nurturing—The Dance of Give and Take

Was this woman an angel from heaven or what? I accepted of course and right away stripped to the skin before I could think about what I was doing. What was I doing? I was lying on Kate's bed, that's what. Naked. With my arms plastered to my sides. My stomach was so tense you could have stretched a net across it and played yourself a game of ping-pong.

Molly crosses her arms and clutches her ribs as she talks on.

I lay there with my eyes shut. I figured that made me less visible, right? I listened to her stoke the stove and set a bottle of massage oil to warm in a pan of water. Then I felt her move behind me on the mattress. She slid her back against the wall and wiggled around until her legs were straddling my head. I guessed it was OK to sneak a peek so I opened up my eyes and looked at her legs. She had on black tights. Her calves and feet were bare and brown. They gleamed like copper and I thought how much more beautiful brown skin is than the white and freckles I got stuck with. She placed her big, incredibly radiant hands under my neck. She held them there and leaned over me and whispered into my ear. Her breath was like sweetgrass.

"Remember to breathe," she said. "Listen for my breathing and then breathe along with me."

Breathe! With this woman leaning over me and tumbling her breast into my ear? I forced myself to take in air and expel it so I'd at least look like I was alive.

Then she sat up and poured some warm oil into her palms. The room filled up with a healing smell I remembered from childhood. The kind that clears out your sinuses in one whiff.

Molly inhales deeply and raises her eyes as if remembering a scene from long ago. The line from Shange's poem runs through my head: *Take a breath so deep your groin senses it....* Then Molly returns to her story.

She slid her hands down my shoulders and arms and somehow still in the same motion she was pulling me up from the waist—all the tight muscles along my backbone, lifting my body and spreading my ribcage so that I finally did begin to breathe. I was gulping in air down to my toes.

I remember opening my eyes and looking up at her, into that honest, strong-boned, upside-down face. The whites of her eyes were so clear they were almost blue. "What are you doing?" I murmured (meaning, "What kind of massage are you doing? It's wonderful!").

Her response is something I've always remembered, because in three words it summed up all the best there is in health care. "I'm doing YOU," she said to me.

I think that must have been the moment I fell in love with her. I fell in love with her confidence and her warmth and her ability to reach me through her hands. She continued moving over me, connecting all my parts to all my other parts. There seemed to be less and less space between us. As if we were becoming one rhythm. I'd never felt so open to any being in my whole life. Or so close, except maybe to my babies when they were tiny. But that was a different kind of close.

Her big, warm hands found my stomach. She began kneading my uterus, rolling over and over it in waves. I heard her giggle and then I felt her drizzle some warm oil into my belly button. She dipped a finger into the oil and drew a line up my body. From my belly, up between my breasts—oh, so slowly—all the way up to my throat and chin and nose and forehead. It was solemn and deliberate, like some kind of initiation ceremony.

She held one finger on my forehead and another just above my pubic bone. I felt tears begin and then I swept off into that state where you float around just sort of touching the edges of the universe. I don't know how long I was there. The next thing I knew, she was sliding her warm body on top of mine and we could feel our hearts beating and our bellies touching and our breath in each other's ears.

It wasn't even so much the feel of her body, it was the electricity between us. We began to move together. And as we moved our hips and shoulders we started making sounds. Now these weren't little bitty squeaks and whimpers. These were out-loud sounds and they would have woken up the wolves or coyotes if there had been any left in the woods. It was as if all the anguish and all the joy either of us had ever felt poured out of us into that room. And then those sounds poured out into tears. And then they poured out into orgasms—the kind that turn your insides into an endless river.

And we hadn't even discovered each other's genitals yet. I can't even begin to tell you what it felt like to reach down and find that sweet handful—and it was just like me! And to reach my tongue out and feel her nipple harden as I sucked. Oh, I was so powerful touching her that night. There wasn't anything I couldn't do. I quoted poems to her. She called me her lyric lover.

Molly has been looking off into the distance as she describes this extraordinary experience. Now she looks at me directly and goes on.

The stove had burned down to embers by the time I woke up. I felt like a newborn baby. Everything was so new. When I opened my eyes, I was opening them for the first time. When I looked at the candle I was looking at flame for the first time. I lay there letting my eyes play with the shadows on the wall by the door. Then it hit me. I had just made love with a woman for the first time.

I checked her breathing to see if she was still alive. I checked mine to see if I was still alive. We were both alive. But what I was feeling inside wasn't anything I recognized. I had this new awareness, this new window in my brain. It was called Trust. Trusting someone else. I realized I trusted this woman whose leg was flung over my thigh. I had always been able to trust myself. And I'd always made sure that whenever I got close to someone I was the dependable one. The giver. In control. And now here was someone—here was a lover—*who was competent to take care of* me.

She was wearing an amethyst on a chain around her neck, and I had the imprint on the side of my breast— for the whole weekend, I think. From that moment on, I was a marked woman!

I crept out from under her leg and wrapped myself up in a quilt and pulled on my boots and went to the porch to get wood for the stove. There was a new moon—a wishing moon—in the sky and billions of stars. The air smelled like wood smoke, and the stillness was huge.

I stoked the stove with chunks of oak and took off the quilt and covered her with it. It was made by her great-grandmother—a daughter of a slave. It had apple green leaves and red strawberries all over it. I crawled in beside her warm body and watched her sleep. That night I made a promise to myself: No harm should befall this beloved woman.

Molly's tone changes as she nears the end of her story. Her voice is still warm and throaty, but it becomes somewhat crisper as she moves into her professional persona, the way I had originally met her.

"Kate and I have been together for eleven years now, and I think we both have the capacity for pleasuring each other—both in and out of bed. Sometimes it's hard to tell exactly what part of the nurturing is sex and what's not sex. I mean, our relationship is a sexual one, with all that that means. So that much of what we do—however we are with one another—ends up being part of how our sex is together and how our sex is ends up being part of everything else. It doesn't always have a lot to do with how often we're genital.

Listening to Molly's story of the ultimate massage renews my conviction that sexual nurturing is more than simply taking care of each other's physical wants or helping each other come to orgasm, although it might include both those actions, as it does for Molly and Kate. There is a complex pattern to balanced sexual nurturing. In the course of all my years as a therapist and workshop leader, I have identified an entire cycle that encompasses the continuum of pleasure, orgasm, and ecstasy and that touches the soul, the mind, and the emotions, as well as the body.[2]

The Cycle of Sexual Nurturing

Women tell me that this cycle originates in the heart, the core of the being. This heart's core radiates energy, just as strongly and palpably as Kate's pot-bellied stove. It is full of desires. It is full of needs. It is full of wanting, wishing, dreaming, yearning, longing. It is full of love. And like Kate's stove, it needs stoking.

"Otherwise it might shrivel up to nothing or turn into a heart that loves too much!" Molly interjects.

I begin to describe how the cycle of sexual nurturing plays itself out: The heart energy radiates out into a number of processes. One of these is the process of reaching out beyond yourself to contact a partner, both to give and to receive. Molly's story illustrates this part of the cycle as she and Kate reach for each other with hands, mind, and feelings—Molly, to fill her need for contact; Kate, to offer a tender, loving, caring experience; both, to howl with the wildness of their first night together. It's hard to say just who made the first moves in the cabin by the winter lake.

"When Kate gave me that massage, I did a lot of receiving from her." Molly understands that a significant part of the dance of nurturing that night was her willingness to open up to the pleasures and comforts bestowed on her by Kate of the warm, strong hands, to fill up her empty places with the warmth of the crackling wood fire, the healing smells of childhood.

This degree of empathic give and take is not necessarily limited to women making love with other women, although some sex-loving lesbian couples assert that this is so. "It's the familiarity," they point out. "It's like making love with yourself. You just *know* what your lover wants. You just *know* how to make each other feel good." But listen to Miriam, a heterosexual woman from the original interviews. She speaks to the possibilities for sexual nurturing between women and men: "He is an elegant, thoughtful lover—and extremely playful and athletic," she relates of her second husband. "In all the years we've been together, one thing I can always trust is his intention. I know we want the best for each other. Our bodies may want different things, but there's no division between our hearts. We're one spirit."

"So after giving and receiving, then what?" Molly asks.

The next process in the cycle of sexual nurturing is bonding. When Molly's tension is released so that she is able to begin breathing again, she feels drawn to Kate in a new way: sexually and with the permission to act on it. She looks into Kate's eyes and bonds with the same immediacy and lack of question that she once bonded with her babies. Attachment and bonding do not always mean falling in love as they do here with Molly and Kate, but they do mean a deep integration of heart and mind and spirit. Sexual nurturing involves more than physical gratification. It involves the whole person and the whole relationship. And, as Miriam suggests earlier, such sexual bonding is not limited to lovemaking with women; it can—and does—also exist between women and men.

Next in the cycle comes a sense of completeness and satisfaction. Molly remembers her full-body lust by the waning fire and loudly asserts: "Now that was a hell of a lot more than what you'd call just a little bitty *satisfaction.* That was *ecstasy.*" Indeed, given the right circumstances, the cycle of sexual nurturing can contain the full power of the ecstasy connection explored in Chapter 3 by Maya and her nieces. Because ecstasy dissolves defenses that keep women divided from themselves and each other, it has the potential to expand perception, to change and transform women's lives. For Molly and Kate, this is the part of the sexual nurturing cycle that moves them to enter into a depth of relationship neither could possibly have envisioned before.

As a natural outgrowth of experiencing some degree of ecstasy connection, the next process in the cycle is a sense of renewal, of growth, of creativity. When Molly opens her eyes after sleep and feels born again, she is filled with new awareness, and new connectedness to her old feelings. Not only has she made love with a woman for the first time, she suddenly encounters a new emotion, trust. She finds herself quite suddenly attached to the woman lying beside her on the bed by the waning fire, and perhaps most importantly, she finds herself suddenly involved in a more aware and caring relationship with her self. Just as Lorie, Maya's niece in Chapter 3, interpreted a similar sense of trust as rightness and resolve in her upcoming marriage, Molly is energized to enter into the next stages of a fruitful—and open—sexual partnership with a woman.

The cycle of sexual nurturing rolls around finally to generosity, the spirit of altruism. Molly exudes altruism when she stokes the stove, tenderly covering Kate with her grandmother's quilt, and vowing to keep her from harm.

"Kate's offering me a massage in the first place—that was the real altruism right there," offers Molly.

And probably if we interviewed Kate, we'd discover that she felt she received as much as she gave during the exchange and experienced the same degree of bonding, satisfaction, and renewal as Molly did. So the dance of sexual nurturing can begin anywhere in the cycle, and it can repeat itself over and over in any order. Like Maya's dance of pleasure, orgasm, and ecstasy, the events can fluctuate and flow and overlap each other in time and space. In the hands of artists like Molly and Kate, the dance becomes a dance of feeling good.

As I outline my ideas about a balanced cycle of sexual nurturing, I have been scribbling on a pad of paper in my lap. I show the results to Molly: a heart with all these elements radiating from it. I ask her to imagine the elements as moving, flowing, pulsing energies that are constantly changing size and shape and importance.

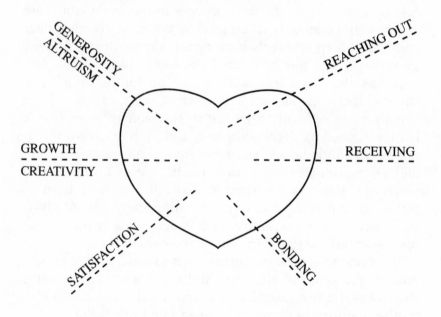

A BALANCED CYCLE OF SEXUAL NURTURING

"This diagram makes it easy to see what you've been saying," says Molly, looking at my picture. "But it looks

174

just a little bit too easy. It's too smooth and creamy. It makes me think of those cartoons in the Sunday papers when I was growing up: What's wrong with this picture?"

I agree that the sexual nurturing cycle doesn't always work exactly as planned on paper. It has a fragile ecology. Its balance can be interrupted. There can be giant glitches.

"For sure," says Molly. "All you need is a klutzy partner. Or one who's into harassment or abuse. Or into patronizing you. If there's really a God in heaven, I just wish she'd protect women from men who turn them into little girls! The person who's your partner has to have your well-being at heart or sex turns into an outrageous act. And even if your partner's wonderful, there can be those horrendous memories that creep into your bedroom and whop you upside the head."

All women in this culture are vulnerable to these interruptions and intrusions, I reflect to Molly. Whether they're nice Jewish girls like her or Spanish, African-American, and Cherokee like Kate; whether they're financially secure or living day to day, all women are to some extent abused and harassed, patronized and infantilized by the system if not by individual partners. Having to deal with racism and poverty greatly magnifies the problems, as Molly is well aware from the women she sees at the center.

Glitches in the Dance of Give and Take

I ask Molly where she sees the difficulties in her own relationship.

"Reaching out and asking is the hardest part for me. When I was married to my children's father, he was stoned most of the time and assumed the world revolved around him. So I never felt I could ask for anything, especially not sex. And if I did, I went through a lot of bobbing up and down and wringing my hands and then I usually didn't get it anyway because he never even noticed me. Whew! That was a whole other lifetime. Of course I thought it was all my fault. Once I bought a lapel button for him. I thought it summed up the situation pretty grandly, but I never quite had the gumption to give it to him. It was hot pink and it said GUILT WITHOUT SEX.

"Even after all the years Kate and I have been together, sometimes I still feel shy about asking for what I want. Receiving is still hard for me, too, but it's getting easier as I do more of it. I guess it takes time to develop that degree of trust."

Molly's difficulty with asking and receiving reflects the cultural conditioning of many of the women who love sex—those with male partners, of course, as well as female ones. Not only is it more blessed in this culture to give than it is to receive, it is also much more familiar, because women are socialized to be the caregivers.[3]

"And it sure is safer," observes Molly, "at least up to a point. If you don't ever ask for anything, you don't have to risk someone saying no. You don't have to hope. That was the biggest agony for me during the cold years. Hoping that someday, somehow, my pathetic little wishes for tenderness and touching would be heard."

"There's something that's even scarier for some women than the risk of not getting what you wish for."

"What's that?" asks Molly.

I explain to Molly the risk of *getting* what you wish for, the fear so many women have of feeling good. When women don't ask for what they want, they cut down on their rejection anxiety and on their pleasure anxiety as well.

"So becoming a constant caretaker spares you all that grief," says Molly, flashing her big smile.

"It spares you *that* grief, but it has some pretty devastating problems of its own," I answer. For instance, taking care of your partner's sexual desires to the exclusion of your own can be red-alert time for lesbian relationships. Because both partners are socialized as women, they may literally try to push each other out of bed as each tries to be the caretaker who gets there first with the most. In heterosexual bedrooms, when there is no space for a woman to ask for what she wants, there is usually a different dynamic: an implicit playing out of the favored patriarchal sexual position: man on top.

When women are unable to reach out in their own behalf—in need or in lust or in love or simply in interest—they are ripe for loneliness and isolation. When they get desperate enough, they may put themselves in positions of danger—emotionally and also physically, whether from abuse, abandonment, or disease. The balanced dance of give and take bogs down to a shuffle. Women find themselves stumbling around in raw, grinding sexual need.

"That's so true," says Molly. "I see women at the center who've given up all their negotiating power just to be with a guy. And this guy usually isn't safe for them—he's a drunk, he's a batterer, he's HIV infected and won't use a condom."

Molly is addressing a self-esteem issue that affects many women who build up sexual needs. Some women drop all sense of protective boundary and fall for impossible promises and any crumbs of warmth and attention that come their way. They may become beggars and victims. Women whose desire for sex is raw and hungry enough can turn manipulative and predatory. They stalk new prey wherever there are warm bodies—in bars or libraries, church socials, construction sites. These are the women who turn into sex and relationship junkies. And they get labeled with names that sound like slaps on their faces: slut, tramp. Even therapists give them a negative name: *sex addicts.*[4]

"The A word—*addiction*," Molly says. "Sometimes I think that's just another way for prudes and moralists to put the blame on any women who have an attitude. Sure, they've got problems, but their problems aren't going away if you neuter them by taking sex away from them."

To reduce the risks precipitated by desperation, some

women close down their sexual responses altogether. They curl their outer leaves around themselves and turn into shrinking violets. They clothe themselves with clanking suits of emotional armor that protect them from feeling confusion and pain but that also prevent them from feeling pleasure. They force their partners to read their minds. Or they sidestep the whole situation by not having partners at all.

"In my case," Molly remarks, running her fingers through her flaming curls, "my suit of armor turned into a chastity belt. It protected me from asking my husband for sex for all those years. But it also prevented me from ever taking deep, full breaths until Kate came along and offered me that amazing massage."

Molly brings up a survival mechanism that may be even harder to deal with than armor. When women need to protect themselves against feeling sexually deprived or hurt or against their memories of feeling deprived or hurt, they may find ways to disappear. They become silent. Like Molly, they stop breathing. They erase themselves, sometimes very early in their lives—as soon as they can talk or walk.

"If you've erased yourself, you don't feel the hurt," says Molly. "But as you say, you may not feel any joy, either. Your angel may visit your bedroom, but you don't know it's perched right up there on the bedpost flapping its wings over you."

Molly is describing the plight of women who are no longer able to love sex. Women who have become nurturance resistant, a hardened species, hybrids. Some women have actually learned to value sexual deprivation and abuse.

"I almost got to that point," remarks Molly. "My husband was a real pill, but hey, I was used to him. I hadn't been turned on to him for a long time. But I valued him the way I value my good old sneakers, because he was, well, *there*—sort of there, anyway. And I have to remember that this was not a labor-intensive relationship. It didn't take anything on my part to maintain it. Being married to Wade for those years was kind of like settling in to watch a real long TV show when you're just too zonked to switch channels."

"So in terms of attachment and bonding," I observe, moving the conversation along to another part of the sexual nurturing cycle that can develop glitches, "it sounds as if it wasn't exactly happening for you."

"Not with old Wade, it wasn't. He was too self-centered and out of it. He was never present for long enough. We hadn't been together a year before he kind of jumped into the bottle and pulled the cork in after him."

When the bonding mechanism is out of balance, sexual commitment lurches out of balance, too. Women feel spun off into space, like Molly. Or, lured by the need for closeness, they find themselves in fused relationships and feel crowded—corralled, roped, and hogtied by the prospect of intimacy. Their sexual responses may short-circuit even before the women are aware there is an intimacy imbalance. A recent client complained: "It's just not fair. I never had any sexual problems before. And now here I am in the middle of falling in love for the first time ever, and I can't even come to orgasm. It's not that he isn't a good lover. He can keep an erection for hours. But I'm so afraid he's going to get bored with me because nothing's happening. It's so frustrating. As if all my systems suddenly went haywire. Now I understand why women fake it."

"Some kinds of closeness can do you in," Molly responds sympathetically. "But women are trained to keep relationships close and feel good about it. Hey, it's our job. No matter how bad it feels. We're supposed to feel incompetent and incomplete unless we're part of a couple. A *close* couple. The kind that does everything together. That finishes each other's sentences. You know, fused at the lip."

Indeed, women are trained to corral feelings, to be the

relationship cowgirls. But when coupleship evolves from societal conditioning and not from the heart, what is perceived in bed is likely to be a sense of control—the energy to constrain—rather than a sense of power—the energy to participate in the fullness of sexual being. Closeness can feel like a prison, to be escaped at any cost.

What makes bonding and attachment grow into power rather than control? Women who love sex say it starts with a healthy sense of self. Molly agrees. She leans forward with her elbows on her knees and looks at me with that gaze that sees the heart. She speaks quietly, but she underlines every word: *"You have to attach to yourself before you can attach to another person."*

She adds that a healthy sense of self requires a sense of history—taking care of the inner child along with the grown woman: "I had been so busy running away from myself that I forgot there was a little girl inside who was hungry and unloved."

Molly relates that recontacting her inner child turned into an excruciatingly difficult job for her: "I never knew it was so much work to learn to play," she laughs. "Before I met Kate, I used to take myself so seriously. I had to. Look at all the clients who were counting on me at the center. Look at my children, my husband I felt so responsible for. If I let up even for one minute, what would become of them?"

In fact, Molly had been assuming responsibility for everyone in her world from earliest childhood when her parents were too soused on corn liquor to be consistently parents. She had acquired some formidable coping skills growing up, but she felt increasingly burdened by having to keep on coping for her younger sisters and brothers, as well as for Wade and countless women for whom she was advocating. By the time she met Kate, she had lost the ability to play, to relax, and even, as was evidenced at the beginning of the massage, to breathe fully.

"So that first summer of my new life I took myself off on a camping trip. Just me. In a tent all by myself up by the lake for four days. Those were long days. First of all, I had to deal with my guilt at leaving Kate taking care of my kids. Then I had to face the terror of spending all that time alone, and it was stormy and windy a lot of the time.

"But what I learned there at the edge of the lake was how to get to know my little girl, the five-year-old who was so needy and so starved. All she wanted was a big person to play with her and teach her how to do things and tell her she was wonderful."

Molly shifts in her chair and strokes her hair with both hands. Then she flashes a smile that makes the lights seem brighter. "Well, I learned who this big person was. It was me. And I found out that the five-year-old was me, too—and that she is one terrific kid if you stop to listen to her. So I taught myself how to take little-girl Molly by the hand and splash in the lake with her and help her brush her teeth by the rocks and sing songs to her by the campfire and hug her when she felt like crying. And I learned how to run naked into the water with her just as the sun was setting. And I learned how to become a one-woman cheering section— pumping the old pom-poms and yelling *Yay! Yay!* to her body for being so strong and freckled. For the first time in all my life, I began to learn to take care of myself."

Stumbling Toward Satisfaction and Growth

As Molly talks, I can see the years drop away from her face, leaving her with a glow of little-girl innocence. "What about satisfaction?" I ask, moving to the next piece of the sexual nurturing cycle. "You seem so calm and contented in your life now. What were you like when you were with Wade?"

"Oh, man!" she exclaims, flashing that smile again. "I was such a bitch. And I honestly think it had to do with sexual frustration. I know that sounds kind of like a dumb

181

cartoon, but during my marriage, I was so disappointed all the time about the lack of sex that nothing could please me—even out of bed. The kids would bring their sweet little clay doodads home from school and all I could say was Grump! I was a leaky bucket. Nothing could fill me up. I felt as if I was dying of starvation."

I ask Molly what she had done to rebalance the satisfaction part of her sexual nurturing cycle.

"I had to open up to change. Take a risk. I guess I always knew I wanted a sexual relationship with a woman, but thinking about it was too scary. Once I allowed myself to imagine it, though, it just seemed to flow. Then Kate took over on that first night, and all I had to do was start to breathe and just enjoy."

Take a breath so deep your groin senses it . . .

Noting how easily she had slid into various states of bliss in the cabin by the lake, I am curious to know if it had continued to be that simple for her to let go into pleasure, orgasm, and ecstasy.

"The sex was out of this world at first. And it still is even though I know lesbians aren't supposed to be able to make it together after the first two years." Molly is referring to humorist Kate Clinton's telling phrase: *lesbian bed death*, the affliction of long-time partners becoming such companionable friends that the sexual part of the relationship gets relegated to the back burner.

"Well, sometimes we do a crossword puzzle in bed," Molly admits. "But yes, we still love each other sexually if that's what you're asking. It's taken some hard work to feel that optimistic about the rest of my life, though." When I press her for details, it turns out as I had suspected, that there have been years of therapy and spiritual work involved in her changing from a perpetual caretaker and malcontent into the serene and loving person she now appears to be. The key areas were communication and her steadfast willingness to give up controlling behavior. "Kate and I know each other almost by heart now so we get along like good old buddies. We know we've got something special going, and we can always depend on it to make everything that's good feel even better. It's as if there's a third presence around called *us*, and when we both respect that presence, we're in harmony."

Molly's statements remind me of another woman from the original interview sample: Maddy was a college professor in her second marriage to a man ten years older than she but very much her peer. When I asked her the most essential ingredient of the peak sexual experience she had just related, she told me, "It was a Saturday afternoon and the children had gone out ice-skating. There was nothing special about what we did together on the sofa by the fire—and that's just it. It's the *ordinariness* of our loving each other that's so extraordinary."

Molly shifts the conversation quite naturally to the next piece of the cycle: growth and creativity. "I keep thinking about my wrestling match with the Angel of Sweetness. Maybe the nurturing cycle started right there with that piece of growth. Being willing to make a move."

She flexes her red sneakers. "Of course every step on the cycle has got to be a kind of growth. But I think the ultimate was my finally owning that the Angel of Sweetness was really me. Once I stopped wrestling with myself, I understood that I had needs, too. I stopped taking care of everyone else like it was some kind of Pavlovian response. I started to relax and enjoy the rest of my life along with the sex. I started to give from my heart."

Self-Fullness and Altruism

Giving from the heart brings the cycle of sexual nurturing full circle to altruism, the generosity that nourishes both giver and receiver. As Molly is quick to point out, this is different from the sexual caretaking she had tried to exert in her marriage, the kind that depletes an already deficit balance and, perhaps saddest to say, doesn't even nourish the person it is intended for. The dictionary definition of altruism is "selflessness," but my own experience of it and Molly's and the stories of other women who love sex do not bear out the notion of self-*less*-ness. Rather, balanced altruism flows from a *fullness* of self, an expansion, a sense of connectedness not only with other beings, but with one's self. Altruism is self-fullness, alive, generative, generous, essential to Molly's notion of remaining in your own skin while getting under somebody else's.

But it is not necessarily self-referential or narcissistic. The self-fullness from which altruism flows moves women to reach out beyond their lives to touch the lives of others— not in order to see their own image reflected back, but to share well-being, perhaps even to change the social structures that keep people stuck in situations that don't nourish them.

Molly points out that it was feeling filled in her relationship with Kate that moved her to apply for her current job as director of the Women's Center: "After all, I couldn't stay in recovery forever. I was getting bored. I kept hearing the same messages in my groups and I thought, well, it's time I begin trying life as a substitute for therapy." It was loving Kate, she says, that helped her understand she could turn her excess energy and emotion into empathy for other women: "It was as if I'd taken what began as my neediness and processed it into feelings of generosity."

Molly's story embodies the breaking of a central paradox about altruism: Women are traditionally cast as caretakers, the earth mothers of the world, yet the world routinely infantilizes, underpays, undervalues, underrepresents, brutalizes them, from their babyhood right through to their old age.

This caretaker paradox greatly confuses the dance of give and take. In sexual partnerships, for instance, selflessness

184

is traditionally idealized, and it passes for nurturance, for giving, for altruism. It is woman's role to please, comfort, feed, heal, clean, pick up the pieces. "Yeah," says Molly, "in most men's minds we get pegged as Nurse Nellie or Florence Nightingale wandering around with a lamp. Or as a Woody Allen fantasy of helium-inflated breasts bouncing across a meadow. But then we get hated for being such capable do-gooders and taking away their precious independence. What are we supposed to do? When are we supposed to get something in return?" In the pages of sexual science, as in most other pages of history, there are no reasonable answers to Molly's question.

"One of my clients at the center told me the saddest thing," says Molly. "She said she felt the women in her family had been genetically depleted. She told me, 'They did the best they could. My grandmother never got enough of what she needed to give enough to my mother, and my mother couldn't give enough to me, and I'm not complete enough to give to my daughter.' "

When nurturing breaks down, the cycle of sexual nurturing breaks down. Then women may fall into a painful relationship trap that accounts for still more confusion and misery in the bedroom. A caretaking pattern may mimic nurturing behavior but it is far from the mutual dance of give and take that has informed Molly and Kate's relationship. It is more a solo shuffle of give and give or of give and give up, a kind of internalized oppression. I have witnessed this pattern in so many women who come into my office for therapy that I have acknowledged it with a name: sexual codependency.[5]

In sexual codependency, women's sexual attitudes and behaviors are habitually determined not by themselves, but by someone else, most often by a partner who reinforces an old, demanding voice from the past. Women focus so entirely on their partners' needs or on fulfilling their Shoulds and Oughts that their own sexual identities cease to exist. When they look into the emotional mirror, they see someone else's image, not their own. It is said in jest that when a codependent dies, someone *else's* life flashes before their eyes.

Molly throws back her head and laughs. "Well, if that's sexual codependency, I did it for years. You know what it feels like? It feels like letting the waiter eat your dinner! You get all salivated up for a big meal. Then the person who's supposed to deliver it to you tucks in and gets the pleasure out of it, and you get called the crazy lady because you complain."

All of the interruptions in the sexual nurturing cycle profoundly affect the spiritual, emotional, and relational aspects of sex for women and the physical aspects as well. If there are enough interruptions, it becomes impossible to reach or receive, to feel attachment or satisfaction, even to grow from the experience (or nonexperience) of sex. Disruption of the give and take cycle can lead to progressive sexual malnutrition and finally to sexual death by starvation.

"Like those 80% of women in our mothers' and grandmothers' generation who never came to orgasm, poor things. Who wouldn't know what one was if it sat up and bit them on the nose." Molly sniffs and smooths her hair with both hands.

But take heart. These interruptions are a matter of degree. Probably, like Molly, most women have experienced one or more of them at one time or another. But not all women experience them all at once or all the time. The good news is that the give and take cycle is infinitely forgiving. And it is possible to repair. Molly's story is testimony that the repairs can begin at any time and at any place in the cycle.

Once again Aphrodite, I run to you fluttering, like a little girl to her mother. The ancient poet voices the age-old desperation of women who love sex: How do we learn to be vulnerable to nurturance without being helpless in the bedroom and in our lives?

Sexual Nurturing—The Dance of Give and Take

"Take a breath so deep your groin senses it . . ."

As Molly rises to leave my office, she pulls her fingers emphatically through her curls: "We have to grow up and change our lives. Let go of a lifetime of training about our sexuality. About what it's acceptable to feel and do. About the fear of what may happen. We have to dare to change our lives to change the world—for ourselves and other women."

What Molly is talking about is letting go. Letting go in the sense of giving in to our own positive feelings, whether what we feel is in the adult world or a return to infant longings. Without such letting go there can be no complete cycle of sexual nurturing. And with such letting go comes the possibility of sexual peace. A peace that passes understanding. A peace that clearly passes orgasm as it is narrowly defined in the literature. A peace that transforms the experience of orgasm into the ecstasy connection, the Big R, a relational knowing of yourself and your partner. A peace, in the words of May Sarton, that will allow us to experience that orgasm "not as a little trick cleverly performed, but as a wave of union with the whole universe."[6]

The dance of give and take. This is an essential part of sexual relationship for women who love sex. It can spell the difference between sex that feels nourishing and slam-bam encounters that create indigestion or worse. It is an essential part of the ecstasy connection. It is ceremonial. It enlivens, invigorates, satisfies. It creates trust. It warms body, mind, heart, and soul.

The cycle of sexual nurturing. Giving from a place of self-fullness, receiving with a glad heart, slowing down, enjoying each other. Clearly this is not a science in any of the quantitative senses of the word. And although it effects changes in society, it is without the machinations of politics. In the hands of Molly, Kate, and other women who love sex, sexual nurturing is an art. The art of feeling good.

7

Rosa

<hr>

Slouching
Toward Intimacy

<hr>

Touch, flesh to flesh, is where the spirits meet.
—*Michael Dorris*

SOME WOMEN EMBRACE intimacy, others lurch unsteadily toward it. Still others slouch toward it unwillingly, as the "rough beast" of Yeats's poem about revolution and chaos slouches to Bethlehem.[1] But however chaotic the road to sexual intimacy may be, most women travel it at some time in their lives, for they crave understanding, closeness, and commitment with their partners. They crave tenderness and meaning, a sense of deep, ongoing spiritual connection. According to many of the women who love sex, these are essential ingredients of the passion that is such a necessary part of sexual ecstasy.

Of her own journey to intimacy, Rosa admits, "I had to drag myself into it kicking and screaming." This is the first time I have had an opportunity to talk with Rosa alone, but I feel I already know her even though I am not yet familiar with the details of her story. Friends have told me about her struggles over the years as a woman, as an artist, and have related how inspired they have felt by her transformation. I have been privileged to witness her spirit through her paintings—voluptuous, shimmering canvases of animals inhabiting an Eden of giant leaves. At her latest show I sometimes felt as if I were in the presence of Kirlian photographs that record electrical energy, the auras of living beings. At the restaurant where we meet, Rosa stands in the doorway with a halo of sunlight around her, ethereal, reaching out her hand, about to speak.

She wasn't always the shining soul she appears to be now. "I used to spend half my life in bed with lovers and the other half agonizing about what on earth I was doing there," she confides over a cup of tea. "I did it for the attention and of course the orgasms, but by the time I got up the next morning, the good feelings were always gone. Evaporated. I usually felt about as empty as this teacup." She drains her mug and holds it upside down to illustrate. Despite these words, the serene woman who sits across from me now seems to be in full ownership of all facets of herself. I guess that her journey to this degree of peacefulness has been complex and that her perspectives will be very different from those of Alice, Molly, and the others; a story about the search for sexual self but filled with different colors, and with valuable information for women who love sex.

"Back then I wanted to be wanted," she continues, beginning to slather some butter on a whole wheat scone and then thinking better of it. "And I'd feel great—as long as I could get someone to wrap their warm arms around me. But the minute they let go, I felt alone and homeless again, and the terror would start. I became a waif without any way to say 'hold onto me or I'm going to dematerialize.' Getting into bed with someone always seemed like a matter of life or death: I'm going to die unless you stay with me. If I could just be close with you for a couple of hours, everything will be all right."

"But that didn't work for you," I affirm, watching a gray cloud form in her eyes.

"Actually, it seemed to work just fine for the first years, say, through most of my twenties. I was the Queen of Chaos. I rode a motorcycle. I slept around. I landed in the emergency room because one of the guys I brought home tried to slash me with a razor he was cutting coke with. Through it all, I drank a pint of peppermint schnapps a day and had about a zillion different jobs to support my painting habit. Hey, things were fresh and exciting!" Rosa flashes me the smile of an imp, not an angel.

"But then I began to notice I was hungry all the time. Hungry here," she brings her hand to her heart. "I was prowling through my days like an alley cat, meowing at anybody I thought might go to bed with me at night. It could be a bartender, a telephone lineman, the guy dressed up in robes preaching the sermon on Sunday, it didn't matter. At one point I sat down and tried to make a list, but I couldn't remember their faces, let alone their names.

I reflect on the capriciousness of timing. Rosa managed to do her prowling before the fact of AIDS, before the threat of HIV burst upon us all. A few years later and the faceless drug-and-alcohol-clouded sexual encounters she is describing could well have been a matter of death for her and not a period she could look back on and chalk up to life experience.

"Finally I just started feeling frantic," she continues. "The schnapps was unplugging me. When I quit that, I realized what was unplugging me was the anonymous sex. My body was going through the moves, but my consciousness was traveling somewhere in outer space—wanting something else, something that could last beyond the next orgasm. I suddenly understood that what I wanted was to like myself. And to wake up next to someone I knew. I wanted to care about the person I was with the next morning and have him care back. At least I wanted to know his name." With the hand that had been pressed to her heart

190

Slouching Toward Intimacy

Rosa reaches for her scone, spreads the butter, and then takes a big bite.

Want, wanting, wanton. As I listen to Rosa, I am struck by the vagaries of the English language. In this pleasure-negative culture, a woman who has sexual wants becomes labeled *wanton*—loose, amoral, immoral. A woman who is found wanting in the right values. Rosa describes her earlier self as a wanton woman wanting to be wanted. A hungry woman. A woman yearning.

Yearning for something more in bed is a feeling most women who love sex have told me they can identify with, at least at some moment in their lives. And many of them can directly identify with Rosa's quandary. In the midst of the search for physical relief and comfort they have found themselves in want because they are somehow bypassing an essential ingredient for satisfaction: intimacy with themselves and with a partner.

I think of Libby, a current client who calls herself a lesbian even though she has yet to have a sexual relationship with a woman. Libby is a social worker who helps place AIDS babies in foster homes. She has spent much of her life as a caretaker of other people, most recently her mother, who is dying of breast cancer. She yearns for excitement, something to mitigate the harshness of her responsibilities. And she yearns for sex: "Maybe I should be a hooker," she tells me in all seriousness. "I can get all the sexual contact I want and get paid for it. And it'll be with men, so I don't have to worry about getting overinvolved— or involved at all." Libby does not seem like a potential hooker to me. She doesn't have the high degree of outgoing energy and resiliency that invites repeated, anonymous sex. Rather, she seems like a woman starved for tenderness and recognition, a woman who would love to love sex but whose life is in too much chaos to let her be fully aware of her own feelings. My job is not to dissuade her from joining the world's oldest profession, however. It is to help her clarify her constellation of wants so that she can move in directions that are right for her life. Perhaps in Rosa's story there will be clues to that elusive piece called sexual intimacy.

What Is Intimacy?

The word *intimacy* derives from the Latin *intima*, which means the innermost layer of an organ, the wall of a blood vessel, about as close to the core as you can get. Many women who love sex maintain that sexual intimacy *is* the core. As I reflect on what these women say satisfies them sexually over the long term, the operational magic word seems most often to be *intimacy*, as if it is the sum of all the sexual parts. Like other areas of positive sexuality, sexual intimacy is a whole-person proposition, powerful and spontaneous. It is more than a pilgrimage to the Big O; it is emotional connective tissue that links body, mind, heart, and soul.

"Touch, flesh to flesh, is where the spirits meet—Michael Dorris said that," remarks Rosa. "It's as fine a definition of sexual intimacy as I've run across."

Surely, sexual intimacy includes touching and being touched, not only flesh to flesh, but emotionally and spiritually, too.

"It's the quality of the touch that's so important," she says. "Intimacy is about *knowing*. Have you peeled an orange lately? I mean so you *know* that orange—the weight of it, the texture of the skin and membranes, the slipperiness of the seeds. The essence of orange, the *spirit* of orange, is in touching, tasting, sniffing, feeling. That's true of human beings, too." I am reminded of Maya's description of sexual ecstasy. She used the same phrase Rosa chooses to describe intimacy: "It's about *knowing*."

We talk about the problems women have understanding the complex concept of sexual intimacy.

192

Slouching Toward Intimacy

"Sometimes it's hard to even be aware of it, let alone understand it," remarks Rosa. "It has a chameleon quality. It's able to change its color so you can't see it lurking there in the branches ready to pounce on you just when you think you're having an uninvolved little fling."

Indeed, intimacy is able to blend with different sexual contexts, and it can take women by surprise. Intimacy can mean love or romance. It can mean nurturing, as it did to Molly and Kate during their massage, that first monumental sexual experience where they melted away any residual reticence and shyness and became fully bonded lovers. Intimacy can mean commitment, as it did to Alice, as she and Frank struggled through their discrepancies of sexual desire, learning to take emotional risks with one another after many years of a marriage patterned by dullness and silence.

"In fact," says Rosa, "don't you think a lot of people use the word *intimacy* when what they really mean is *sex?* It keeps them from having to say the S word when that seems too close to the bone."

"As in: 'I had *intimate relations* last night?' " I respond. "You know they're not talking about having their cousins over for a cozy little dinner at home!"

Semantics help create the layers of confusion women feel about what sexual intimacy means. To compound matters, women tend to have few positive (and powerful) models for intimacy, especially sexual intimacy. I ask Rosa where she began to develop her own patterns.

"I suppose I started by mimicking my mother and my aunts," responds Rosa. "I learned how to do the caretaking and pleasing and flirting things before I got into junior high. Beyond that, well, I read magazines and romantic novels like any other horny adolescent."

"What kinds of tips did you pick up?" I ask.

"I learned that romance was a sexist trap and that marriage amounted to prolonged domestic violence or profound boredom."

193

"Not exactly a model for equal, honest, open relating," I observe.

"What about our inner images of intimacy?" Rosa asks me.

Intimacy is a whole lot more than the ability to remember a lover's name. It is a sense of sharing the same images of pleasure or at least being able to respond fully to each other's images.

"I mean, if we don't have the picture, how can we see what intimacy looks like?" She agrees, drawing intersecting vine leaves on her napkin with the handle of her spoon. "I think we need a media blitz on long-term snuggling. Let's get the government to fund it with some of the billions they spend on nuclear warheads."

Essential as intimate connections may be, they are not always easy to make, even for women who love sex. "I didn't fall into intimacy by doing exactly what comes naturally," quips Rosa, "because what came naturally to me was to flirt and please and caretake and then build a wall around the rest of me—guard my emotions like the queen's jewels. My body might be right out there smiling, but not *me*, not my *self*."

Why does intimacy not come naturally to all women? Why are we bound up in emotional armament, even in our sexual relationships where we are most naked and vulnerable, closest, it would seem, to the core?

"My core wasn't anything a partner would want to get close to," says Rosa. "Even I didn't want to be close to it. It was all hurt and fear and porcupine quills. The fear of being seen. The fear of never being seen. The fear of dislocation. And all the years of anger that went with it."

As Rosa speaks, my memory floods with clients who have come into my office bristling with their own brand of porcupine quills and rattling their rage and hurt at the very partners who might have offered them the closeness they craved. Mona was one of these women. She had never been able to talk directly about her feelings of betrayal about

194

her husband's affair, and she stabbed out at him continually with daggers of sarcasm. Karima was another woman enraged at a philandering partner. She had turned to alcohol to dull the pain, and by the time I saw her in therapy, she had swallowed her anger until she could barely speak. When she did, she spoke with a controlled rage that reminded me of a turn-of-the-century etching I had seen of a woman walking on a tightrope while juggling knives. Karima was not a woman you wanted to get too close to.

Rosa continues her story: "I come from a long line of adventurers—the men, anyway. The women all wore black dresses and became depressives and suicides. My grandparents were Costa Rican, but somehow they ended up on Cape Cod, nobody talks about why. As far back as I can remember, even when I was six or eight years old, I felt like I was playing a bit part in a melodrama. I knew I was supposed to come in and curtsy on cue, but I just never learned the lines."

I ask her to explain her feeling of dislocation. "Well, I didn't fit into my family because I refused to grow up to wear black and wait on the men. I didn't fit in with the nice white kids in school either. Their birthday parties weren't like mine. So we finally just left each other alone, and I'd spend weekends in my room drawing pictures of dragons and flying horses. There wasn't anyone else around like me. It was as if I'd been dispossessed."

"It must have been a terribly lonely childhood for you."

"And oddly freeing, too. Right from the beginning I knew I had to invent myself. But I was always longing for something else—excitement, passion, I don't know. By the time I was thirteen, I was fantasizing about a Mr. Macho who'd sweep me away on his Harley-Davidson. And nobody suggested I fantasize anything else. There was not a single clue in my family as to what it takes to create a close relationship, let alone a close sexual relationship. I grew up with totally unrealistic ideas."

"You must have had *some* outside influences," I say.

"Well, there was the Church. But you have to understand my family. They isolated their women. Except for Sunday mass, they kept them at home until they molded or went mad or did themselves in."

"What about television?"

"The first rule of the family was to worship Grandfather—Popo. And Popo wouldn't allow us to have a TV, which I suppose I ought to be thankful for, because I'd probably never have learned to amuse myself by drawing. On the other hand, television might actually have helped someone as cut off as I was learn a little more about the world."

Rosa's description of her childhood underscores how difficult it is for some women to begin to understand the qualities necessary to create intimacy, especially with men whose experience tells them they have little to gain from it. The plain fact is that in order to find models, most women, like Rosa, have to look outside their families, outside themselves.

The problem is that the keys to sexual intimacy aren't outside us. They're on the inside, even though there may not always be enough light inside to find them there. Like other aspects of positive sexuality, intimacy is characterized by empathy—the ability to reach out fluidly to a partner in acceptance and generosity and also in desire. But the reaching toward a partner is rooted in the full acknowledgment of self, of how you are feeling, thinking, remembering, *being*. So reaching out in sexual intimacy is far from a selfless act. It bespeaks the kind of self*full*ness so eloquently described by Molly in Chapter 6.

Sexual intimacy is something that is learned, bit by bit, from risk and experience and sometimes in spite of risk and experience. In therapy sessions I am often privileged to witness couples striving to equalize power balances and create win–win situations. My clients Sharon and Ted are a case in point. It was clear that they had learned zero intimacy skills growing up in their admittedly alcoholic families. For them, intimacy meant the heart-throbbing closeness they remembered feeling together as they escaped from the senselessness and brutality of their respective homes. They had fallen wildly in love as teenagers: "It was so easy. We both felt cherished for the first time ever. We got married the minute we could." In striving to repeat those glowing feelings *ad infinitum,* however, they each drifted off into extramarital junkets, escaping now from each other, because escape was the only way they knew to move toward intimacy. By the time I saw them, their marriage was deeply shaken. Doubly shaken in that they still remained clueless about how to show each other their feelings of hurt and anger—and of love.

When I became their communications coach (as they called me), I likened their learning process to a poker game, encouraging each of them to stay in the game, to raise the level of engagement by upping the ante until all their emotional cards were out on the table. But willing as Ted and Sharon were, upping the ante wasn't easy for them. They had to learn that long-term sexual intimacy is a fluctuating journey traveled over time rather than a series of hormone-drenching affairs. Moreover, they had to learn that there are no easy formulas for success. It is impossible to quantify or measure intimacy by objective standards. Like many of the ingredients essential for sexual ecstasy, its definition depends on the ebb and flow of energy, and so far, energy ebb and flow defies statistical analysis.

From Chaos to Connection

"Come home with me," invites Rosa. "I have something to show you." We finish our tea and agree to carry on our conversation at her house.

The hall outside her studio is a mass of framed photographs arranged around six of her sensuous, steamy jungle paintings. The walls breathe and pulse with the prowl of panthers and slither of cobras. We seem oddly civilized in our city clothing. "This is me at eight," she says pointing to a snapshot of a skinny, grinning kid with her arms wrapped around a black labrador puppy. The eyes of both girl and dog stare unflinchingly back at me.

"It's actually me and the first being I ever remember loving without fear," Rosa unhooks the picture from the wall and hands it to me. "His name is Bolivar. When Bolivar was a pup, I used to take him to bed just to have a warm body there. My mother would yell and scream and carry on when she caught me as if there was some sort of primal scene going on that was out of her control. But I could always count on Bolivar to sneak back upstairs again with his tail wagging!"

Rosa turns to me and suddenly asks, "Do you think Bolivar was an intimate relationship? I'm not talking bestiality or anything, but if it hadn't been for Bolivar, I don't think I would have known how to begin to have any other closeness in my life."

Before I can answer, Rosa points to another photograph: "This is the only one I have of our family all together." It is blown up from a snapshot taken sometime in the fifties in front of a shingled house with a pillared porch. Nobody is touching. Nobody is smiling. The men are moustached and have hats on. Rosa's mother is looking down into her hands, which are clasped against her black dress. Rosa is the only child. She crouches on the grass, wearing shorts and holding onto Bolivar.

"I started being sexually active quite young—ninth grade. Back then, they called it *fast*. I didn't care what they called me. I was so crazed for affection or attention or *something*, I'd do whatever it took. You know the story— I was good at it. And it was fun—exciting—for years. Then I began having all those feelings I was telling you about in the restaurant—the longings for something more."

Rosa describes this period of her life again as a dark

night of her body and soul. "I actually got quite ill," she continues. "Fevers and flu symptoms that wouldn't go away. Ironically, I literally couldn't get out of bed. I was too weak to go to work. I couldn't paint. I just lay there and brooded about my zapped-out immune system. One day it occurred to me that being so sick was actually fallout from all the years of sicko sex. I made a list of the kinds of relationships I was having to maintain to keep on having that kind of sex. And the relationships I was missing out on, the ones I was having to do without. Close woman friends, for instance, that kind of loving support that keeps you in balance. And I wanted a dog, but I couldn't trust myself to be home enough to feed it."

"How did you begin to heal?" I ask.

"I made some changes in my life. Gave up alcohol. Gave up no-name sex. Gave up sugar and caffeine. When someone suggested I give up white flour, I decided: Enough!"

I empathize with Rosa. "There's only so much you can give up before you feel like you're giving up your*self*."

"Eventually, I asked myself, What does sex have left to teach me? I figured I already knew everything I cared to know about except the intimacy. But whenever I tried to make myself concentrate on intimacy, I spaced out or fell asleep. How's that for defensiveness?"

"So what happened?" I ask, seeing nothing of a defensive Queen of Chaos in the glowing, self-possessed woman showing me pictures of her family.

"I made myself look around at people I knew who were in long-term relationships. Most of them looked, well, pretty miserable to me. I began to figure out what intimacy isn't. It isn't role playing. It isn't being the compliant person your partner wants you to be because you don't know how to be anybody else. It isn't playing mommy games and controlling your partner to keep him out of trouble. It isn't swallowing each other alive to keep yourself from dying of loneliness. And," she says with a flourish, "intimacy certainly isn't never having to say you're sorry."

Rosa is talking about some of the dynamics that are intimacy killers, especially when they are played out in the bedroom: violence and isolation, codependency and fusion. All of them can be born of the traumas and skewed psychosexual messages women typically grow up with. They can be born also from the cultural myth that says sex is a power play, not a balanced relationship dance.

"Surely not all the couples you looked at were either sparring partners or locked into *American Gothic*," I challenge her, visualizing Grant Wood's classic painting of the dusty, tight-lipped duo, defined by a pitchfork the size of their heads.

"Oh, no. I've known people who've been with the same husband or wife or lover for thirty-seven years," responds Rosa. "My old painting teacher—she still holds her husband's hand and lights up when he comes in the room. When they're not together, they tell you loving little stories about each other. And I envy them, admire them. But when I was doing this piece of life research, I thought, Nope, that one's just not in the cards for *me*.

"I actually got quite politicized on the subject. Well, politics is what we were doing in those days."

I assured Rosa that I remembered. The mid-'70s, after all, was when I was beginning to raise my own consciousness as a feminist—as a woman—in the male-dominated field of human sexuality.

"I kept agitating for change. You know, that female superior position in and out of bed. I don't think it had a whole lot of effect on the men. They just seemed to absorb it and keep on doing their thing."

"Wasn't the thing they were doing usually rolling over and going to sleep—at least where our lives were concerned?" I interject.

"Right. And I got tired of being mad. So I learned about sex with myself."

"Sex for one," I comment, thinking of Betty Dodson's

liberating book by that name.[2] "You started to masturbate?"

"Yeah." Rosa laughs, raising her palms for me to see. "And talk about breaking taboos. I mean these hands were never allowed under the covers when I was a kid. Ever. Even in the dead of winter."

"So what happened?"

"I learned I could take care of myself very nicely, thank you. These hands can do more than make paintings. Well, I discovered I have a clitoris."

A mist of silence begins to rise gently between us as it will in an open meadow to signal an abrupt change in temperature. I do not break the silence. Rosa clears her throat and continues. "I discovered that there were parts of me that no man had ever touched. It was more than just my vulva, though that was pretty terrific. It was the focus on myself, taking the time, making the comfort."

"Learning to love yourself?" I offer.

"Learning to respect myself and respond to my sexual feelings directly instead of going out to a bar and rubbing up against some guy's leather jacket. I took a mirror and actually looked at myself, looked deep inside my vagina when I was menstruating. Do you know how many different colors a vagina can be?" Her painter's eye comes to rest on the voluptuous blossoms cascading down the canvas behind a panther's shoulder.

"Then when I'd got my genitals down, I thought I'd like to discover some more about the rest of myself. So I took myself off to a retreat center. They advertised that in only a week there I would learn to live more gracefully and productively. Well, I don't know about the grace, but I did find something that has turned out to be of enormous value to me. Actually, two things.

"The first thing was the calming effect of sound. Especially the sounds from a singing bowl they used during the meditations, one of those Tibetan jobs that makes incredible vibrations when you rub a dowel around the edge. I'd never heard anything like it. The sound seemed to stay with me and rearrange all my cells. Sort of as if I were getting an interior massage.

"Then there was this poster on the kitchen wall, which kept staring at me whenever I went in to get cups of tea, just as if it had eyes that followed me. It was one of those homilies about living in the middle of mess. I related to it strongly because it had fly specks all over it. It was just like my life." She laughs. "I wrote the message down and stuck it in my wallet. Later I had it laminated, so it's still there, next to my driver's license. The saying goes like this:

Show up
Pay attention
Tell the truth
Be open to the outcome

"This saying kind of hummed to me at the same vibration as the singing bowl. Actually, it became like a beacon of light at that time. Or maybe like a lightning rod that helped me ground out the chaos. Because I was just beginning to realize that intimacy isn't about holding on, holding tight, belonging to someone else, or owning them. It isn't about trying to change them either. Intimacy is about letting go. Letting go of expectations. Letting go of attachment so you can *be* in bed with someone else.

"But you know, such an interesting thing happened. Just as I thought I'd let go of the whole sexual intimacy fever forever, I met Roberto." Rosa points midway along the wall of wild paintings and framed photographs of her life. A slim, massively maned man bends over a drawing board, grinning at the camera, grinning at Rosa.

"He was from Guatemala, not so far from Costa Rica, you know, where my family lived for so many generations. He was five years younger than I was. There seemed to be an immediate understanding between us, almost a genetic one. He got what I was about. I didn't have to raise his consciousness, he was already there. I never had to explain my life to him. For the first time I felt I was with someone and I belonged."

"For one thing, it sounds as if he linked you to your cultural roots," I affirm.

"And without being in any way a controlling, macho pig." Rosa laughs.

I take note again of the glow that emanates from Rosa and reflect on how drastically her energy must have changed since her days of prowling from one spacy bedroom scene to another. She appears to be walking proof that personal growth is imbedded not only in the self, but in relationship. Like Molly and Alice, Rosa's lessons about life and sexuality have been ultimately learned by working them through with their partners.

Rosa shows me another picture of Roberto. He is splendid in a white linen suit, his eyes dark and limpid—I resist the temptation to compare them to Bolivar's, just a few feet down the wall.

Rosa's hand is over her heart. "He was totally romantic. My Latin lover. At first I was skeptical that he was for real. I've always thought of romance as a plot of the patriarchy to hide women behind thick walls and hook them into bearing male children. But Roberto—he had a gift for it. It was part of his being. And it's what won me over. More than that, it's what kept me interested when things got shaky later.

"For him, romance was much more than a bunch of flowers on Valentine's Day. He had a true sense of ceremony. When we first met, I had described to him the haunting sounds of that singing bowl. And on the morning of our wedding day, he brought me a singing bowl—he'd found a perfect one. Utterly simple with no decoration and a voice that opened up the heart. Whenever we had something to celebrate we'd reach for that bowl. It diffused the passion, Roberto said. Sent it back into the universe. It was

203

one of our ways of keeping ecological balance with the planet. We'd breathe together and we'd listen until the sound reached our bones. Roberto called it the celebration of his feminine side. And he kept on being a romantic, even after we were married, like when he had to be away in Guatemala, sometimes he'd fly home for the weekend, just so we could be together."

"So Roberto whooshed into your life and you became instantly bonded," I comment. "But I sense there's much more to the story."

"I'd fallen in love before—maybe once a month in fact, for years. But this was different. We cared about each other in a permanent way. He loved me, he loved my art animals, especially the jungle series." She waves her hand at the wall crawling with luminous primates and felines. "Suddenly I was with this one man and I wasn't constantly looking over his left ear wondering about the next encounter with somebody else. Then something really weird happened. The more focused and deep I became with Roberto, the more unfocused and scared I was getting when we went to bed together. It was as if I had all I ever wanted and still it wasn't enough. I got crazy if we couldn't make love once or twice a day, and I'm talking full-blown lovemaking, not just a little cuddling—a couple of hours of intense struggling, topped off by intercourse."

"What kind of crazy were you getting?" I ask.

"I needed him to be with me, to be in bed with me all the time. I needed all that heavy physical action or else I got really skitzy. I couldn't stand my feelings. I started spacing back to my past, to my childhood. It was as if I was not "showing up" with the man I loved, with Roberto. I begged him to be with me then I picked fights and threatened to leave him. I blamed him for how scared I was feeling."

"What were you blaming him for?" I ask. "I thought he was the archangel from south of the border who swept into your life and gave it meaning."

Slouching Toward Intimacy

"That's just the point," Rosa tells me. "I wasn't responding to *Roberto*, I was responding to all those people I felt took advantage of me in the past. To show up in the present with Roberto I had to resolve all that part of my life where I was sleeping around and not relating. I had to go back even further and show up in the past. And to do that, I finally realized I had to come to terms with my family."

Rosa leads me back to the photograph of her fifties family posing before the pillared house. "*He* drank himself to death by the time I was twelve." She points to her father, perpetually shadowed under his wide-brimmed Panama. "*She* overdosed on pills while I was still in college." She points to her mother, perpetually watching her life leaking through her clasped hands. "How could I get close to anyone? Look what love like mine does to people."

"What was your fantasy about how destructive your love could be?"

"If I loved someone who loved me back, they'd kill themselves. I didn't want to do that to Roberto."

I wanted to ask Rosa: How did you know it was your love that was so very powerful? Given a family like yours, how did you grow up knowing anything about love? Then I remembered it is the nature of children to love and often to express love by taking blame for love sickness in the family, as if drafting off the negativity of others gives them a measure of power and control over their young lives in an otherwise impossible situation. Many of these children grow up to become compliant, self-effacing women who love "too much." But for others, this extraordinary ability to love through the abuse and craziness of those who are supposed to be taking care of them eventually produces a profound healing of the spirit and immense strength. I suspect that Rosa is one of these.

"Of course"—Rosa breaks into my thoughts—"I wasn't consciously thinking this all out while it was going on. But with hindsight, I know that fear of losing Roberto was behind what was happening for me in bed."

Rosa continues her story: "I had to unlearn a lot of old lessons. I had to listen to that saying I kept in my wallet: *pay attention, pay attention.* Pay attention to the dynamic, to my self, to the *roles* Roberto and I were playing when we thought we were making love. I think I must have been playing Miss Piggy—so needy and self-centered and hungry. I was wanting him inside me all the time. You know, a day without simultaneous orgasms just wasn't a day worth living. I never let up. Gosh, I suppose that makes me a woman who comes too much." Rosa flashes another one of her big grins.

I grin appreciatively back. "How was Roberto responding to all this?"

"Of course, he got more and more into playing Shrinking Violet. He was backing off from my grabbiness, but I mean he was literally shrinking, too. After a few months of being with me, this lusty Latin lover, he started having migraines when I came on to him. And he had trouble getting it up, too."

"That must have made life interesting for you," I offer, wondering how Rosa and the splendid Roberto had resolved this dilemma in their bedroom.

"Interesting and agonizing. We had to learn to communicate our feelings instead of just grunting and pointing. We had to talk about what we wanted and didn't want. We had to go to the next part of my Zen saying and start *telling the truth.*"

"What was the truth for you?"

"The truth was, we were both making ourselves miserable by some pretty rigid definitions. I thought the love I wanted was something I could get only through intercourse. And of course Roberto thought the only way he could be a man to me was to be turned on all the time and have a constant erection. I was giving him that message, of course, but that was his conditioning, too. How he thought he ought to be. I began to feel so depressed. At one point I remember rolling over and telling him I might as well turn into a good Latina mama or grandma—*mamacita*—and slip into a black dress and blend into the woodwork."

"Do you think that's what had happened with the women in your family?"

"You know, I began to wonder. Behind all that swaggering *machismo*, maybe Popo and my papa and all the uncles, well, maybe they couldn't get it up with their wives either."

"Maybe that's why they acted so controlling and the women got so depressed and suicidal," I respond. "They were playing out the old patriarchal sexual equation."

"What's that?" asks Rosa.

"Love equals intercourse. Power equals intercourse. The sexual trip that's been going on for centuries. Man on top. It's the politics of power played out in the bedroom. It keeps everybody stuck in the missionary position in and out of bed."

From my experience as a therapist, this intercourse equation makes for major sexual problems, the kind that are labeled dysfunctions—for both women and men. Because these dysfunctions can't always be talked about with ease, they can eat into the psyche and make people feel crazy. Sonya is one in a long line of clients whose ability to love sex has suffered from the intercourse equation. At a highly energized age fifty-six, she was already in deep mourning over the loss of her sex life because her husband's erections were becoming less and less reliable. She accompanied him into therapy with the fury of a woman scorned. Like Rosa and Roberto, this couple had to learn to talk together about their desires and feelings of inadequacy. Then they had to risk moving beyond their sexual conditioning. They had to learn how to express love, closeness, and erotic energy in other ways, to discover that some of the methods of outercourse mentioned by Iris and company can expand the sexual universe for men as well as women.

Rosa continues with her story: "While I was being so nuts, Roberto was busy running his own scene. He got self-accusing and maudlin. He said all he wanted was to make me happy, to give me everything I had ever wanted in bed."

"But he felt he couldn't give it to you because he couldn't control his erections?" I offer.

Rosa nods and laughs softly as if she is conversing directly with Roberto now. "Poor guy. He felt like a total flop. The truth was, what it turned out I wanted didn't have a whole lot to do with his penis. What I really wanted was for Roberto to stop being all mad at himself and be his tender, sensitive self. I wanted him to look at me and hold me, not necessarily stick his thing in me. And when we pulled off all the emotional masks, it turned out Roberto didn't care if I was all over his body every hour of the day. He just wanted to be seen and heard and appreciated. Not adored. Just sincerely *seen* by me for who he was."

"You had to figure out what you wanted. So you could see it, visualize it, taste it."

"And paradoxically, at the same time, I had to let go of really specific goals, like we're going to spend three hours tonight making love. I had to follow my Zen saying. I had to be open. Somehow, serenely open to the outcome."

"That one's hard," I say, "especially if you grow up in a family like yours where you learned about control and depression instead of intimacy. Being open to the outcome implies trust in a benevolent universe. After all, what was the outcome of your so-called intimate relationships in the past—from your parents on up through all those anonymous lovers?"

"Exactly," replies Rosa. "All I could think of was the disappointment."

"And disconnection?"

"And disconnection," she agrees. "I was in terror. There

were months there when I thought I was losing it entirely. One minute my life was fortified like a Moorish castle and the next minute I had demilitarized. I felt fragmented, blown apart. Indescribably vulnerable."

"The old patterns weren't making it anymore. You had to change."

"Oh, God, intimacy was so much work," Rosa sighs again as if Roberto were standing next to us.

"Sure," I respond. "But I hear you telling me that once you put in the work, the relationship changed."

"It was uncanny," she says. "It was sorcery. Like magic."

"This *is* the magic of sexual relationships," I agree. "Use your words: If you show up, pay attention, tell the truth, the outcome has got to change as apparently it did for you and Roberto."

"So I made an amazing discovery working all this through," says Rosa.

"What's that?"

"I learned that sexual misery is optional."

Exchanging Vulnerabilities and Learning to Love

When I ask Rosa just what techniques she and Roberto had used to break through their stalemate to sexual intimacy, she says simply, "We started to listen to each other."

"Once two people start telling the truth, listening becomes a lot easier," I remark.

"Because," says Rosa, "you're not spending all that energy defending and blaming. You can use it to see what life feels like on the other corner of the sheet."

When Rosa says this, that wonderful phrase of Fritz Perls flashes into my consciousness: "Contact is the appreciation of *differences*." By listening to one another—body, mind, heart, and soul—Rosa and Roberto were able to appreciate each other's *sexual* differences. And they were able to learn by themselves what some other couples can learn only through months of intensive therapy—if ever. I am remembering Alice and Frank, who had to struggle so hard to hear each other's words, let alone the context of each other's deep desires.

"One of the things I hadn't understood," continues Rosa, "is that sexual intimacy begins way long before you get to the bedroom."

"You mean it's in the day-to-day relationship?"

"I mean it begins right here." She taps her heart energetically with both palms. "I learned that all that chaos in my life—the pre-Roberto sleeping around, and also the sexual fights with Roberto—all this was a whole lot worse when I tried not to do it, when I tried to control it. I kept thinking I could compartmentalize those behaviors, keep them separate from my life. I tried to office-manage my way around them."

"And never have to look at your anger, which was always bubbling away under there keeping the chaos alive and well."

"And never look at my anger," Rosa agrees, glancing at the panther coiled above her on a branch twined with brilliant green vines.

"So, being open to the outcome meant being willing to quit tap dancing and shuffling to keep your feelings at bay . . ."

"The weekend I finally burst through to my rage and beat the stuffing out of the sofa, we made love after that as if we couldn't stop. There was so much tenderness between us. So much whispering and touching. I remember us waking up and lying side by side in the morning just gazing into each other's eyes. We weren't saying anything. Just observing and accepting. Just being there. It was pure, open connection."

"Uncritical," I offer.

"And I learned there are certain conditions that make sex sing," she says. I wonder for an instant if this will be like the list of dos and don'ts Alice evolved for Frank. But as Rosa starts to elaborate on her conditions for sexual intimacy, I remind myself that even though she and Alice are both women who love sex, they are very different beings at different places in their lives.

"Chemistry, for one." Rosa begins her list. "Well, Roberto and I never had any problem with that. And affection. No problem there either. We were immediate best friends as well as lovers."

"Are you talking about love?" I ask.

"Without doubt," says Rosa. "But I mean love beyond my training as a good girl who was supposed to grow up to wear black dresses and wait on the men."

"But you say you spent most of your adult life being a bad girl wearing a black motorcycle jacket," I counter.

"Yeah," responds Rosa. "But I always felt guilty for breaking the rules. So when I met Roberto, I was still a good Catholic girl at heart, see? Only I was trapped in a bad girl's body. Six years of relative abstinence hadn't erased the guilt, just arrested it. So speaking of love, I had to learn to love myself. First I had to forgive myself for all that running around with guys. Then I had to learn to love *him.* And not in that smarmy, adoring way you read about in novels or in the depriving way my family doled out love."

When Rosa tells me love is essential to her satisfaction in bed, she is echoing stories of many other women who love sex. And, like these women, she is talking about unhooking love from its family limitations and social constructions. She is talking about amplifying it.

"And tenderizing it," Rosa adds, smiling again at the apparent presence of Roberto. "Tenderizing it by letting down the guardrails."

To describe the process of letting down guardrails so that couples can move closer and more appreciatively toward each other sexually, Masters and Johnson coined a delightful phrase: *exchanging vulnerabilities.*[3] The process

Rosa describes with Roberto illustrates this phrase exactly. Love that fosters intimacy is not a process of fusion, but of letting go. "And taking a risk," says Rosa. "It's beyond romance. Those risks aren't always about making nice. Sometimes they're about saying the things your partner does that make you nuts. And sometimes they're about exploding toxicity."

"As a couples therapist," I offer, "I call that dumping garbage."

"You know, a lot of people scoff about women having to have love before they can have sex. I'm not even sure I know exactly what that means, but I think it's one of those pat phrases that puts women down and keeps rage going between women and men. It says to me that all women want to do is hook men into marrying them and that men are much more pure and able in terms of anything that has to do with their bodies. That isn't how Roberto was. After knowing him, I don't believe those easy gender distinctions any more. He needed love as much as I did, and he was willing to put out to help it happen between us."

"What about falling in love?" I ask.

"Isn't that mostly a product of overactive adrenal glands?" laughs Rosa.

"More than that," I answer. "It's also hooked into societal conditioning. Take a look at the signs. Obsessing after your lover, dancing to his moods, being immobilized unless you're together—sounds like a textbook for addiction and codependency."

"Hey, wait a minute!" Rosa laughs. "You're describing the first year of life with Roberto. Such meetings and partings. Such sweet, *sweet* sorrow!"

"But the falling-in-love signs can also be symptoms. Symptoms of love sickness," I argue. I am thinking particularly of the notion of limerence, the turbulent, buoyant, aching passion of new love so well known by most women, and so deftly explicated by psychologist Dorothy Tennov.[4]

"OK, so love is many splendored," quips Rosa. "It's also

multidimensional. Sometimes it's multidifficult, too. Roberto and I found out the hard way that falling in love isn't the same as being able to love over the long term. Before we got into this, we thought it would be so simple. But we found out that love and marriage don't go so easily together like a horse and carriage. In fact, marriage can do in the horse. It nearly did us in."

Finally Touching the Spirit

Signs and symptoms notwithstanding, for women who love sex, life is filled with opportunities to experience healthy love and intimacy in all of the challenging contexts of relationship. These contexts include commitment, cohabitation, marriage, and marriage equivalency. To meet the challenges, women say both partners need to be open, trusting, and trustworthy. Sheila, one of the women from the original interviews, told me of an exact, gentle moment when she knew that she and her partner had reached a point of mutual trust: "We had just made love and were breathing together in each other's arms. We had no needs, no agendas. There was nothing separating us." Karla spoke of a different sort of trust test: "We're very confrontive and our sexual warm-up often starts with some kind of wrestling match—he's bigger and stronger, but I win the verbal battles. What makes it fun, what makes it incredibly close and sexy, is that it's never a real competition, it's more like a celebration. We *know* we're not trying to hurt each other. This is how we play."

"Partners need to be equal, too." Rosa smiles, reminding me that sex is not only a source of celebration and play, but also of balance. This is what leads to what one sex researcher calls "peer bonding" in bed—the intimate connection of two grown-up individuals who are able to respect the needs of both self and other.[5]

"Roberto and I had an astounding sense of cooperation," Rosa interjects. "Once we got through our blue period, we also seemed to possess a spontaneous sense of letting each other know where we were at, especially while we were making love. We cared about each other so much that sometimes we seemed to be in kind of a cosmic dance where we could intuit each other's moves, each other's wishes.

"Even doing the most ordinary things," Rosa continues. "We worked together on children's books—he wrote and I illustrated. So we spent a lot of our time together focused on details. Often he was able to express what I was visualizing before I could see it myself and, of course, vice versa."

"You did children's books together, but did it ever bother you not to have children?" I ask this tentatively, not wanting to probe a spot that might be too tender. Rosa answers in her most forthright manner:

"I never dared have children. I'd known so little parenting myself. We decided to have dogs instead. Cato, the old black lab who greeted you at the door, is our all-time favorite.

As if Rosa is remembering something from long ago, she gestures to the wall of pictures. "This is the last photo I ever took of Roberto." He is smiling with his arm around Cato, both dog and man alert, in their prime. "One month more, and we would have been celebrating our ninth anniversary."

"What happened?" I knew Roberto had died quite suddenly, but I had never heard the full story.

"He was in Guatemala visiting his sisters and there was a tropical storm—one of those flash floods that wipes out whole villages. He was helping to pull children out of the basement of a church and a boulder crushed his head and shoulder. It was almost instantaneous . . ."

Rosa looks down at her hands. For a moment she becomes the despairing mother in the family snapshot. Then she looks up at me. Her face is not sullen like her mother's.

It is wide and generous and glows with light. "He helped save fifty-nine children. I have letters and testimonials from people in the town. That was almost five years ago. But I still feel his spirit with me."

"How did you cope with the news?"

"At first, I thought I'd die, too. How could I go on living when this unspeakable thing had occurred? I had loved him and he had died. That was the central fact of my life. The old curse still haunting me. I was totally bereft. Enraged. I felt like scourging my flesh. Tying myself to a rock and letting birds pick me apart piece by piece.

"Then I realized, how could I *not* go on living with all I have to live for? But after a few months, a new kind of despair set in. I went through a period where I thought I'd die of not having Roberto next to me in my bed. Of not having sex in my life anymore—his sex. I couldn't imagine going back to the old way and I couldn't imagine ever finding a match for Roberto. Of course, I knew how to bring myself to orgasm, but that wasn't what I was missing. Finally, I asked myself the question again: Does sex have anything left to teach me?"

"Did you get an answer?"

"Yes. A very clear one. In the midst of my despair, I went for the singing bowl again. The one we'd used so often together."

"And it spoke to you?"

"It did, although I must say it surprised me."

"What did it say?"

"It said: 'Surrender.' "

"Surrender? You mean, give up? Give up sex? Give up hope?"

"No, not that kind of surrender. The kind of surrender that means relax. Breathe. Smell. Feel. Allow what is. Let go of control. Like my Zen saying: After you've done everything you possibly can, then it's time to slow down and let yourself *be open to the outcome.*"

"So by surrender, you don't mean that old bugaboo for women? You don't mean submission?"

Rosa looks again at her hands—wide and strong, capable of moving great weight. "I remember when I met Roberto I was determined to get control of my life. I wasn't going to land in another one of those rotten little romances where I soften up and then get left. Not me. Even when we first kissed, I wouldn't let myself feel anything—here's how I held my lips." Rosa prisses her lips against her teeth in a caricature of the grooming primate in the painting over her shoulder.

"But how was that making my life better? What I was controlling was my own feelings, as if I was playing all the roles in my family, not allowing Rosa to have any pleasure." I glance at the photograph of her father, shadowed under his Panama hat; her mother, wringing her hands.

"That was my first notion that surrender was a possibility—a positive possibility—for me. It had to do with valuing myself, honoring myself really. It meant giving in to my hungers, listening to my internal metronome. I started remembering all the places on my body I'd ever wanted to be touched. I started feeling. I started leaping on Roberto and lavishing him with my body. I started having fun. Maybe I got obsessive about it for a while. And we both had some work to do about that, but the fun gave us a start."

Rosa is speaking of the kinds of experiences that begin in delight and may lead to a wisdom beyond delight, of sexual encounters that are paths to the pulsing energy of the universe. She is describing vulnerability from within, a personal readiness to open up, to submit to the sensuality of experience. When Rosa talks about surrendering control, she does not mean that she was giving up and giving over to the will of an Other. Like Alice, she means she had learned to let go of barriers that kept her separated from herself and therefore from the fullest of sexual possibilities. She means she was surrendering the chaos with which she had shrouded her life. She means she was slouching at last toward intimacy.

Without such surrender, Rosa tells me, she cannot imagine fully knowing sexual connectedness, sexual ecstasy. Perhaps without such surrender there can be no women who love sex by their own definition. No Saint Teresa invested with the flaming arrow of God, no Alice with the courage to confront an abuser, no Iris to reveal pleasures beyond the jade gate, no Suzanne with the fiery imagination to orchestrate orgasms in every chakra.

"But did surrender help with the despair?" I ask.

"I started feeling again. Feeling what it was like to be alive and sexual."

"You mean you started showing up and paying attention."

"I mean I felt the rage and grief of losing Roberto's flesh. And I also felt the urge to paint again. To dig my hands into color and cover canvases with energy, with things that breathe and move and eat and prowl after one another during their rutting seasons."

In such surrender to the force of life is power. Not power in the sense of control over others, but in the sense of affirmed lust and connectedness. In the sense of humming with the rhythm of the universe. "It's the kind of power that doesn't come from the ego," says Rosa, "but that wants to share.

And it's the power that's in our nature," she muses, "if we're not messed with somewhere along the way." Rosa looks at me straight on. "Sex isn't compartmentalized any more than the rest of living is. It's not just the body. Sex isn't dead just because Roberto's body isn't here anymore. The energy is still here. The spirit we created still survives. I learned that sexual intimacy doesn't mean you've got to have a partner on the premises."

Rosa sees my skepticism and continues. "It's not so hard to understand. Come downstairs." She beckons. "I have something else to show you."

Rosa reaches over to the mantel and picks up the Tibetan

bowl that Roberto had given her on their wedding day. It glows with the softness and sheen of silk. "This bowl was crafted in the high mountains from seven holy metals. It's said it takes on the voice of the prayers that are chanted over it while the metals are still molten.

"I see this bowl as a symbol of woman," she continues. "The monks put the music in, but they borrowed the design from us. Women are strong like bowls. We're round. Just look at our bottoms and breasts and bellies. Our arms when we're nurturing a child. The nature of a bowl is that it has no corners or projectiles. It's powerful like an open hand, not a closed fist.

"Listen to this bowl," she says. "It retains its own integrity absolutely, yet it's able to reach out to others. *Listen . . .*"

Rosa balances the bowl in her palm and begins to stroke the rim with a wooden dowel she holds between the thumb and index finger of her other hand. With the late afternoon sun behind her, she is haloed again, an angel. Her breathing is deep and expectant, her lips parted, her throat flushed. Like the singing bowl she cradles in her palm, she is a splendidly crafted alloy, a blend of holiness and heat.

Slowly, from the measured stroking of the seven holy metals, the pulse of the universe arises. It is a barely audible contralto, yet vibrant enough to waffle the eardrums, to wring tears from the eyes, to strip the paint, it would seem, off the very woodwork. "Listen," she says. "This is a woman's voice. A voice of heartbeat, of connection, not of aggression. Its song isn't Bang or Whiz. It's Hummmmm. The hum the earth sings."

As Rosa strokes the song from the bowl, each of my bones, each of my muscles seems to soften and expand. I imagine I can see the vibrations as well as hear and feel them. They are in astounding color, like the sapphire rays that emanate from a healer's hands in Kirlian photographs. Rosa and I breathe together, meeting each other's eyes. We allow the energy to reverberate in our consciousness and beyond.

8

Reflections on Self, Spirit, and Social Change

It is this aspect of a woman that has heat. Not a heat as in "Let's have sex, baby, baby." But like a fire underground that burns high then low, in cycles. From the energy released there, a woman acts as she sees fit. A woman's heat is not a state of sexual arousal but a state of intense sensory awareness that includes, but is not limited to, her sexuality.
—Clarissa Pinkola Estés

WHEN I FIRST started researching this book in the early 1970s, the women's movement was in full flower along with the so-called sexual revolution. *The Female Eunuch, Open Marriage,* and *The Joy of Sex* were among the reading du jour. Women were getting in touch with themselves (as the saying went), experimenting with behaviors that ranged from bra burning and skinny-dipping to swing parties and butch–femme relationships with other women. Couples were turning each other on by smoking dope. Affairs flourished. The divorce rate skyrocketed along with hemlines—the miniskirt was in. The Pill was into its second decade,[1] abortion was about to be legalized,[2] homosexuality was about to be declassified as a disease.[3]

As a fledgling therapist, I was particularly aware of what was occurring on the personal growth front. Masters and

219

Johnson had recently published their theories of sexual response and inadequacy,[4] and the push to be more sexually adequate was surfacing as a presenting concern in therapy offices all over the country. The National Sex Forum was instituting its first SARs (Sexual Attitude Reassessments), multimedia encounters that confront prejudices about a plethora of sexual lifestyles.[5] Books by Betty Dodson and Nancy Friday were making the rounds of women's consciousness-raising groups; Lonnie Barbach's and Shere Hite's books were soon to follow. Translated into numerous languages, these would help liberate women worldwide to assert their fantasies and capacities for self-pleasure—and turn their partners on without necessarily relying on dope.[6]

It was an age of sexual possibilities, with orgasms enough for everyone (we thought); the sexual revolution had not yet been deconstructed as a way for men to get more women into the sack. The repressive fifties were gone forever (we thought); the New Right morality of the Reagan–Bush era had not yet hit. Family values were something discussed at the dinner table and not at political conventions on prime-time TV. AIDS, substance abuse, sexual harassment, incest, date rape, and sexual misconduct by doctors, therapists, lawyers, and clergy were not yet issues of public awareness and concern.

As I write today, women have become increasingly visible and vocal at least in public life, much more of a political force than twenty years ago. From Hillary Rodham Clinton, the "presidential partner," to grass-roots organizers, women are, at last, having some say in the shaping of public policy. Women even earn a few cents more on the dollar than they used to, although they may have to work harder for it.

But has the picture really changed for women? Some women's lives have eased, to be sure, and certain ideas and conventions of society have altered. But the basic social structure is still in place. While some of us are making money and noise, many, many more of us are out of work, abused, homeless, or powerless at subtler levels of our lives. This is also, remember, the age of backlash. It is the distinct purpose of the ongoing, undeclared war against women, as Susan Faludi calls it, "to push women back into their 'acceptable roles'—whether as Daddy's girl or fluttery romantic, active nester or passive love object."[7]

The media still depict a feminine ideal. She is slim, white, young, affluent, heterosexual, and alluring to men. Sexy, but not too *sexual*. Certainly demanding nothing for herself that doesn't also please her man. The courts continue to disregard women's needs for protection against sexual assault ("she brought it on herself").[8] The medical system and pharmaceutical industry continue to pathologize our reproductive cycles, creating expensive illnesses out of natural shifts and changes from PMS to menopause.[9] And the pleasure killers are always with us. Right-wing religious groups continue to heap hellfire and damnation on women's attempts to take sexual initiative. Moreover, since women gained the legal right to abortion, these groups have stepped up their hate campaigns against our ending unwanted pregnancies. In a blatant example of spin control, Operation Rescue has, in the name of life, family values, and Christian love, bombed scores of clinics and assaulted thousands of women.[10] Whenever it looks as if women might gain an inch of constitutional right, attacks accelerate. Dr. Jean Baker Miller observed as long ago as 1976: "It is almost as if the leaders of backlashes use the fear of change as a threat before major change has occurred."[11]

The social structure cuts across roles and classes, constantly pressuring women to adjust to someone else's notion of health and sexual health, of what we *ought* to be. If a mother openly loves another woman she may lose her children (along with her job, and status in the community). If a feminist openly loves a man, she may be castigated by what Susie Bright calls "retrofeminist posturing" from groups who hold that all men belong to the evil empire.[12]

221

If a woman seeks recovery from various substance abuses and codependencies developed as survival mechanisms in a confusing and hostile world, she may be roundly blamed for bringing on her own "disease." If she admits to hungering for the warmth and excitement of sexual relationships, she's more than likely to be tagged as a sex addict.[13] I have even had a client accused of sexual abuse for breast feeding her baby.

The backlash message is: Women love too much, eat too much, want too much. The backlash reality is: Women are still the second sex. It's no coincidence that women held up as standards of Western beauty are ones who have been rendered essentially powerless (quite literally in some instances: the Venus de Milo and the Winged Victory of Samothrace have no arms).[14] And all through history, to survive hostility, confusion, and despair, mortal women, including sex goddesses like Marilyn Monroe (the world's first Playboy centerfold),[15] have played out this image by finding ways to disarm themselves. Many of us still pooh-pooh our talents, undermine our successes, wear washed-out colors, make as little noise as possible, keep the neighbors from finding out.[16] If we are making history, it is still framed as a history of men. *"Half* of everything taught should be about women,"* asserts feminist educator and author Dale Spender. "This is about the most radical demand that one could make."[17] On the eve of the twenty-first century, we still live in a world in which it is a radical notion to ask for equal time, especially in bed.

I look back on the years that span my research on women's sexuality and see that all the major underlying repressions that divide women from their sexual experience are still in place today. Despite the sexual revolution (or maybe abetted by it), sex, and how we think about sex, is still male defined. Way back, when lines of ownership were drawn, it seems that women got to keep the kitchen utensils, while men walked away with the brightly colored box containing sexual pleasure. Centuries are invested in keeping that box intact. It's part of the social fabric.[18]

At the heart of today's backlash is the age-old sexual oppression of women. From the very beginning, the men who owned women as their property knew that the one thing they couldn't control was the sexual energy of their women—the pleasures, orgasms, and ecstasies that invested those women's lives with vitality and creativity. Maintaining the power position over women requires power tactics. Just as neo-Nazis now say the Holocaust never happened, or homophobic surveys have pared the gay male population down to a measly 1%,[19] men in power have systematically tried to erase women's sexual experience. They have done so violently, by sexual abuses, and insidiously, by creating a model of sexuality that abnormalizes much of what women love about sex. And often women have capitulated here, too. In need of male protection from male violation, they have spent their sexual capital on their husbands and lovers. Or in seeking autonomy, they have rejected their femaleness and their erotic energy. However you slice it, in losing control of their sexuality, these women have lost a primary source of their power.

It is virtually impossible to talk about ecstatic union and emotional involvement, those elements of sex that women most often find most gratifying, without receiving a defensive response. Most often the response is from men, but sometimes it is from women who have bought into the system. Disbelief, diminution, dismissiveness, jokes, changing the subject—one way or another the conversation will spin. The level of defensiveness, of not getting it, is a measure of the threat. "Women don't experience *more*," a male colleague announced as I was pointing out some of the shortfalls women were reporting about the goal-oriented pursuit of sexual intercourse, "they just experience something *different*."

For women who love sex, there is a triple bind. If we keep silent, we stay in the same place. If we speak up, show

ourselves, we risk attack. And in a context of social powerlessness, if we talk about personal power, let alone sexual
power, we seem downright escapist. The messages are
carved deeply into stone: *It's OK to be sexy, but don't claim
ownership of your sexual energy. Women energized can disrupt the way things are. Women aroused are dangerous.* The
structure of society depends on status quo, and for centuries, the status quo has depended on the downplaying of
women's energy. Any shift in the sexual ecology could precipitate a landslide.

Toward Social Change

Henka, the Japanese call it. In Hebrew it's *Shinui*. In
Spanish, it's *transformación*. It means *change*. Every culture
has a word for it—and we fear it utterly.

The concept that women who love sex can make a serious
impact is new because we have learned to associate sex-
loving women not with spiritual growth and societal
changes, but with the same old stereotypes—bad girls, ma-
nipulators, nymphomaniacs, addicts, ballbusters, cunts,
women who love sex *too much*. The very words are putdowns, oaths against all that's good and holy.

But women who love sex are neither bad girls nor armless statues. Maya, Rosa, Dr. Suzanne, the women whose
stories are in this book, and the many others with stories
as yet untold are women with attitude, women who dare—
proactive, outspoken. They are warm, embodied, and, even
if every sexual encounter is not perfect, they are capable of
enjoying a full range of experiences in the bedroom and
beyond. Some of these women are fully grounded in this
world. Some, like Molly, whose revelatory dream allowed
her to begin to let down her guard and trust, are touched
by the power of angels, not so much the sanitized saints of
organized religion, but more the deities of the earth, per-

haps what Jungian analyst Clarissa Pinkola Estés calls the "dirty goddesses," who laugh out loud from their bellies and create heat and well-being.[20] Belly laughs like these can have far-reaching implications. From the sensory awareness they create, "a woman acts as she sees fit."

So, women who love sex laugh and move to redefine themselves. Their laughter, their delight, also redefine sex, broaden it to fit their own complex lives. The sexual response cycle that derives from their stories could never be crammed into the box owned by men. It's a different shape—circular and spherical instead of triangular and hierarchical. It is mobile and self-renewing rather than static and goal oriented. Its effect is not to tone women down, but to invest every aspect of women's lives with more energy. Ultimately, of course, men benefit, too. When women's lives change, everyone's lives change.

Is it true that women can use their fullness, their released sexual fire, to move beyond backlash? Yes, but not alone. Social changes don't happen by the efforts of individuals acting in isolation. The world remains unsafe for all of us, no matter how careful we are to stay off the streets at night or how often we change our locks and phone numbers. Our lives are at stake, here, not just our egos. Our task is to act collectively, dare to set trends.

We can tell our stories. We can acknowledge the energy we can take out of the bedroom. We can encourage each other, set boundaries, learn to trust, keep reaching out in love. We can change the rules about who makes the rules.

We can spread the news that shame is someone else's problem. We can choose and relate to our partners from a place of self-worth. We can inform each other of all the safe-sex knowledge that will keep us healthy—physically and emotionally—and we can practice sexual safety.

We can learn to turn fear into rage. Then we can learn to turn the energy of rage outward into energy that moves us forward. We can cherish our outrageous acts and understand that "outrageous" (which to the people in power means beyond the pale) is often another name for high-hearted and freeing. And we can keep on telling our stories.

What was your most outrageous sexual experience? I asked this question of many women who talked with me. When Alice drops her inhibitions (along with her petticoat) and steams up a rental car with Frank, she is breaking the myth that a faithful wife and mother can feel no lust. When Iris prowls out the primal pleasures of her female–male–animal nature, she is moving well beyond the constraints of acceptable femininity. When Molly and Kate melt away their shyness and nurture each other as fully bonded lovers, they are affirming themselves and their right to relationship and sexual ecstasy. That these women can tell their stories helps make it possible for others.

When I look back at stories like these, and many more, I see that they are outrageous acts of sexuality. They are also outrageous acts of courage and celebration, of self and spirit—high-hearted and freeing. And because Alice, Iris, and Molly are not dissociating the energy informed by their sexuality from their other energies, they are also acts of *henka*, social change.

I can no longer view sex as I was taught to in my proper Bostonian upbringing—sex as contained in that too small box owned by men. Out of the myths and coercions, out of the moral proscriptions, out of the media hype, new patterns emerge. I see more now. It's like putting my eye to a kaleidoscope. At each turn, the glittering bits of information rearrange themselves to tell a different story.

The core story of women who love sex is this: Broadening our understanding of sexuality is a model for social change. Acknowledging the spirituality of pleasure allows us new, life-enhancing rituals. Valuing women who love sex narrows the gender gap—we can't afford to do without half our resources. We have to take ourselves seriously before others will. We are singing for our lives.

It is not a matter of belief or even of logic, but of finally seeing the pattern as it emerges. As the information shifts,

Reflections on Self, Spirit, and Social Change

I see us safe. Safe to enjoy ourselves in a culture that respects and nurtures women.

What's the social significance of women who love sex? I ask this of a colleague who edits a national sexuality newsletter.

"We're the missing link between pleasure and power," she says.

"What do you mean?"

"Once we start defining pleasure for ourselves, we can't be controlled in the same way anymore. Even the language will change. But the culture is unprepared to deal with us."

"We can't wait for the culture to catch up with us," I reply.

We can suspend disbelief. We can listen to each other. We can create a critical mass of support.

The real sexual revolution has got to start with us.

Afterwords
and Acknowledgments

This project has now occupied over a third of my adult life. In that respect, it feels somewhat like my grown children— it has a personality of its own, has moved several times, and has collected its own friends over the years. Although I was necessary for the birth, there is more to the development of the concepts in this book than just me. Even if I were so inclined, I cannot claim total ownership.

If ownership belongs to anyone, it is to the women interviewed, the women who love sex. But we live in the kind of culture where they have to remain nameless in order to protect them from the moralists who would attack their reputations and others who would attack their beings. To those who, when they hear the title of the book say, "Heh! Heh! Can you give me their phone numbers?" let me take this opportunity to remark: That's what we mean when we say, "You still don't get it." So these women must remain anonymous—the fifty "easily orgasmic" women from the original interviews and the hundreds more from other contexts. Historically, they are in good company—"Anonymous was a woman," as Virginia Woolf remarked in *A Room of One's Own*. But as long as we keep on talking to each other, that imbalance will shift. The unnameable—women who love sex—will be safely nameable, out loud and clear.

The Institute for Advanced Study of Human Sexuality gave me carte blanche to begin asking questions. Wardell Pomeroy, Margot Rila, Phyllis Lyon, Ray Stubbs, and Charles Moser all contributed greatly to my learning there.

Afterwords and Acknowledgments

Ed Brecher, in his gentle way, mentored the beginning of the interview process: "Don't ask them about how many times they did it," he suggested. *"Ask them what they did."* Ed was a man who loved women who love sex, and we who loved him greatly miss him. Jim Ramey, along with Betty Ramey, not only encouraged me to keep writing over the years, they all but adopted me into their family for a time. Amie Morgan-Stebbins, an East–West soul sister, traveled with me, read, enjoyed, suggested, and even taught me to fish for trout one Adirondack June. Beverly Whipple opened up her lab to me as well as her home. My sister, Elaine Lavalle Freeman, has been a consistent cheerleader. For inspiration and thought provocation along the way—in somewhat chronological order—I thank Eleanor Hamilton, Tee Corinne, Pepita Seth, Sonia Johnson, Anne Zevin, Jean Swan, Fritjof Capra, Hazel Henderson, Jane Claypool, Honor Moore, Mimi Katzenbach, Dell Williams, Beau-Janette Feldman, Philip Feldman, Sidney Abbott, Ellen Cole, Leonore Tiefer, Karen Hicks, Annie Sprinkle, Judy Tobin, Betty Dodson, Rae Larson, Peggy Clark, Melanie Brown, Mary Ann Williams, Wendy Kaminer, Galen Brandt, Barbara Lambert, and Deborah Tolman. Heide Lange, my long-suffering agent, guided me through many versions. Sally Peters, my first Pocket Books editor, asked the quantum questions that focused the book. Denise Silvestro, who inherited me at Pocket Books, guided me with immense enthusiasm and good humor through the daunting prepublication period.

Kaye Andres deserves a paragraph all of her own. From the beginning of this project, she moved me to push boundaries, to redefine, reconsider, reconceptualize. Even now, she helps me look farther than the horizon, and she never laughs at a new idea.

Many of the ideas in the book were stimulated by interaction with audiences during the presentation of papers and workshops. Thanks to the U.S. Journal and Interface Foundation and to the regional and national conferences of the

Afterwords and Acknowledgments

Society for the Scientific Study of Sex; the American Association of Sex Educators, Counselors and Therapists; and the American Association for Marriage and Family Therapy for providing a forum for me all over the United States and Canada. The women for the original research project were gathered at the annual Focus on Women Conference in Pittsfield, Massachusetts. Focus has disbanded, but the National Organization for Women has asked me to speak in the very same auditorium at Berkshire Community College where it all started. The more things change, the more they stay the same. Thanks to *Berkshire Women's News* for a forum in print from 1982 to 1987.

Jo Chaffee, my partner of twelve years, helped me write the original draft of the manuscript—a journey from pencil and yellow foolscap to a 286 laptop computer. That our relationship has survived and flourished and that the manuscript is finished and published, I count as two of the mysteries, indeed blessings, of the universe.

The honing of this material over the past three years could never have happened sanely without the solidarity beyond friendship of my writer's group: Bernardine Hayes, Jane Redmont, Elena Stone, Debra Cash, and Ellen Hansen. Poets, scholars, and consummate *women*, they were always ready to tackle yet another draft.

Notes

1

1. An interesting twist on the exclusion of women in research is offered by Carol Tavris, *The Mismeasure of Woman* (New York: Simon & Schuster, 1992), p. 99: "... experimenters often exclude females from research—even female rats in studies—because it is simpler and cheaper to use male animals. The female's estrus cycle disrupts responses in certain behavioral and biological tests, and increases variation...."

2. Betty Dodson, *Sex for One* (New York: Crown, 1987), Shere Hite, *The Hite Report* (New York: Macmillan, 1976), Lonnie Barbach, *For Yourself* (New York: Signet, 1975), Sheila Kitzinger, *Woman's Experience of Sex* (New York: Putnam, 1983), JoAnn Loulan, *Lesbian Sex* (San Francisco: Spinsters Ink, 1984) and *Lesbian Passion* (San Francisco: Spinsters/Aunt Lute, 1987).

3. Loraine Hutchins, from a plenary presentation "The Expanding Middle Ground—Being Bisexual: Both/And, Not Either/Or," June 11, 1993, State College, Penn., at a regional meeting of the Society for the Scientific Study of Sex.

4. The Sexual Climate: Pleasure, Power and Politics, April 3–5, 1987, Philadelphia, Penn., a regional meeting of the Society for the Scientific Study of Sex featuring leading East Coast sexologists.

5. The Sexual Liberals and the Attack on Feminism, April 4, 1987, New York, N.Y. a conference featuring leading feminists: Kathleen Barry, Susan Brownmiller, Phyllis Chesler, Andrea Dworkin, Shere Hite, Sheila Jeffries, Robin Morgan, Mary Daly, Sonia Johnson, and others.

6. The resulting dissertation is "Perception of Touch in Easily Orgasmic Women during Peak Sexual Experiences" (Institute for Advanced Study of Human Sexuality, San Francisco, Calif. 1981).

Notes

7. Focus on Women, June 10, 1980, Pittsfield, Mass.

8. Fifty-two women at the Pittsfield conference signed up for the interviews. I had already completed pilot interviews with five women (professional colleagues), and not all of the Pittsfield women could schedule an interview. But those women sent friends or friends of friends, so aside from the pilot study, the sample of easily orgasmic women was generated one way or another from the speech in Pittsfield, Mass.

9. For a discourse on how Madonna has shaken up traditional social roles and hierarchies, see Laurie Ouellette, "Let's Get Serious: The Attack on Madonna Scholarship," *On the Issues*, Vol. 26 (Spring 1993), pp. 30–33.

10. Samuel S. Janus and Cynthia L. Janus, *The Janus Report on Sexual Behavior* (New York: Wiley, 1993).

11. Two eloquent calls for redefining women's sexuality are by Shere Hite in the last half of *The Hite Report* and Sheila Kitzinger, *Woman's Experience of Sex*, in the introduction. A third is by Leonore Tiefer in various academic presentations and journal articles over the years, e.g., "New Perspectives in Sexology: From Rigor (Mortis) to Richness," *The Journal of Sex Research*, Vol. 28, No. 4 (Nov. 1991), pp. 593–602.

12. Several sex researchers have hypothesized universal sexual response cycles: Wilhelm Reich, *The Function of the Orgasm* (New York: Orgone Institute Press, 1942); William Masters and Virginia Johnson, *Human Sexual Response* (Boston: Little, Brown, 1966); Helen Singer Kaplan, *The New Sex Therapy* (New York: Brunner-Mazel, 1974) and *Disorders of Sexual Desire* (New York: Brunner-Mazel, 1979).

13. For instance, the "Hot and Horny" workshops for gay men (information available at any AIDS Action Center).

14. Alfred Kinsey et al., *Sexual Behavior in the Human Female* (Philadelphia: W.B. Saunders, 1953), p. 590. (This book is popularly known as *The Kinsey Report*.)

15. Hite, *The Hite Report*, p. 426.

16. Beverly Whipple, Gina Ogden, and Barry Komisaruk, "Physiological Correlates of Imagery-Induced Orgasm in Women," *Archives of Sexual Behavior*, Vol. 21 (1992), pp. 121–133.

Notes

17. A raft of self-help books, spearheaded by Robin Norwood, *Women Who Love Too Much* (New York: Jeremy Tarcher, 1985), examine the relationship traps women can fall into in and out of bed by focusing on their partners instead of on their own needs and desires.

18. Wendy Kaminer's *I'm Dysfunctional, You're Dysfunctional* (New York: Addison-Wesley, 1992), points out that the oversimplified prescriptions in the self-help literature not only insult the intelligence of its readers, most of whom are women, but create a victimization model that can damage relationships. Katie Roiphe takes this thought a step further in "Date Rape's Other Victim" (*New York Times Magazine*, June 13, 1993, pp. 26 ff.). She deconstructs the victim model, asserting that women's sexual passivity harks us back to the desexualized 1950s.

19. Samuel S. Janus and Cynthia L. Janus, *The Janus Report on Sexual Behavior*, defining sex as physical and intimacy as emotional, report that the majority of the men and women they polled by questionnaire consider sex and intimacy to be separate from one another.

20. Alfred Kinsey et al., *Sexual Behavior in the Human Male* (Philadelphia: W.B. Saunders, 1948), discourses eloquently on the effectiveness of one-on-one interviews in sex research. Almost half a century later, Phyllis Mansfield, Ann Voda, and Patricia Koch concur. In their study, "Midlife Sexual Response Changes: Effects of Menopausal Transition and Context," 1992 (in press, *Health Values*, 1994, p. 19), they state that personal interviews offered them an unparalleled opportunity to listen to *women*.

2

1. Sharon Olds, "Greed and Aggression," in *The Gold Cell* (New York: Knopf, 1987), p. 56.

2. The Stone Center for Developmental Services and Studies at Wellesley College was created in 1981 for research in women's psychological development and the prevention of psychological problems. Its theories about relationship are informed by ongoing group process among its investigators and are shared as works in progress in a yearly colloquium series open to the public.

Notes

3. Judith V. Jordan, "Clarity in Connection: Empathic Knowing, Desire and Sexuality," *Work in Progress No. 29.* (Wellesley, Mass.: Stone Center for Developmental Services and Studies, 1987).

4. Helen Singer Kaplan's *Disorders of Sexual Desire* is only one in a long history of titles that pathologize sexuality, well in line with forebears such as Richard von Krafft-Ebing's *Psychopathia Sexualis* (U.S.A.: Pioneer, 1939—12th edition, 1986), and William Masters and Virginia Johnson's *Human Sexual Inadequacy* (Boston: Little, Brown, 1970).

5. For more information on desire discrepancies, see Bernie Zilbergeld and Carol Rinklieb Ellison: "Desire Discrepancies and Arousal Problems in Sex Therapy," in Sandra R. Lieblum and Lawrence A. Pervin, ed., *Principles and Practice of Sex Therapy* (New York: Guilford Press, 1980), pp. 65-101.

6. Elise Boulding, *The Underside of History* (Boulder, Colo.: Westview Press, 1976), p.3.

7. Marilyn French's *The War Against Women* (New York: Summit Books, 1992) is a chilling cross-cultural compendium of crimes perpetrated and perpetuated in the name of sex.

8. For an in-depth discussion of the sexual roles of women through history, see Vernon Bullough and Bonnie Bullough, *Sin, Sickness and Sanity* (New York: Meridian, 1977).

9. Memory researchers Elizabeth Loftus and Katherine Ketcham in their *Witness for the Defense: The Accused, the Eye Witness and the Expert Who Puts Memory on Trial* (New York: St. Martin's Press, 1991) have studied the phenomenon of false memory, actually creating false memories in research subjects to test the hypothesis that one's current belief about past events is more important and "real" than what actually happened.

10. Wilhelm Reich, *Selected Writings* (New York: Farrar, Straus & Giroux, 1973), pp. 136 ff.

11. A note on the distinctions among desire, lubrication, and orgasm: According to Helen Singer Kaplan (*Disorders of Sexual Desire*), sexual response progresses through three interconnected phases, each with its own neurological hookup. The desire phase is controlled by the limbic system. The excitement phase, which triggers lubrication, is controlled by the parasympathetic nervous

system. The orgasm phase is controlled by the sympathetic nervous system. The emotional concomitant to function and dysfunction in these areas is not spelled out in the literature, but it stands to reason that when a woman is holding onto anger she is, in effect, blocking the expression of impulses from her limbic system—in other words, inhibiting the possibility for sexual desire—which may in turn disrupt her parasympathetic response of sexual excitement and inhibit lubrication during intercourse.

12. A blow-by-blow discussion of the effectiveness of role reversal in dislodging stuck emotions can be found in Jonathan Fox, ed., *The Essential Mareno* (New York: Springer-Verlag, 1987), pp. 81 ff. See also psychodramatic techniques used in sex therapy in Gina Ogden, *Sexual Recovery* (Deerfield Beach, Fla.: Health Communications, 1990), pp. 72–74.

13. For complementary perspectives on the sexually devastating effects of incest, sexual abuse, and other traumas experienced in childhood, see Charlotte Kasl, *Women, Sex and Addiction* (New York: Tichnor & Fields, 1989), pp. 246–275, and Judith Herman, *Trauma and Recovery* (New York: Basic Books, 1992), especially Chapter 5, pp. 110 ff.

14. For a full, official description of PTSD, see *The Diagnostic and Statistical Manual of Mental Disorders, Third Edition, Revised* (DSM-III-R) (American Psychiatric Association, Washington, D.C., 1987) pp. 247–251.

15. In "A Feminist Critique of the Sexual Dysfunction Nomenclature," in *Women and Therapy*, Vol. 7, Nos. 2/3 (1988), pp. 5–21, Leonore Tiefer challenges the nosology of sexual dysfunction, stating that it focuses on body parts and performance issues rather than on the holistic and relational issues important to women.

16. Masters and Johnson's *Human Sexual Inadequacy* and Helen Singer Kaplan's *The New Sex Therapy* define sexual dysfunction by the inability to achieve orgasm on intercourse. These are the standard texts upon which the contemporary mainstream theories of sex therapy are built.

17. Jean Baker Miller, *Toward a New Psychology of Women* (Boston: Beacon Press, 1976).

18. Carol Tavris ("Beware the Incest-Survivor Machine," *New York Times Book Review*, January 3, 1993, pp. 1, 16 ff) reasons

elegantly for the incest (and other) "survivors" to shift from a victim stance, prevalent in the recovery literature, to an emphasis on social change.

3

1. Alfred Kinsey et al. *Sexual Behavior in the Human Male*, p. 648, and *Sexual Behavior in the Human Female*, p. 470, describe a seven-point scale, or continuum, of heterosexuality through homosexuality. The point (radical for the era) was to show that most human beings are neither totally heterosexual in fantasy and behavior nor totally homosexual but fall somewhere along a continuum in between. Describing yourself as a "3" on the Kinsey scale is, in effect, saying you can swing both ways.

2. Mary Daly, *Gyn/Ecology* (Boston: Beacon Press, 1978) coined the term *re-membering* to mean the process of women owning all the fragments of their experience, including the past.

3. William Masters and Virginia Johnson (*Human Sexual Response*) propose a four-stage cycle of sexual response based on laboratory studies (including intravaginal monitors) of the physiology of sexual arousal in men and women. These stages are excitement, plateau, orgasm, and resolution. Helen Singer Kaplan's *Disorders of Sexual Desire* proposes a triphasic model of sexual response based on clinical observation and physiological research. These stages are desire, arousal, and orgasm. Both of these sexual response cycles are oriented to the "achievement" of the signs and signals of physical orgasm and are widely accepted as a gauge of sexual normality.

4. Some of the influential books in the popular self-healing movement are O. Carl Simonton, Stephanie Matthews-Simonton, and J. L. Creighton, *Getting Well Again* (New York: Bantam, 1978); Bernie Siegel, *Love, Medicine and Miracles* (New York: Harper & Row, 1986); Joan Borysenko, *Mending the Body, Mending the Mind* (New York: Addison-Wesley, 1987); Louise Hay, *You Can Heal Your Life* (Carson, Calif.: Hay House, 1987); Melody Beattie, *Codependent No More* (New York: Harper/Hazelton, 1987); Deepak Chopra, *Quantum Healing* (New York: Bantam, 1990). Magazines such as *Prevention, New Age Journal,* and *East West Journal* deluge

the public monthly or bimonthly with up-to-date information on healing everything from cancer to your relationship.

5. The "real thing" is, of course, intercourse, carved into stone as a medical reality by authoritative sex researchers such as Freud and, more recently, Masters and Johnson and Helen Singer Kaplan.

6. Ashley Montagu, *Touching* (New York: Columbia University Press, 1971), p. 219. Also Harry I. Harlow, "Sexual Behavior in the Rhesus Monkey," in Frank A. Beach (ed.), *Sex and Behavior* (New York: Wiley, 1965), pp. 234–265.

7. Niles Newton and her husband, Michael Newton ("Psychological Effects of Lactation," *New England Journal of Medicine*, Vol. 277: 1967, pp. 1179–1188), discuss the role of oxytocin, the pituitary hormone that causes the let-down reflex in nursing mothers: Muscle fibers in the breast contract, expelling milk into the channels leading to the nipple. The sensation is designed by nature to be extremely pleasurable for the women experiencing it, especially since it is accompanied by concomitant contractions in the muscle fibers of the uterus. (Women have reported to me that this is not only pleasurable, but that after a cesarian section, the pain of surgery is completely relieved during these contractions.) The Newtons also discuss "breast feeding frigidity" among women who have suffered psychosexual disturbances.

8. James Prescott, "Body Pleasure and the Origin of Violence," *The Futurist* (1975), pp. 64–74.

9. Montagu, *Touching*, pp. 219 ff.

10. For Reich's analysis of pleasure anxiety, see "Pleasure (Expansion) and Anxiety (Contraction): Primary Antithesis of Vegetative Life:" in Wilhelm Reich, *Selected Writings*, (New York: Farrar, Straus and Giroux, 1951), pp. 124–135. His opinions on the cultural effects of pleasure-repression can be found in "The Sexual Rights of Youth" in Wilhelm Reich, *Children of the Future: On the Prevention of Sexual Pathology*, (New York: Farrar, Straus and Giroux, 1983—by Mary Boyd Higgins as trustee of the Wilhelm Reich infant trust fund) pp. 161–221.

11. Philip Blumstein and Pepper Schwartz, in their *American Couples* (New York: William Morrow, 1983), found that sex in married couples diminishes over time. Among couples married for

Notes

two years or less, 45% had sex three or more times a week. Among those married ten years or more, 18% had sex that often.

12. Gioia Timpanelli, personal communication, Omega Institute, Rhinebeck, N.Y., June 8, 1985.

13. Elizabeth Dodson Gray, personal communication, Omega Institute, Rhinebeck, N.Y., June 8, 1985.

14. Statistics on rape and incest can differ, depending on the authority consulted. Feminist academicians, such as Carol Tavris, argue that statistics quoted in the self-help literature are inflated and misleading. Sue Osthoff, director of the National Clearinghouse for the Defense of Battered Women, Philadelphia, Penn. says that statistics vary wildly; oversimplification is largely a function of the media. She makes the point that no matter what the statistics, the reality is that women are hurt (personal communication, February 22, 1993). The sexual assault statistic is from Andrea Parrott from a personal communication at the Eastern Region Meeting, Society for the Scientific Study of Sex, Philadelphia, Penn. April 12, 1992.

15. Beverly Whipple, personal communication, April 1991.

16. Maya is referring to the turn-of-the-century fathers of the science of sexology like Iwan Bloch, inexorable researcher of homosexual anomalies and "inversions"; Magnus Hirschfeld, whose brainchild, the Institut für Sexualwissenschaft in Berlin, was crammed with sexual secrets of high officials, among others, and was an early target for obliteration by the Nazis; and Richard von Krafft-Ebing, whose best-selling *Psychopathia Sexualis*—each edition more lurid than the last—foisted moralist and misogynist values upon an entire generation.

17. Robin Morgan, *The Anatomy of Freedom* (New York: Anchor Press/Doubleday, 1982), pp. 100–146.

18. Daly, *Gyn/Ecology*, p. 67.

19. From Saint Teresa's *Vida* as quoted in H. W. Janson, *History of Art*, 2nd Ed. (New York: Harry N. Abrams, 1977), p. 487.

20. See Richard Bandler and John Grinder, *The Structure of Magic* (Palo Alto, Calif.: Science & Behavior Books, 1975).

21. For a delightful anecdotal analysis of the importance of anecdote to science, see the account of Gregory Bateson on the role

of joking, poetry, and other forms of storytelling in Fritjof Capra, *Uncommon Wisdom* (New York: Bantam, 1988), pp. 77–79.

22. Fritjof Capra, *The Turning Point* (New York: Bantam, 1982).

23. Abraham Maslow, *On the Psychology of Being* (New York: D. Van Nostrand, 1968), pp. 71 ff.

24. Charlene Spretnak, *The Politics of Women's Spirituality* (New York: Anchor/Doubleday, 1982), p. xviii.

25. Audre Lorde, *Uses of the Erotic* (Trumansburg, NY: Out and Out Books/Crossing Press, 1978), p. 3.

4

1. Alice Walker, *Possessing the Secret of Joy* (New York: Harcourt Brace Jovanovich, 1992).

2. Advocates of the vulva over the years: Robert Latou Dickinson, a gynecologist in the first half of the century, wrote and copiously illustrated his *Atlas of Human Sexual Anatomy* (Melbourne, Fla.: Krieger, 1933), a moving document of the need for clitoral stimulation for women. Other researchers who have championed the importance of clitoral stimulation are William Masters and Virginia Johnson, *Human Sexual Response*, Mary Jane Sherfey, who outlined an entire clitoral *system* in her *Nature and Evolution of Female Sexuality* (New York: Random House, 1966), and Shere Hite, whose *Hite Report* politicized the clitoris with landmark interviews of women. Beverly Whipple has been the principal researcher of the Grafenberg spot, or G spot, and is coauthor of *The G Spot* (New York: Holt, 1982).

3. Betty Dodson's most recent book is *Sex for One*. An astounding documentary videotape of her two-day Bodysex workshops is titled *Selfloving*. (New York: Betty Dodson Productions, 1991).

4. Throughout history, groups have been safe arenas for women to talk about what is on their minds as they gathered to do necessary chores like pounding corn or sewing quilts. The women's consciousness-raising groups and other peer groups of recent decades have borne out the empowering effect of focus groups, even without the chores. In the last decade, such groups have

had a profound effect on women—in particular, the so-called recovery groups, such as Alcoholics Anonymous (AA) and its many spin-offs: Alanon, ACoA, and groups for survivors of sexual abuse.

5. Alfred Kinsey et al.'s *Sexual Behavior in the Human Female* mentions (but only *mentions*) full-body contact on page 196. Alex Comfort in *The Joy of Sex* (New York: Simon & Schuster, 1974) alludes to full-body contact not as a staple of sexuality but as a kinky afterthought he calls "Goldfish," where couples tie each other up and make love no-handsies. Comfort asserts that a good many women get their orgasms this way "simply by struggling" (p. 193).

6. Jolan Chang, *The Tao of Love and Sex* (New York: Viking, 1977), pp. 47 ff.

5

1. Beverly Whipple is known for research on the G spot, an intensely pleasure-sensitive area some women are able to locate through the anterior of the vagina. She is coauthor, with Alice Ladas and John Perry, of *The G Spot*.

2. Beverly Whipple and Gina Ogden, *Safe Encounters: How Women Can Say Yes to Pleasure and No to Unsafe Sex* (New York: McGraw-Hill, 1988).

3. Alfred Kinsey et al., *Sexual Behavior in the Human Female*, p. 590.

4. Shere Hite, *The Hite Report*, p. 426.

5. William Masters and Virginia Johnson, *Human Sexual Response*, p. 21.

6. Some of the research that led up to the study of physiologic correlates of imagery-induced orgasm in women is described in Beverly Whipple and Barry Komisaruk, "Elevation of Pain Threshold by Vaginal Stimulation," *Pain*, Vol. 21 (1985), pp. 357–367, and "Analgesia Produced in Women by Genital Self-Stimulation," *The Journal of Sex Research*, Vol. 24 (1988), pp. 130–140.

Notes

7. See a transcript of the guided imagery tape in Appendix B.

8. Blood pressure was measured in millimeters of mercury and was recorded via a Biolab system (Stoelting, Inc., Chicago, Ill.). The blood pressure cuff, placed on the subject's left calf, automatically inflated every two minutes. Heart rate was measured in beats per minute and was recorded via a photocell on the right great toe every two minutes throughout the experiment and when the subject reported that she reached orgasm.

9. Pain thresholds were determined by applying a gradually increasing force to each finger of one hand, using a Ugo Basile Analgesia Meter (Milan, Italy). During each resting control and experimental condition, the subject placed her finger on the one-millimeter-diameter point of the analgesia meter, and a controlled, steadily increasing force was applied, ranging from zero grams to a maximum of one kilogram over a twenty-six-second period. The linear scale is from zero to twenty-five units; these correspond to a linear increase of 0 to 1,000 grams.

10. Tactile thresholds were determined by applying a graded system of twenty nylon monofilaments of varied stiffness (von Frey fibers, Stoelting, Inc.) to the dorsal surface of the subject's hand between the thumb and index finger. These fibers are graded along a log scale, yielding a linear function of force required to bend each fiber over a range of forces from 4.5 milligrams to 447 grams. The tactile threshold was defined as the minimal force to bend the fiber during which the subject correctly stated that she felt the tip of the fiber three out of three times using an ascending/descending method of limits.

11. Pupil diameter was determined using a pupilometer (BioLab system, Stoelting, Inc.) consisting of an infrared-sensitive video close-up camera and a variable infrared source that is directed at the eye. Relative changes in pupil dilation were displayed on an analog meter and monitored via a BioLab system.

12. Whipple and Komisaruk, "Elevation of Pain Threshold by Vaginal Stimulation."

13. Beverly Whipple, Gina Ogden, and Barry Komisaruk, "Physiological Correlates of Imagery-Induced Orgasm in Women," *Archives of Sexual Behavior*, Vol. 21 (1992), pp. 121-33.

Notes

14. John Money and Anke Ehrhardt, *Man and Woman, Boy and Girl* (Baltimore: Johns Hopkins University Press, 1972), pp. 149 and 253.

15. Money and Ehrhardt, *Man and Woman*, p. 246. Also John Money, "Phantom Orgasm in the Dreams of Paraplegic Men and Women," *Archives of General Psychiatry*, Vol. 3 (October 1960), pp. 373–382.

16. Judy Grahn, *Another Mother Tongue* (Boston: Beacon Press, 1984), p. 252.

17. Nancy Friday's books on women's sexual fantasies include *My Secret Garden* (New York: Pocket Books, 1973), *Forbidden Flowers* (New York: Pocket Books, 1975), and *Women on Top* (New York: Simon & Schuster, 1992).

18. Money and Ehrhardt, *Man and Woman*, pp. 148 and 187.

19. For example, Jane Rule, whose books include *Desert of the Heart* (New York: Arno Press, 1964—reprinted in 1986 by Naiad Press, Tallahassee, Fla., and adapted for the film *Desert Hearts* in 1985); artist Judy Chicago, whose *Dinner Party* (1982) merged images of everyday accomplishment and images of sexuality; Betty Dodson, artist of the woman's body and the vulva in *Liberating Masturbation* (New York: Body Sex Designs, 1974); Tee Corinne, who drew the variety of vulvas in the *Cunt Coloring Book* (San Francisco, Calif.: Pearlchild Productions, 1975) and photographed the body mandalas in *Yantras of Woman Love* (Tallahassee, Fla.: Naiad, 1982); Suzie Bright, author and sometime editor of the explicitly sexual woman's periodical, *On Our Backs*; Nancy Friday, collector of sexual fantasies in *My Secret Garden*, *Forbidden Flowers*, and *Women on Top* (New York: Pocket Books).

20. For example, Candida Royalle, articulate, innovative, feminist president of Femme Productions, New York, N.Y., and Annie Sprinkle, whose film *Sluts and Goddesses* helps earn her the self-proclaimed title of "post-porn feminist."

21. The Kensington Ladies Erotica Society wrote *Ladies Home Erotica* (Berkeley, Calif.: Ten Speed Press, 1984) and *Look Homeward Erotica* (Berkeley, Calif.: Ten Speed Press, 1986).

22. This model of women's response to sexual imagery was first presented for peer review as a paper, "Women, Imagination, and

Imagery: Implications for Sex Research and Therapy," at the annual meeting of the Society for the Scientific Study of Sex, Minneapolis, Minn., November 11, 1990.

23. Recent studies are showing that while all kinds of childhood sexual abuse can be devastating to an adult woman's self-esteem and sexual functioning, there may, in fact, be little functional difference between women who have been abused as children and the rest of the population. Carol Tavris's *The Mismeasure of Woman* points out that the symptoms reported as a result of sexual abuse are also characteristic of women who are not abused. She proposes the political argument that sexual abuse is a metaphor for all that is wrong in women's lives.

24. Jean Kilbourne et al., *Killing Us Softly* (Cambridge, Mass., Cambridge Documentary Films, 1979) a film exposing the assault of advertising on women's self-image.

25. Candida Royalle, "Eroticism and Sexuality: Views from the Trenches," presented at the Society for the Scientific Study of Sex, Eastern Region Meeting, Philadelphia, Penn., April 12, 1992.

6

1. Ntozake Shange, *Sassafrass, Cypress & Indigo* (New York: St. Martin's Press, 1982), pp. 14–15.

2. This model of sexual nurturing was first presented for peer review as a paper, "Need, Nurturing and Altruism in Lesbian Relationships," presented to The Academic Group, Cambridge, Mass., February 3, 1991, and later developed into a series of workshops presented at Interface Foundation and throughout the United States and Canada for Health Communications/U.S. Journal.

3. Judith Jordan, from a speech at the Stone Center, Wellesley College, March, 1992. That women have traditionally done most of the world's work and reaped the least of the world's bounty is an observation echoed by Marilyn French in *The War Against Women* and many feminist writers from Robin Morgan to Sonya Johnson.

4. Charlotte Kasl, *Women, Sex, and Addiction* is outspoken about the role of culture in creating sexual oppression for women. She

sees the term *sexual addiction* as a form of internalized oppression stemming from white male privilege rather than from a defect of women's character. Ultimately, of course, that means that women have taken on the responsibility for pleasuring their partners without the rewards of pleasure for themselves. From "Many Roads, One Journey," presented at Interface Foundation, Cambridge, Mass., November 6, 1992.

5. *Sexual codependency* is a term I first presented for peer review in a paper, "Co-dependent Couples: Challenges for Sex Therapy," presented at the Society for the Scientific Study of Sex, Eastern Region Meeting, Boston, April 8, 1989, and later developed into a book: *Sexual Recovery* (Deerfield Beach, Fla.: Health Communications, 1990).

6. May Sarton, *Journal of a Solitude* (New York: W.W. Norton, 1973), p. 113.

7

1. William Butler Yeats, "The Second Coming" (1921) in Mack Maynard et al. (ed.), *Modern Poetry* (Englewood Cliffs, N.J.: Prentice Hall, 1960).

2. Betty Dodson, *Sex for One*.

3. Virginia Johnson, personal communication, June 15, 1986.

4. For a comprehensive list of the signs and symptoms of being in love, see Dorothy Tennov's *Love and Limerence* (New York: Stein & Day, 1979), pp. 23–24.

5. James Ramey, *Intimate Friendships* (Englewood Cliffs, N.J.: Prentice-Hall, 1976), p. 28.

8

1. Oral contraceptives gained Food and Drug Administration approval in 1960. (Although the birth control pill was developed in Worcester, Mass., it was illegal in Massachusetts and Connecticut until 1972.)

Notes

2. With the *Roe v. Wade* decision on January 22, 1973, American women gained the constitutional right to abortion.

3. In 1973, the American Psychiatric Association declared that homosexuality could no longer be classified as a disease.

4. William Masters and Virginia Johnson, *Human Sexual Response* and *Human Sexual Inadequacy*.

5. The first SAR was presented in 1969 by the National Sex Forum, 1523 Franklin Street, San Francisco, Calif.

6. Betty Dodson, *Liberating Masturbation*; Nancy Friday, *My Secret Garden*; Lonnie Barbach, *For Yourself*; Shere Hite, *The Hite Report*.

7. Susan Faludi, *Backlash* (New York: Crown, 1992), p. xxii. This book, along with Marilyn French's *The War Against Women*, details the systemic, inexorable undermining of women's attempts to advance toward political, economic, and personal power.

8. One recent and chilling reminder of the inequities of the court system is recounted in Bella English's "Sorting Out the Suffering," *Boston Globe*, July 12, 1993. A woman calls the police to protect her from a violent attack from her husband, only to be handcuffed, jailed, and brought to trial for defending herself.

9. A controversy rages about which of women's reproductive cycles are a natural course of events and which ones warrant medical intervention. A stunning collection of stories of abuses of women by the medical system can be found in Karen Hicks (ed.), *Misdiagnosis: Woman As a Disease* (Allentown, Pa.: People's Medical Society, 1994).

10. The spin is the same in many cultures, but the methods may differ. Compare Operation Rescue's bombing attacks in the name of life and love to clitoridectomies done in the name of health and holiness.

11. Jean Baker Miller, *Toward a New Psychology of Women*, pp. xv–xvi.

12. Susie Bright, "She Knows What She Likes," *New York Times Book Review*, July 11, 1993, p. 13.

13. The trend for pathologizing sexual desire as sexual addiction was greatly furthered by Patrick Carnes in *Out of the Shadows:*

Notes

Understanding Sexual Addiction (Minneapolis, Minn.: CompCare, 1983), which formed the basis for treatment at the Golden Valley Health Center's facility for sex addicts in Minneapolis, Minn.

14. The armless Venus de Milo and Winged Victory of Samothrace can be seen in the Louvre Museum in Paris, dramatically displayed, and of course on pedestals.

15. Marilyn Monroe appeared as the Playmate centerfold in *Playboy* Magazine, December 1953. According to Playboy Products, a copy of this issue now sells for $8,000.

16. Katie Roiphe in her feminist analysis of the feminist analysis of rape hype calls for action: "It is the passive sexual role that threatens us still, and it is the denial of female sexual agency that threatens to propel us backward." "Date Rape's Other Victim," *New York Times Magazine*, June 13, 1993, p. 68.

17. Dale Spender, "An Alternative to Madonna," *Ms.*, (July/August 1993), p. 45.

18. John Updike constructs a striking argument about the historical permanence of sexual repression in his article on lust: "Even the Bible Is Soft on Sex," *New York Times Book Review*, June 20, 1993, pp. 3 and 29.

19. According to a recent Roper poll, 20% of Americans believe the Holocaust may never have happened (as reported in James Carroll's, "The Barriers Obliterated by the Holocaust," *Boston Globe*, July 20, 1993). A survey of 3,321 men between the ages of twenty and thirty-nine conducted by the Battelle Human Affairs Research Center in Seattle and published April 15, 1993, in the Alan Guttmacher Institute's journal, *Family Planning Perspectives*, reported that 1% considered themselves gay (as compared with the long accepted Kinsey figure of 10%). The Battelle survey has been criticized by the scientific and gay communities for methodology that is both manipulative and naive.

20. Clarissa Pinkola Estés, *Women Who Run with the Wolves* (New York: Ballantine, 1992), p. 33.

Appendix A

Interview Questions Asked of Women Who Love Sex

Questionnaire from Dissertation Study: "Perception of Touch in Easily Orgasmic Women During Peak Sexual Experiences"

These questions were asked of fifty self-described easily orgasmic women in one-on-one interviews. Note that many of these questions are open-ended, allowing for descriptive information (each interview lasted between one and two hours). Note also the absence of questions about safe sex, abuse, and substance abuse. This study was completed in 1981 before the threat of AIDS was known and before there was extensive research on abuse and substance abuse.

I. Demographics

How old are you?

What do you do for work?

Do you have children? If so, how many? What are their genders and ages?

How many times have you been pregnant? Please comment on infertility problems or miscarriages if any.

Appendix A

Are you presently married or in a committed sexual relationship?

How many times have you been married or in a committed sexual relationship?

How many male sex partners have you had? How many women sex partners?

How many male love partners have you had? How many women love partners?

How many times have you been in love with men? With women?

II. Orgasm

Please describe your experience of orgasm with a partner. What does your orgasm feel like to you?

If you have had partners of both genders, is there a difference in the orgasms you experience with male partners and female partners?

How many orgasms during each sexual encounter do you typically have with a partner? Do you have a different number of orgasms with male and female partners?

How many seconds (minutes, hours) from the beginning of lovemaking would you say it takes for you to come to your first orgasm with a partner? Is the timing different with male and female partners?

Please describe your experience of orgasm with yourself, that is, on masturbation.

How many orgasms do you typically have with yourself each time you masturbate?

How many seconds (minutes, hours) from the beginning of masturbation would you say it takes for you to come to your first orgasm with yourself?

Appendix A

What is your surest route to orgasm with yourself?

What is your surest route to orgasm with a partner?

What is your most pleasurable route to orgasm with yourself?

What is your most pleasurable route to orgasm with a partner?

Do you use any kind of erotica or pornography to arouse yourself to orgasm with yourself and with a partner? Please describe.

How important to your experience of orgasm is emotional feeling? Please describe.

Have you ever come to orgasm on extragenital stimulation alone, that is, with touch on various parts of your body but with no touching of your genitals? Please describe.

Have you ever come to orgasm spontaneously, that is, with no touching of your body at all?

Were these spontaneous experiences while you were asleep (wet dreams), while you were awake (fantasies), or other? Please describe.

What do you mean by "easily orgasmic"? Describe how you consider yourself an easily orgasmic woman.

III. Peak Sexual Experience—Perception of Setting and Other External Factors and Conditions

Note: The set of questions in Sections III, IV, and V was repeated two to four times, depending on the experiences of the research subject. Each woman was asked to describe at least two peak sexual experiences, one with herself (on masturbation) and one with a partner. Twenty-six percent of the women had had sexual experiences with both men and women; they were each asked to describe a peak sexual experience with a man and with a woman as well as with themselves. Sixteen percent of the women had had group sexual experiences; they were asked to describe a peak experience with a group of sexual

Appendix A

partners as well as with themselves and with an individual partner.

Please take a minute to remember a time in your life when you experienced sexual ecstasy, an encounter that you would call a peak sexual experience. This might be far back in your memory or it may be very near to the present time. Whenever it occurred, please allow yourself to reexperience it now as if it was happening right now in the present. You can close your eyes if you wish and simply enjoy reliving it as I ask some questions about it.

Is this experience that you are remembering a sexual encounter with yourself, a partner, or a group? (If partner:) Is this a man or woman? Lover or husband? Committed or casual? (If group:) Is this a known and trusted group or new and untried?

Where is this peak sexual experience occurring?

How old are you when this experience is occurring?

Is it day or night?

Is it light or dark?

Is it cold or warm?

What sounds are you hearing?

What textures are you feeling?

What tastes and smells?

Is there food involved in this experience?

Drink?

Drugs of any kind?

Are you using any kind of contraception?

What is the duration of your experience from beginning to end?

Appendix A

IV. Peak Sexual Experience—Perception of Touch

Now I'm going to ask you some specific questions about how you are perceiving the touch during this ecstatic experience. I'm going to ask you to focus on every part of your body as you remember exactly how you were touched by your partner's hands: Are those hands gentle, firm, or rough? Is there stroking, rubbing, slapping, or pinching? What about your partner's mouth—sucking, blowing, licking, nipping, tongue fluttering? Does your partner use anything else to arouse you—hair, feet, genitals, sex toys? Anything else? Allow yourself to feel it all now as I ask you specifics.

The women were asked to rate their pleasurable perceptions of touch on a 0 to 7 scale (7 being orgasm). The matrix on pp. 254–55 was used both to guide the specific questioning and to make notes. By the end of the interview some women had virtually filled the matrix; others reported touch only on hot spots like genitals, breasts, lips. Some women reported more overall touch in experiences with other women or during group sex.

EXTRAGENITAL MATRIX
AREAS OF BODY AND KINDS OF STIMULATION

	Hair	Face	Eyes	Nose	Lips	Tongue	Ears	Lobes	Neck	Throat	Shoulder	Breasts	Nipples	Armpits	Upper arms	Behind elbows	Lower arms	Wrists	Hands
Hand Stroke																			
Hand pinch																			
Hand slap																			
Lips suck																			
Lips blow cold																			
Lips blow warm																			
Tongue lick																			
Tongue flutter																			
Teeth																			
Hair																			
Feet																			
Genitals																			
Other																			
Toys																			

Fingers	Sternum	Stomach	Abdomen	Upper back	Lower back	Coccyx	Buttocks	Mons	Clitoris	Outer lips	Inner lips	Urethra	Perineum	Introitus	Vagina	G spot	Anus	Outer thighs	Inner thighs	Behind knees	Calves	Ankles	Feet	Toes	Whole body	Other

Appendix A

V. Peak Sexual Experience—Perception of Emotions and Other Intangible Factors

Taking all the elements into consideration, what would you say is the essential ingredient of this peak sexual experience?

Do you come to orgasm during this experience? On a 0 to 7 scale, please rate the importance of your orgasm(s) to this experience.

Are you and your partner committed to one another beyond this experience? On a 0 to 7 scale, please rate your degree of commitment.

Do you use fantasy during this experience? On a 0 to 7 scale, please rate the importance of fantasy to this experience.

Do you and your partner love one another? On a 0 to 7 scale, please rate the importance of love to this experience.

Does romance play a part in this experience? On a 0 to 7 scale, please rate the importance of romance to this experience.

What is the greatest sexual turnoff for you?

What is the most outrageous sexual experience you ever had?

Appendix B

Guided Imagery
for Women Who Love Sex

Transcript of a Tape for Laboratory Study:
"Physiological Correlates of Imagery-Induced
Orgasm in Women"

*This ten-minute tape was played during the laboratory studies of
orgasm in women who could come to orgasm on imagery alone with
no touching of the body (see Chapter 5, "Thinking Off and Other
Thoughts on Sexual Imagination").*

First of all, be aware of your breathing . . .

Let yourself take a deep breath in . . . and let it go . . . being
aware that your inhale breath is the breath of control and taking
charge of your life. And the exhale breath is the breath of letting
go—the breath of pleasure, the breath of orgasm, the breath of
ecstasy.

So be aware of your own breathing now, your own rhythm.
And as you breathe, let yourself walk down inside yourself, taking
yourself now to your place of images—the place where you keep
your imagination, your memory.

Feel what it feels to be inside that place of images. What do
you see? What do you hear? What's the space like? The textures?
The light? Is it big and expansive or is it small and intimate?
Whatever it's like, simply let yourself experience it now. And if
you experience distractions, simply let them go on your exhale

Appendix B

breath. *[Note that during the laboratory study, the blood-pressure cuff is constantly inflating and deflating. Also, twice in the course of this tape I will interrupt the woman to take finger-pain assessments and pupil measurements on the pupilometer.]*

And as you breathe now into your place of images, let yourself walk around and become more and more familiar with them. And when you're ready, begin to move toward the ones that turn you on.

Begin to be aware now of the images that excite you. There may be a picture. There may be a sound or a feeling. There may be a special memory. Or there may be a body sensation. Whatever it is now, let yourself breathe it in. All the way in. And breathe it out. As if you could allow this image to move through you at your will.

And as you breathe, allow yourself to become aroused . . . as you imagine more and more fully the image that turns you on. And be aware of your breathing, and know that in this place inside you it feels as if you have all the time in the world.

This is a place where you can feel in charge and yet perfectly open, perfectly aware. . . . As you allow yourself now to feel, to see, to hear, to sense, in every cell of your body, that aroused feeling that comes when you allow yourself to be fully in your imagination. . . . As you breathe in and as you breathe out. And allow yourself now to feel in your body, in your mind, in your soul, in every part of you, what happens when you let yourself be aware of the images inside yourself that arouse and excite you. And let yourself simply feel what it feels like to be so turned on as you see and hear and feel and sense the images that arouse you.

You begin to feel like a flower opening. You begin to feel like the sea, moving in and moving out, over the sand. Like the sun opening her arms and encircling the green earth. And know, as you feel these feelings, that you're *good*. And be aware of your breathing. As you breathe in . . . and as you breathe all the way out.

Allow yourself to stay in this place for a while longer. Being aware of this place and aware of your breathing. And when you

Appendix B

feel ready, allow yourself to look around one last time and prepare yourself to walk back into the present, into this room.

Do what you need to do to say good-bye for now to these images, knowing that you can return whenever you want. And in your own good time, bring yourself back into this room, refreshed, aware, and feeling good about yourself.

Selected Readings

Abbott, Sidney, and Barbara Love, *Sappho Was a Right-On Woman* (New York: Stein and Day, 1972).

Anand, Margo, *The Art of Sexual Ecstasy: The Path of Sacred Sexuality for Western Lovers* (Los Angeles: Jeremy Tarcher, 1989).

Barbach, Lonnie, *For Yourself* (New York: Signet, 1975).

—— (ed.), *Pleasures* (New York: Doubleday, 1984).

Blumstein, Philip, and Pepper Schwartz, *American Couples* (New York: William Morrow, 1983).

Boston Women's Health Collective: *The New Our Bodies, Our Selves* (New York: Touchstone, 1992).

Boulding, Elise, *The Underside of History* (Boulder, Colo.: Westview Press, 1976).

Brecher, Edward, M., *The Sex Researchers*, 2d Ed. (San Francisco: Specific Press, 1979).

Bullough, Vernon, and Bonnie Bullough, *Sin, Sickness and Sanity* (New York: Meridian, 1977).

Capra, Fritjof, *The Turning Point* (New York: Bantam, 1982).

Chang, Jolan, *The Tao of Love and Sex: The Ancient Chinese Way to Ecstasy* (New York: Viking Press, 1977).

Chopra, Deepak, *Quantum Healing* (New York: Bantam, 1989).

Corinne, Tee, and Jackie Lapidus, *Yantras of Womanlove* (Tallahassee, Fla.: Naiad Press, 1982).

Daly, Mary, *Gyn/Ecology* (Boston: Beacon Press, 1978).

Dickinson, Robert Latou, *Atlas of Human Sexual Anatomy* (Melbourne, Fla.: Krieger, 1933).

261

Selected Readings

Dodson, Betty, *Sex for One* (New York: Crown, 1987).

Estés, Clarissa Pinkola, *Women Who Run with the Wolves* (New York: Ballantine, 1992).

Faludi, Susan, *Backlash* (New York: Crown, 1992).

Ford, Clellan, and Frank Beach, *Patterns of Sexual Behavior* (New York: Harper & Row, 1951).

French, Marilyn, *The War Against Women* (New York: Summit Books, 1992).

Friday, Nancy, *My Secret Garden* (New York: Pocket Books, 1973).

———, *Forbidden Flowers* (New York: Pocket Books, 1975).

———, *Women on Top* (New York: Simon & Schuster, 1992).

Grahn, Judith, *Another Mother Tongue* (Boston: Beacon Press, 1984).

Greer, Germaine, *The Female Eunuch* (London: MacGibbon & Kee, 1970).

———, *The Change* (New York: Knopf, 1991).

Griffin, Susan, *Pornography and Silence* (New York: Harper & Row, 1981).

Freud, Sigmund, "Three Contributions to the Theory of Sexuality," in A.A. Brill (ed. and trans.), *The Basic Writings of Sigmund Freud* (New York: Random House, 1938).

Herman, Judith Lewis, *Trauma and Recovery* (New York: Basic Books, 1992).

Heyn, Dalma, *The Erotic Silence of the American Wife* (New York: Turtle Bay Books, 1992).

Hite, Shere, *The Hite Report* (New York: Macmillan, 1976).

———, *Women and Love* (New York: St. Martin's Press, 1987).

Janus, Samuel S., and Cynthia L. Janus, *The Janus Report on Sexual Behavior* (New York: Wiley, 1993).

Jordan, Judith V., "Clarity in Connection: Empathic Knowing, Desire and Sexuality," *Work in Progress No. 29* (Wellesley, Mass.: Stone Center for Developmental Services and Studies, 1987).

Selected Readings

Kaminer, Wendy, *I'm Dysfunctional, You're Dysfunctional* (New York: Addison-Wesley, 1992).

Kaplan, Helen Singer, *The New Sex Therapy* (New York: Brunner-Mazel, 1974).

———, *Disorders of Desire* (New York: Brunner-Mazel, 1979).

Kasl, Charlotte, *Women, Sex and Addiction* (New York: Ticknor & Fields, 1989).

Kensington Ladies Erotica Society, *Ladies Home Erotica* (Berkeley, Calif.: Ten Speed Press, 1984).

———, *Look Homeward Erotica* (Berkeley, Calif.: Ten Speed Press, 1986).

Kilbourne, Jean, Joseph Vitagliano, and Patricia Stallone, *Killing Us Softly* (Cambridge, Mass.: Cambridge Documentary Films, 1979). Video recording.

Kinsey, Alfred, et al., *Sexual Behavior in the Human Male* (Philadelphia: W.B. Saunders, 1948).

———, *Sexual Behavior in the Human Female* (Philadelphia: W.B. Saunders, 1953).

Kitzinger, Sheila, *Woman's Experience of Sex* (New York: Putnam, 1983).

Ladas, Alice, Beverly Whipple, and John Perry, *The G Spot* (New York: Holt, 1982).

Lorde, Audre, *Uses of the Erotic* (Trumansburg, N.Y.: Out and Out Books/Crossing Press, 1978).

Loulan, JoAnn, *Lesbian Sex* (San Francisco: Spinsters, Ink., 1984).

———, *Lesbian Passion: Loving Ourselves and Each Other* (San Francisco: Spinsters/Aunt Lute, 1987).

Maslow, Abraham, *Toward a Psychology of Being*, 2d Ed. (New York: D. Van Nostrand, 1968).

Masters, William H., and Virginia Johnson, *Human Sexual Response* (Boston: Little, Brown, 1966).

———, *Human Sexual Inadequacy* (Boston: Little, Brown, 1970).

Selected Readings

Mies, Maria, *Patriarchy and Accumulation on a World Scale* (London: Zed Books, 1986).

Miller, Jean Baker, *Toward a New Psychology of Women* (Boston: Beacon Press, 1976).

Money, John, and Anke Ehrhardt, *Man and Woman, Boy and Girl* (Baltimore: Johns Hopkins University Press, 1972).

Money, John, and H. Musaph (eds.), *The Handbook of Sexology*, Vols. 1, 4, and 5 (New York: Elsevier, 1978).

Montagu, Ashley, *Touching* (New York: Columbia University Press, 1971).

Morgan, Robin, *The Anatomy of Freedom* (New York: Anchor Press/Doubleday, 1982).

Newton, Niles, and Michael Newton, "Psychological Aspects of Lactation," *New England Journal of Medicine*, Vol. 277 (1967), pp. 1179–1188.

Norwood, Robin, *Women Who Love Too Much* (New York: Jeremy Tarcher, 1985).

Ogden, Gina, "Perception of Touch in Easily Orgasmic Women during Peak Sexual Experiences." Doctoral dissertation, Institute for Advanced Study of Human Sexuality, San Francisco, Calif., 1981.

————, "Women and Sexual Ecstasy: How Can Therapists Help?" *Women and Therapy*, Vol. 7, Nos. 2/3 (1988), pp. 43–56.

————, *Sexual Recovery* (Deerfield Beach, Fla.: Health Communications, 1990).

Ramey, James, *Intimate Friendships* (Englewood Cliffs, N.J.: Prentice-Hall, 1976).

Reich, Wilhelm, *The Function of the Orgasm* (New York: Orgone Institute Press, 1942); (New York: Farrar, Straus & Giroux, 1973).

————, *Selected Writings* (New York: Farrar, Straus & Giroux, 1973).

Sarton, May, *Journal of a Solitude* (New York: W.W. Norton, 1973).

Selected Readings

Shange, Ntozake, *Sassafrass, Cypress & Indigo* (New York: St. Martin's Press, 1982).

Sherfey, Mary Jane, *The Nature and Evolution of Female Sexuality* (New York: Random House, 1966).

Spretnak, Charlene, *The Politics of Women's Spirituality* (New York: Anchor/Doubleday, 1982).

Steinem, Gloria, *Outrageous Acts and Everyday Rebellions* (New York: Holt, Rhinehart & Winston, 1983).

———, *Revolution from Within* (Boston: Little, Brown, 1992).

Tavris, Carol, *The Mismeasure of Woman* (New York, Simon & Schuster, 1992).

Tennov, Dorothy, *Love and Limerence* (New York: Stein & Day, 1979).

Tiefer, Leonore, "A Feminist Critique of the Sexual Dysfunction Nomenclature," *Women and Sex Therapy*, Vol. 7, Nos. 2/3 (1988), pp. 5–21.

———, "New Perspectives in Sexology: From Rigor (Mortis) to Richness," *The Journal of Sex Research*, Vol. 28, No. 4 (1991), pp. 593–602.

Walker, Alice, *The Temple of My Familiar* (New York: Simon & Schuster, 1989).

———, *Possessing the Secret of Joy* (New York: Harcourt Brace Jovanovich, 1992).

Whipple, Beverly, Gina Ogden, and Barry Komisaruk, "Physiological Correlates of Imagery-Induced Orgasm in Women," *Archives of Sexual Behavior*, Vol. 21, No. 2 (1992), pp. 121–133.

Whipple, Beverly, and Gina Ogden, *Safe Encounters* (New York: Pocket Books, 1990).

INDEX

INDEX

INDEX

271

INDEX

INDEX

INDEX